SCHOOL OF THE AGES

The War Against Love

SCHOOL OF THE AGES

The War Against Love

Matt Posner

Vitasta

Let Knowledge Spread

Published by
Renu Kaul Verma for
Vitasta Publishing Pvt Ltd
2/15, Ansari Road, Daryaganj,
New Delhi - 110 002
info@vitastapublishing.com

ISBN: 978-81-925354-5-6

Layout and Cover Design by Vitasta Publishing Pvt. Ltd.
Character Design by Dipjyoti Lahkar
Printed by Vikas Computer and Printers

For Morris Posner
The man with the courage to
stand up to the bullies

Contents

Preface

This is the third book in the School of the Ages series. In this book, Simon faces challenges and changes that will ask him to act as a man rather than a boy. Some of these—going to war against deadly enemies at age fifteen—are, sadly, far from uncommon in the world. Others like having an offer of marriage to someone really amazing while still in high school are wonderfully strange. In the story, Simon does seem to go back and forth between being grownup and being a kid. Working as a teacher, I see my students going through such changes all the time as they grow up when tough times force them to do things they don't feel ready to do. As you work hard to find your way, you sometimes make mistakes. Growing up is hard. Even at 43, I often find it hard to be a grown-up! I hope you never have to deal with the kinds of problems Simon faces, and as you get older, you must not ever be afraid of change. I like to draw up good plan that will help solve the problem, try to take care of other people as best I can, and then move forward boldly.

Readers are welcome to write to me at my website (http://schooloftheages.webs.com) and to my Facebook page (http://www.facebook.com/schooloftheages) and to follow me at http://www.twitter.com/schooloftheages. As a teacher, I am always happy to hear from young people.

Happy reading.

Mind's Eye

This story doesn't start happily. It also doesn't end happily. In between, there is some happiness, but it isn't easy to tell. Stories aren't easily finished, and they rarely reach an ending that doesn't leave a feeling that more could be told. Some storytellers spend so much time getting ready for the end that when it comes, the reader just blinks and misses it. That won't happen here. Maestro Morgan, our meditation teacher at School of the Ages, taught us that the universe continues to expand since the Big Bang. As it expands, the changes that occur, its growth, are perceived by living creatures as time. Expansion of the universe has no predictable end, and so time has no predictable end, and stories definitely don't end. When I was a child, my Indian grandmother Devi taught me that just as living things die and are reborn, the Universe also dies and is renewed. Lord Shiva destroys, Lord Brahma recreates, and Lord Vishnu protects from evil. The story begins again, as it always has, beyond the range of human understanding. I can't imagine or understand other variations of the universe, before or after the version I know. And though this story is in my past, beginning when I was fifteen going on sixteen, it has never ended, and I understand no more now than I did then about the beautiful and impossible questions of why, how, and what next.

I'm called Simon Magus. That's my magician name; my birth name is Leicester S. Moore. I was in my parents' house in Bayside, Queens,

New York, a two-story brick home on Bell Boulevard with basements and bedroom balconies. It was 5:30 PM on a winter night, with darkness and ice outside. Inside with me were five cats and my half-brother, Peter Murasaki, who was eighteen and mad at the world

My parents were expected home soon.

The doorbell rang. Peter was watching TV. I got up and went to the door and checked the peephole, and saw outside a nightmare.

A girl in a black coat, black leggings, black boots ,wild hair barely contained by a fuzzy red *fedora*. Her hair had blondish-silvery highlights. Her eyes were so intense, so savage, as she looked into the peephole, that I felt as if she could see me on the other side. Her face, unpleasantly pale, had become leaner and harder. It was Hélène La Méduse, the girl magician from Paris who had decisively beaten me in our previous encounter, and who had tortured my dreams since.

"Hello, Simon Magus," she called in a mocking tone. "We have come to see you!"

A young man came up the steps to stand beside her. He was as I remembered, with wavy hair, grey coat, grey eyes, gaudy rings on each finger of his right hand. But now his left hand had rings as well. He was Yves le Maître, the henchman of Hélène, who could knock you out by counting to three.

Quickly I considered the possibilities. In an attempt to prevent a fight in Paris, I had invited them to visit the school, so there was a very slight chance that it was a friendly visit and they weren't here to cause trouble. But that was unlikely. They were wicked magicians, and the greater likelihood was that the other two members of Hélène's gang, the thugs Gautier Le Malveillant and Arnaud le Vampire, were also in the area.

I wasn't alone. It was worse than being alone. I had to protect a non-magician, Peter Murasaki, who neither liked nor respected me. He hadn't even come invited; he was there supposedly because he was mad at his mother, Kotone, for refusing to pay to get his car fixed, and he needed a place to cool off and watch TV. I had only one advantage, and that was being at home. A magician's ability is always greatest in his own home. This might help me hold out for a while against a stronger magician, but four stronger magicians would still be too much for me. And then, there was one more problem. My parents would be home soon, and they were non-magicians.

I would somehow have to deal with Hélène's whole gang by myself without any time to plan or prepare. First, I'd call for help. I did this using the sorcerous power called thought trading, in which I shared a thought with a person and then heard a response indirectly, in the form of one of my own thoughts. Thought trading wasn't a power of all magicians–only a few of us could do it and fortunately my partner could.

Goldberry, those French kids we fought are at my house.

So that was what it was, she sent back to me. She'd already been out and about just in case.

You might wonder why I would endanger my partner by calling her for help. The answer is, it's a rule at School of the Ages–FPTA, "first partner, then advisor." As far as she was concerned, if I didn't call her first, our partnership wasn't worth anything. With her power as a diviner, getting strong hints of the future, she might well have shown up anyway. Anyway, first partner, then advisor.

Dr Archer, those French kids we fought in Paris are at my house. I need help.

He was not certain that help was needed. He encouraged self-reliance.

I sent back that I really needed help.

Dr Archer was in Europe but would try to help from where he was.

I wasn't going to open the door. I stepped back into the living room, which was right next to the foyer by the door. The stairs were opposite the door. An "old witch" Halloween costume hung on a coat rack in the hall.

"Peter," I said to my brother.

He grunted.

"Call my father."

He grunted again. His father too.

"Tell him he and my mother should stay away from the house until I call them."

Peter said, "Why?"

"Peter, some bad magicians are going to attack the house. You and I are in trouble, but we can save my parents."

"Yeah, right, Leicester." he said. He wouldn't say Simon, and only used my real name.

The doorbell rang again.

"Call him, Peter."

"I'm not doing that."

The doorbell rang.

"Peter, someone is out there that I don't want to let in. Believe me, it's a couple of bad people. At least two, probably four. They're very tough, and we're in trouble. I need your help."

He picked up the remote and began flipping channels.

Jag, the striped tabby cat who had been a kitten when I first joined School of the Ages, came barreling down the stairs. Was someone up there? My balcony door was locked, but my parents' maybe wasn't. Jag was nervous by nature and could also have been startled by the doorbell.

Banging on the door. Rapping on the window. The shades were down.

"What?" said Peter. He switched off the TV and dropped the remote. "You should call 911."

"Make the call, Peter. My… our father."

"Whatever."

"Use my phone." I tossed it to him.

Meanwhile I was putting a part of my mind on defense. My

imaginary cylinder, the defensive visualization School of the Ages students used to protect themselves, was in good shape, as it normally was, even when I was sleeping. Now, however, alert to the beginnings of a combat, I imagined it turning into solid stone with protective spikes. Then I began to visualize the outside of the house. I saw all parts of it, each wall, each window, the roof, in my mind. This wasn't easy to do, but two years of training in meditation and visualization from Maestro Morgan, plus daily practice maintaining the cylinder had prepared me and my magical abilities were increased at home.

I added another cylinder around it. I couldn't protect the whole house at once -- my mind wasn't sharp enough for that–but maybe I could get some idea of what was going on. I imagined that cylinder with three surfaces, stone inside, fire on top of that, and on the outermost surface, eyes and ears.

At once I got more information. Someone was at our back door looking in through the window. I couldn't see the person but I could feel the slimy shadowiness that I recognized as being Malevolent Gautier, who wielded a bullwhip and had the ability to "drift"–a kind of teleport that happened only when you weren't looking at him. Besides Gautier, I could also feel that someone had slipped inside before I made the house cylinder. Jag had fled I feared because someone was upstairs.

"Let us in, little one," Hélène called through the window. The house cylinders and my personal defenses remained in my mind while I took stock of my surroundings. Peter was on the phone.

"Yeah, there's someone here. I don't know. They're banging on the window. He says stay away. Yeah, okay." He hung up.

"Peter," I said. "Someone's inside, upstairs. I'm going to go up and fight him. Anyone who comes downstairs except me, jump him and beat him till he doesn't move."

"How do you know who's upstairs?"

"I'm a magician, Peter. I didn't make that up. There's two in front, one at the back door, one upstairs. Any of them can kill us. Just trust me."

He rolled his eyes. "This is the last time I come over here."

There was no sound from outside any more. Arnaud the vampire was upstairs. He must have climbed up onto the balcony long before Helene rang the doorbell; they had surprise on their side. He was dangerous and tough for me. They all were. The four of them had beaten eight of us School of the Ages kids just six months ago.

I went to the stairs. Leo, our big Maine coon cat, was sitting on the middle steps looking at me with an intelligence I'd never seen before. He looked up the steps and made a deep, frightening growl. It lasted ten seconds and was surely audible all through the house. In answer came growls and yowls from all parts of the house. Leo puffed out his fur, looked at me as if to tell me to follow him and started up the steps. I followed. He had become big and moved not like a housecat stalking a mouse, but like the lion he was named for: a lion entering battle.

We came to the top of the steps. My room was on the right, a bathroom directly ahead, and my parents' room on the left. Arnaud was there. I looked at Leo, whose intelligent expression told me he was waiting for me to make the first move. I nodded, and he began to growl again.

Once, as a child, I had lain in a bathtub listening to a howling tornado pass not far from our Long Island house. Leo's growl sounded like that. I had known Leo since he was a kitten. He had slept in my bed hundreds of times but now I didn't feel safe that close to him. That growl would have made anyone uncertain.

There was a bang on one of the doors downstairs. Switching to my house cylinder, I perceived through the eyes and ears Yves Le Maitre making hand motions. What were they doing? Be quiet Peter, be…

No good. He'd freaked out and was yelling at them to go away.

Leo mewed at me, then turned back towards my parents room.

A thought-trade: Dr Archer hoped he had been helpful.

…………………………………………………………………………

Thank you, Dr Archer.

My parents' bedroom door was ajar. In a quick motion, I shoved it open and stepped back. Inside, the drapes were drawn even on the balcony doors and there was little light. Still, I saw a shadowy figure standing by the dresser fumbling with something. My mother's jewellery, probably.

Leo snarled.

A heavy crash on the front door and a blow to the glass of the back door. Peter cursing. Someone fiddling with the basement window. Too much going on for me to track. I had to attack, now, and hold onto my defense, but my opponent wasn't waiting for me. He turned towards me, and even in the sliver of illumination from the lights downstairs, I saw vampire fangs glinting.

Melee

"On your knees!" I shouted, exerting my will, and he yelled his own war cry, "*Allahu Akbar*!" as he flung up his cape and lunged.

He dropped to his knees and shrieked when a gigantic cat leapt growling at his head. Leo bounced off the cape but ripped through it with his claws. I couldn't see Arnaud's face or his hands behind the cape, in the darkness, so I tried to visualize them as I had last seen them, more than half a year ago. Scorpion stings in the hands, in the eyes. Maybe they didn't hit solidly, but they hit him, and he wailed something in Arabic. Leo clawed at the protective cape as I reached behind me. Cool air on my palm preceded the arrival of a rock. I rushed up and began pounding him with it. He lashed out hard, catching me on the jaw and throwing off Leo as well. The blow shocked me so that I lost the cylinder of eyes around the house, exposing the fire. Someone outside yelled, and the cats yowled. More bangs downstairs. I fell to the floor on my side, hurt my elbow badly and lost my grip on the rock. Arnaud was up now and stood looming over me, his torn cape over his face leaving his eyes free. They had to be hurting still.

"Leo, go help Peter," I said quietly.

Leo made a purr like a lion, almost a scolding noise, and then bounded over me, leaving me alone with Arnaud.

The glass broke downstairs at the back door.

Fire!

....

The fire layer of the cylinder startled whoever it was, probably Gautier, but it was imaginary fire and wouldn't injure him. "Cougar, Cheetah!" I shouted. "Back door!"

Two answering noises showed they had heard and understood me.

The little monster was done trying to intimidate me and he lunged. He was a small man, but I was a small kid, and he was too tough for me to wrestle with. I reached back for more rocks, one in each hand, throwing both. One bounced off his cape; the other grazed his temple. He stumbled.

"On your knees!"

He went down on his knees.

Scorpion sting! I aimed this hex to pass in one ear and out the other.

"*Allahu Akbar*!" he shouted again, defying me.I knew he was hurt when he lost his grip on his cape. That was my opening. I could see him, could visualize his whole body. The knee was my target.

"*Yeishu ben Pandeira*!" The name of the ancient Jewish heretic was my activation for a magical blow. This magic had knocked out several of Yakov Mermelstein's teeth. If it hit hard enough, it might shatter Arnaud's kneecap. I hoped so because I had three more magicians to fight.

No luck. He shrugged off the blow and backhanded me across the face. I had never been hit in the face before and never been hit so hard anywhere. I staggered back into a dresser. He grabbed me by the collar and threw me against the wall. I landed on the bed. All my cylinders were gone, including the one for my personal defense.

"*Allahu Akbar*!"

I was stunned but not beaten. Apparently I was physically tougher than I thought. All the same I played dead as I blocked out pain from my face, jaw, and elbow and rebuilt my personal cylinder. He was shuffling towards me, humming. What could I use against him? My strongest weapons had already been tried. How had he obtained so much physical power through magic? Vampires weren't real so but how could he be so much like one?

Intuition and logic, *chokhmah, binah*. He thinks he's a vampire and uses vampire weapons. I visualized his chest on his left side, where his heart might be. Then I imagined a wooden crucifix with a sharp point at the bottom. Then I sat up and met his eyes.

"*Allahu Akbar*," I said, and mentally pushed the crucifix inside his heart.

He dropped. Slowly, I rolled off the bed. Then using one arm I dragged him to the open balcony door and hauled him outside. Checking his pockets, I found jewellery and put it in my pocket instead. Then I locked him outside.

I had little time to take stock of the small victory. I had beaten a strong adult magician who was way tougher than me. Why didn't he win?

Downstairs there was roaring, hissing, spitting, crashing. Standing in the doorway of my parents' room, I remembered I had three opponents remaining downstairs. Leo was with Peter, and Cougar and Cheetah were delaying whoever had come in the back way. I didn't know where the other cats were, but it didn't matter for the moment. I had to stay on offense, and that would be easier if the French magicians couldn't see me. Hélène was the leader and taking out the leader was good strategy but … she'd beaten me the last time. Better to pick off her henchmen first. I formed a mental image of Yves as I had seen him through the peephole. I visualized hands going around his neck and squeezing.

Immediately I heard yelling downstairs but he shook off the attack. He was inside already! He must have knocked down the door. Now listening, I heard him counting. Could he knock me out without seeing me? I had to counter his power. It was based on counting.

Un. Deux.

Cinque, I thought, (one... two... five), and pushed that thought outward spoiling his count. It worked.

Peter: "Ow! Get off!"

Hélène, with annoyance: "Stop struggling!"

The whip of Gautier crashed into something. There was no room in the house where he could swing it fully and I counted on my cats to be too agile to get hit.

Footsteps on the stairs. Up came Yves. I had seconds to act while he climbed. Time to help Peter. I would have no trouble visualizing Hélène La Méduse. I had been dreaming about her since I met her. What had worked against Arnaud might work against her. The Medusa's eyes turned people to stone. What if she saw her own face? I visualized a big oval silver mirror, with flames dancing in the back. Mentally, I slid this in front of her real face. I heard a thump and a smashing sound but didn't know what had happened. The cats' yowling came again and echoed as if the house were a gigantic cave.

"Yoo hoo," came the voice of Yves from the hallway outside my bedroom. He was fresh; I was hurt. I needed help. I sent out my thoughts.

Jag.

An answering screech from downstairs must have shocked even Yves. Huge claws clicked up the stairs. I couldn't see but I knew Jag was at the head of the stairs, staring down my opponent. Jag was our smallest cat yet sounded like a bull. I decided it was time to build on Yves' nervousness. I got up and went into the hall. There he was, facing our now-gigantic cat, his hand held up to count.

"*Un,*" he said, chopping the air, watching Jag nervously. "*Deux.*"

"*Cinque,*" I said. I didn't pronounce it very well.

He turned. "No one can block the count," he said flatly.

"I just did," I said. "You don't belong in my house. Ask your vampire when he rises from the grave."

His lip quivered. "I laugh at your threats. *Un. Deux.*"

"Cinque. Try something else."

He kept grinning. "Okay. Something else." He spun his hand

around. I felt weariness, dizziness pushing at my cylinder, trying to spin me around. I spun my cylinder the opposite way from his attack. The dizziness passed.

"Okay" I said. "The Basic Hex. On your knees!" I saw fear in his eyes. "Jag, bite his hand."

As Yves dropped to his knees, the huge cat leapt catching his coat with both claws, and at the same time I moved grabbing one hand as Jag's jaws closed on the other. He whimpered. I chopped with the hand I was holding and counted. "One. Two. Three."

Yves fainted.

"And I didn't even practice," I said. "Jerk. You can let go, Jag." My cat released him, licking the blood from his lips. Kneeling, I pulled off several rings from Yves' slimy hand but again there was little time. Mentally I scanned the house. Hélène had overcome Peter. Leo was also in the living room, alert but not moving. Gautier was in the kitchen, throwing things at Cheetah. I couldn't find Cougar or Pink Panther.

Then I felt something bad. My mother was coming up the yard.

I ran down the stairs and Jag followed.

"What the hell happened?" she shouted.

"Run! I called out. "Get clear, before…"

But she was already entering the living room in her red woolen coat, where Hélène waited for her. I couldn't get there in time.

Aftermath

"Get the hell out of my house!" my mother shouted at Hélène. Her voice cracked; she was not used to yelling. An attractive woman in her mid-forties, she was tall and slim, with ginger hair and light eyes, and always looked supremely professional.

The living room was wrecked. Two normal-sized cats, Pink Panther and Leo, lay on the floor, one out cold, the other seemingly hypnotized. Peter lay unconscious on the floor bleeding from his mouth and nose, with Hélène sitting nearby holding him down. I couldn't make her go down on her knees; she was already there. The TV was off, its screen cracked.

Next to me, Jag mewed. He was also normal-sized now. Neither was Cheetah now large enough to restrain Gautier as he walked into the room squaring off with my mother as Hélène did with me.

Now I was in the worst possible position facing two deadly opponents with two non-combatants in the room. "This is Hélène La Méduse and this is Malevolent Gautier. They're my enemies."

"How did they get here?" my mother demanded.

"I don't know," I said. To my surprise, the French magicians weren't attacking. They had to be sizing up my mother. I knew she had no magical ability, but maybe they didn't.

"The spell you put on the cats worked," I said. "You have to teach it to me."

"When you're old enough," she said, picking up my bluff.

Then I heard two more voices coming up the steep hill to our house.

Goldberry: "Oh, bloody hell."

Clive Tinker: "I hope they haven't brought an axe."

"Come in," I called to them.

They did. Goldberry three inches taller than a year before, was wearing one of her mother's silver fox furs. She looked gorgeous. Her father, tall and hard-faced, wore a blue trench coat and a Homburg hat.

"You left two for us," my partner said shaking out her hair. "Good. I want this rotten girl for myself."

Hélène stood. "Stupid. You are all talk, you British fool."

I looked at Mr Tinker. "Feel free to help."

He nodded. "That will cost you one service from our bargain."

"No," Goldberry said. "*I'm* asking you to do it."

He gave his daughter a black look. Raising his right hand, he gave his extended fingers a slight twist. Gautier immediately flew up to the ceiling where he was splayed like a squashed spider.

"Hélène," Gautier squeaked.

"Now to you," Mr Tinker said. "If you know Simon Magus and my daughter, then I trust you know who I am, don't you?"

Hélène nodded, swallowing.

"Then you know a curse from me means something. If you threaten my daughter again, I'll curse you so strongly you'll forget to breathe." He twisted his hand again and Gautier fell face-first, his head clipping the edge of the already collapsed coffee table.

"You can stop damaging my house," my mother said.

"Of course, Ms. Gale," said Mr Tinker giving her the magician name she used as the Dean's executive assistant.

"I can beat you," Hélène said to me. "I beat you before. I haunt you."

It was true. I didn't respond.

"It wouldn't count with my father here," Goldberry said to the

French girl. "But we'll meet again, and I'll knock you out." "She is a mean little one, eh?" Hélène said nervously to Mr Tinker.

"That makes me proud every time I see her," Clive Tinker replied. "She's daddy's girl and it's only out of respect for her claim on you that I haven't fed you to the tiger at the Bronx Zoo. Now take him and go," he commanded her, looking at the reeling Gautier.

Hélène hauled her companion to his feet and soon they were walking over the splintered front door and headed down the hill for the darkness of Bell Boulevard.

My mother went to help Peter. Leo woke up and licked himself. Jag ran up the stairs again.

"Where's the basement door?" asked Mr Tinker. "Someone's down there."

I showed him. We went down together. There was a young girl there, maybe ten, blond and dirty, wearing tattered jeans, a dirty sweater, and beret. Her eyes were hollowed. She was eating the last of a bag of cookies from our basement pantry.

"Who are you?" I demanded. "I'm called Delphine," she said. "I told them not to attack you in your house, Simon Magus, but the Teacher said to, and they made me come."

"The Teacher? Who is that?"

"Not Duparc?" Clive Tinker asked.

"No. The Teacher doesn't work at Citadel d'If." (That was the name of the Paris magic school that had trained the other four.)

"You're not a member of that gang?" I asked.

"Oh, *no*! But the Teacher sent me anyway."

Mr Tinker nodded. "Go to sleep," he told her.

Delphine fell asleep.

"We'll question her later. Let's secure the other two." He picked up Delphine, and in the living room deposited her on one of the couches. Peter, his face cut and bruised, was on the other.

"Who's this?" my mother asked, lowering her cell phone.

"A prisoner," said Mr Tinker.

"She's so young," Goldberry said. She was also on a cell phone–mine, which she must have found on the floor after Peter dropped it. "You didn't hurt her," she accused her father.

"Of course I didn't hurt her," he replied. "You know me better than that."

"Dr Pierre is on her way back to her clinic," Goldberry told my mother.

Avery's mother, Dr Pierre, was now the vet for all five Moore family cats. Presumably, all five were going to see her. Harlem was inconveniently far but she was the best so far as we were concerned.

Mr Tinker and I went upstairs. "Good job on this one," he said as he examined the unconscious Yves with his shoe nudging the young man's cheek. "Take the rest of the rings. Where's baby Dracula?"

"On the balcony, through there." I gestured.

"No. Seems he's made his escape with the others. How did you beat him?"

"I staked him."

Clive Tinker laughed. "That's rich. Generally you are too kind but that has potential."

I continued pulling off and pocketing the rings. If I had him alone, I was going to settle something else.

"Mr Tinker, is William Goodenough spying on Goldberry for you?"

"What is that knowledge worth to you?" he asked.

"I don't want to bargain for it. Just tell me or refuse."

He considered, then said, "He's not my creature. He has his own will and treats me the same as he does everyone else except with more tolerable manners. William is sincere about my Goldberry, I believe."

"And you approve?"

"He's powerful and he cares for her. If he has a touch of the devil, that will help him help her against those who are worse. Why do you ask? Have you someone in mind for her? You've not expressed an interest that I know of."

"No. I love her, but she's my partner. It's different. I know you understand how that works."

He nodded, but there was something strange about how his eyes crinkled.

I got the last ring from Yves' right thumb. I had been thinking about another question and decided it was time to ask it. "Mr Tinker, who was your study partner at School of the Ages?"

He snorted. "You don't need to know that. Now, let's tend to this one." He grabbed Yves by the foot and dragged him down the stairs, his head thumping on each carpeted step.

My father had arrived. He was holding my mother around the shoulders and talking on the phone.

"What was this about?" my mother demanded. "How does that minor scuffle in Paris turn into this?"

Goldberry was now helping Peter to sit up. His eyes were only half-open with grogginess, but he opened them wider to stare at me.

"I hate you," he told me coolly.

"You'll get over it," I suggested.

"Take it easy," my father said to Peter. "It's because of your brother that you know where you got your handsome face." He was off the phone looking at my mother. Martin Moore, my father had even features and a slightly dark complexion that reflected my Asian Indian grandmother. He was wearing a dark suit, with his tie loosened. He looked at my mother.

"Who gets Dr Pierre and who gets the people to hospital, sweetie pie?"

"When my mom sees what happened to me she'll sue you," Peter said. "It's all his fault, your stupid son." He pointed at me.

"Don't be rude," I said. "I took a beating too. And you will need my help if they come back."

"He's right," Goldberry said.

Peter took a deep breath as he took her in for the first time. He was groggy but he still knew a gorgeous girl when he saw one. "Okay, I can make up a story to tell Mom on one condition." He touched Goldberry's arm. "You have to go out with me."

"Pardon me?" said Clive Tinker. "How old are you?"

"I'm eighteen."

"You're too old for her."

Peter rolled his eyes at that. "Are you kidding me? She's a magician, right? Well, I'm not. So I figure she's safe."

Clive Tinker looked him over, looked at my father. My father shrugged. "He's from a good family."

"All right," said Mr Tinker. "It's a fair bargain. Up to you, Goldberry."

Now it was her turn to look Peter over. "I want to see *The Producers*. Then eat at *Daniel*."

He blinked. That was three or four hundred dollars right there. But he said, "You got it. And Leicester is still a jerk."

I could see through the front doorway that a white SUV had pulled up the hill into our driveway.Moments later, my mother's boss the Dean was standing next to her; she must have called him. We hadn't seen him enter but the Dean's arrival and departure were always difficult to observe. A medium-sized, balding man with a goatee, he wore a tweed coat and a concerned expression.

"Maybe you can explain this to me," she said flatly. No preliminaries. "After you apologize."

He was her boss the head of my school, and a strong magician. Not one of those things seemed to slow her down at all.

"I am deeply sorry," said the Dean hanging his head. "While I drive your family to the hospital, I will answer your questions."

"I'll go to Dr Pierre then," my father said. "If you wouldn't mind holding the fort?" he asked Mr Tinker.

"Not a problem, Moore," said Mr Tinker. "Leave the prisoners to me."

My father went for the cat carriers.

Simon Warrior

My mother sat in the front seat. At the back, I sat between Goldberry and Peter, who quickly fell asleep. The Dean explained.

"School of the Ages is at war with a cabal of European magicians called *Gott im Himmel*," he said. "They are traditionally anti-Semitic. As School of the Ages is globally known for its instruction in the field of Cabala, we believe this is a motive for their aggression against us. Their current leader is Kaiser Petrus. Gott im Himmel and School of the Ages have been opposed from the beginning of their existence. It seems as if the two organizations, which were founded within a few years of one another, are likely always to be enemies. I dislike terms such as good and evil. I admit that School of the Ages has produced more than a few disagreeable graduates. However, our intentions are good, and we are supportive of the aims both of individuals and of democratic society. Of Gott im Himmel, the opposite may be said. It is dedicated to the belief that might makes right, and that no one can be trusted.

"Dr Archer, our school defender, is presently in the Czech Republic with Dr Chatterjee, attempting to locate and defeat Kaiser Petrus. I think that the gang of Hélène are under the influence of our enemies, and perhaps this was also the cause of their prior brawl with our students in Paris.

"However damaging this attack was to your home and family, we can however take some comfort from the fact that we have two individuals to question."

"Dean," my mother said, "you know that I like working for you. But I've told you before that I don't like seeing my son endangered."

The Dean sighed. "And I have told you, Ms Gale–Mrs Moore–that he is going to be endangered in some capacity regardless of what I do. Astrologically speaking, he is facing various perils. School of the Ages is empowering him to face threats that are inevitable. He has today fought alone and held his ground against four magicians who defeated him along with his seven comrades a few months ago."

"Not really alone," I explained. "Dr Archer helped me. He made the cats into panthers, so they could fight with me."

"He what?" said my mother.

"All the same," said the Dean. "As you begin your third year, Simon, your capability is increasing very rapidly."

"Yes sir," I said. My elbow was throbbing and my jaw was sore. "But the Rambal told me power isn't important." If you're new to my story, the Rambal is Rabbi Moshe ben Lichtman, a rabbi over a hundred years old who teaches Cabala at School of the Ages a man wise, famous, and holy.

The Dean was silent for a moment. Then he said, "In terms of spiritual health, power, as you say is not required. But there is also the task of serving others. To fight evil, Simon, is in your character."

"My son's not a warrior," my mother said. "Don't try to brainwash him, Dean."

"I'm not that easy to brainwash," I argued.

"He really isn't," Goldberry added, leaning forward suddenly. "He's a stubborn fellow. Takes even really good advice a long time to penetrate."

My mother looked at Goldberry. " Do you like seeing him get mixed up in a magical war?"

"Well, I'm mixed up in it as well so I don't mind the company. Honestly, ma'am, I can't imagine him not doing it. And I think you would fight, too, if you had to. He's more like you than your husband."

My mother sat back in the seat, and fiddled with something. Then she extended her hand towards my partner. Goldberry took it then let go holding something. "What's this?"

"I was saving it for a daughter," my mother said. "But I never had one till now."

Goldberry flipped on the dome light.

It was my mother's diamond engagement ring.

"I can't," Goldberry said.

"You're not just Simon's partner," my mother said. "Now you're mine, too. Okay?"

"Okay."

Goldberry wiped her eyes with her coat sleeve as she switched off the dome light.

We arrived at Queens Hospital Center on 164th street. The Dean swung his car into the roundabout by the emergency room. I woke up Peter and Goldberry then helped him out of the car and towards the emergency room. I was starting to follow when the Dean called me back to the car to sit next to him.

"Simon," he said, "do you genuinely want to help us in the conflict with Gott im Himmel? I do not wish to compel you and I do respect your mother's view. I relieve you now of any pressure that you may feel from me. Act with free will."

I didn't feel any different. "Dean," I said, "I don't think I'm being forced. It's not that I like to fight but Goldberry was right. I can't imagine not doing it. No sane person wants to fight in a war, but what else could I do?"

"There is a path of peace, a path of love instead of war. One of my own teachers, Mr Dancer, taught me of this path when I was myself a student at School of the Ages. As he said, it is a truth that war never ends. People enter and leave war, and there are always others ready to fight in their places. In the end, it is a paradox: war is something that will always have a cause but will also be without sense."

"It doesn't matter. I can't back out of this fight, Dean. They attacked me, and they'll attack me again."

"You can indeed back out. There are consequences, of course, to a path of peace. It is harder than fighting, to be attacked and not to fight back."

"No, I'll fight."

"I thought you would make that choice."

"Why?"

"Astrological reasons. But consider also who is your mentor. Dr Archer fights constantly against evil men."

"And so I will always be fighting and won't ever have peace and love?"

"I hate to think that," the Dean said. "My regard for you and your mother makes me wish you both peace and love in abundance. Nor is there anything in astrology that rules them out. Yet you will be scarred."

I saw my mother coming back to the car to fetch me so I got out to meet her, reminded by the ache of my elbow and the sting of my facial bruises that I had been injured in a fight less than an hour ago. I realized then that I would call this war that would take away my peace –the War Against Love.

Advice from an Archer

Dr Archer arrived at JFK Airport the next morning with Dr Chatterjee, who was shaken up. The Smoot Prep bus delivered them to our home. Neither teacher had visited my home before, and they arrived just as the workmen from my father's company were installing our new front door. We sat at the dining table with tea and danishes. Dr Chatterjee spoke on his cell phone, telling someone he was all right and to get the maya (that's Sanskrit for magic or illusion) ready for school. Dr Archer listened to our story without comment.

"Something bothers me," my mother told him. There was a bang as the workers removed the ruined hinges of the back door. "I'm certainly glad that you helped but three of our cats are hospitalized now. Did you have to get them involved?"

"I could not devise nor obtain a more effective agency in such limited time," said Dr Archer. "I merely gave the animals increased capability. Their actions were free-willed. Their loyalty to your son must therefore be considerable."

She shook her head. "You're not telling us the truth."

"We've all survived, Magdalene," my father said, touching her hand gently where it rested on the table. I'm much more concerned about future attacks than about laying blame for this one. What do we have to do to prevent a repeat performance?"

"I do not wish to be deceptive," Dr Archer said. "My primary attention is given to the elimination of Gott im Himmel, but they are dangerous adversaries, and I cannot promise there will not be further attacks. Simon and Goldberry are assisting me and the best help you can give me is to allow your son to continue the task so long as he wishes to do so."

"And what about those kids that Clive took out of my house last night?"

"We intend to exploit the advantage of having them to question," said Dr Archer. "To have prisoners is regrettable, of course."

"This is America," my mother said. "Citizens don't take prisoners."

"I agree," said Dr Archer. "However, just as the United States is at war with terrorists worldwide, School of the Ages is engaged in a covert war of magicians. These two shall, however, be treated kindly and released swiftly."

"The boy is no good," my father said, "but that young girl–she's not as bad as the others."

"I respect your judgment," said Dr Archer. "I have not seen her yet. After I have stopped at home and my office briefly and have questioned the girl myself, I shall be leaving again for France to locate her family."

"You need to get some sleep, Dr Archer," I told him. "You don't look good."

"Meditation is a good compensation for lost sleep," he said.

"But not for lost rest," my mother said. "Why don't you two take naps here before you leave for the school?"

"Not necessary," Dr Chatterjee mumbled.

"On behalf of the Dean," she said, "I insist."

❖ ❖ ❖

After Dr Archer's nap, he called me to meet with him privately. We sat together on my balcony. He did look a little better–his eyes were clearer–but he still didn't look good. He questioned me about the details of the fight, specifically how I had managed the magic. "Ambitious," was his comment at the end of the story. "You were aided by being in your home territory and by some camouflage and concealment. The eagerness of your pets to fight was also helpful. Naturally, I shall speak to Dr Pierre about effective treatment for them."

"Thank you. But my parents could be attacked again without me there," I said. "How can I protect them?"

"You do not need to protect your parents," he said. "Neither is as vulnerable as you suppose. Indeed, before you became my protégé, your parents were your guardians. I think you may still consider them able to protect you and manage your affairs."

"But they can't do magic."

"Perhaps not. Yet to be a non-magician is not necessarily to be vulnerable. Your parents are as capable as they were before you had even heard of School of the Ages.

"Now, I wish to instruct you in a matter of magicians' protocol. Your strategy to combat the gang was well-done. However, it is typical for a magician approached in his home to take a defensive posture. More typically, he confronts the visitor and admits or dismisses that person. To defend at once is a posture of weakness which will be reported as weakness to our enemies. It will be seen, not that you overcame four to one odds, but that you called for help because you were outmatched."

"I was."

"No, Simon, you were not. Left alone, you had an excellent chance to win."

"Against all four of them?"

"Yes."

"I'm not that powerful, Dr Archer. I have studied numerology and construction but it still seems like I always have to improvise." He looked at me coldly. "You perceive your need to improvise as a weakness."

"Well, not really. I mean I'm glad I can but I feel I should have more things to pick from."

"Too many choices can slow decision-making," he said. "I advise allowing your talents to develop gradually and in pace with your schooling. For now, I assign you to construct various objects for your use during the war against Gott im Himmel. First, scribe a nonsense poem on a small scroll, place it in a small tube and wear it around your neck."

"A small scroll in a small tube?"

"It will be for mental defense."

"Any nonsense poem?"

"One you can memorize. Next, you will need an object for opening what is shut. Incorporate metal and oils. Understood?"

"Yes."

"Third, a protective device against physical wounds. These generally do not work well and can at best divert a wound to a less lethal location but it is best to make one."

I nodded. "Finally, prepare a weapon of offense for specific use against embodied spirits."

"What kind of weapon?"

"Handheld, easily concealed and non-metallic. It should be a reusable object that can be carried on an airplane."

"I'll get to work."

He offered me a handshake. "You are remarkably brave. Now it is time for me to go." He started to get up.

"One more question, Dr Archer."

He sat down. "I must go to the school, and then to France."

"Quickly. Who was Clive Tinker's study partner at School of the Ages?"

When I saw his face, I was sorry I had asked. His eyes grew wet and his lips tightened. I tried to explain. "Was it you? I'm trying to figure out why you guys don't like each other."

"I suppose," he said, "I should be content that a protégé of mine should pose a question so sharply relevant to my circumstances when few would see the connection. But you must excuse me."

Before I could decide what to say next, he was out of the room. I woke in the middle of the night. My cell phone rang. "Hi, Simon." It was the calm voice of Donovan Archer, my teacher's son, and a good friend. "What do you want to know?"

When I asked my question he explained that Clive Tinker's study partner was Ada, his mother and Dr Archer's wife. Both men Clive and Archer were in love with her but she chose Archer. Clive Tinker felt betrayed and the men became enemies henceforth. Another girl involved in this mess was Colette Leveque, the daughter of the French master magician I had met in Paris the year before. Colette had loved them both and went a little crazy as her love was reciprocated by neither of the two men.

The Palace

The next day I went to see Goldberry at her home on the Upper East Side. It was my first visit. They were fourteen stories up, just below the penthouse. The Tinkers' home was an entire floor. Rosemary Tinker, tall, lovely, greeted me and gave me a tour of the lavish premises. There were eight bedrooms, four baths and two kitchens, one for the family's food, one for the servants'. A gigantic dining table and a crystal chandelier. A study with a huge library. A den with a whole wall of CDs and a massive flat-screen TV. A hot tub and a sauna.

It didn't look like a private home but resembled what I decided to call it from that point on: The Palace.

They had a butler, three housemaids, and a French cook who asked me what I would like for lunch. The servants wore black suits or dresses like in a British manor house. The cook was a middle-aged lady.

"How about quail?" I joked. "I never had that."

I expected her to roll her eyes, but she nodded. In a moment she had retreated to the kitchen.

"I didn't mean it," I began to Rosemary.

"No, no, it will keep her busy," Goldberry's mother said.

"Or else she'll gossip all day," Goldberry added.

"Why don't you children play in the study?" said Mrs Tinker. She knew we were going to talk magic.

"Is the study private?" I asked Goldberry as we headed there.

"Nowhere is private here so we'll be careful what we say."

She shut the door and we sat together on the sofa. "Now, what's up?"

"Donovan told me the story of why your father and Dr Archer are enemies."

"*Did* he?" she said menacingly.

"Yes, he did."

"And I suppose Dad looks rather bad."

"I think they both do. "Well, they were all youthful fools," she concluded. "But we aren't, though."

"No?" I asked.

"We're smarter," she said.

"Smarter than your father and Dr Archer?"

Doubt flickered over her features. "Well anyway *I* am. And no one's separating us." She patted my hand, and I saw that she was wearing my mother's ring, now her ring.

"No," I said. "We're family forever.

"Something I need your advice about," my partner said. "In absolute confidence. Just the two of us, right?"

"Right."

"If you've anything to say that isn't *completely* stupid."

"I'll try."

She nodded. "I was with William yesterday, having a carriage ride round the park."

I didn't like that image in my mind. William Goodenough, her boyfriend, was a tallish, handsome, fair-haired young man, a year older. His manipulative smoothness and mind games made me hate the sight of him. Also, he had created a nasty nickname for me, 'Ladybug.' In response, I called him 'Jack Good'. Even though my love for Goldberry was like a brother's love for a sister, I thought Goodenough was a creep and not good enough for her.

"He said he wanted to be more serious with me."

"More serious?"

"His parents know my parents and he thinks we'd make a good couple."

A pause. "So what can I help you with?"

"Well..." She waved her hand. "I mean to say–does it really make sense to be that serious with him?"

I admitted, "You know I hate the guy. But you have been dating him a long time."

"I really should consider it then."

"Maybe he's different with you when I'm not around. But there's another problem. You're going out with Peter, aren't you?"

"Yes, this weekend. Don't worry about that. However he may be with you, he won't be any trouble when he's with me."

Late Night Call

I fell asleep early on Friday night. I dreamt that I was with friends from School of the Ages, although their faces blended and changed. I fell backwards, and above me loomed the smoking towers. Small dots sprang from the summit and plummeted–the distant specks that I knew to be people, I saw their hair flowing as they sped downward through the choking clouds–my parents, my grandmother Devi, Dr Archer, the Dean, Peter, all falling to their certain deaths.

Then I saw Leah's face blocking these visions, filling my field of vision . Glancing over her shoulder, she spoke sternly. "Enough. Get out." She turned to me and smiled, and when she smiled, from her mouth came a loud jangling sound.

The jangling noise was my cell.

"Get to Manhattan now," intoned Clive Tinker.

"Is that my last service to you?" I asked, bleary-eyed. "No, you imbecile. Goldberry's been attacked!"

I was up and dressed in minutes. I banged on my parents' bedroom door.

"What?" my father called sleepily.

"Goldberry's been attacked. I have to go to the Tinkers'. Will you drive me?"

Soon we were in the car, on the Long Island Expressway, bound for the Midtown Tunnel. It was 3 A.M. Traffic was light. There was dampness in the air perhaps rain or snow was imminent.

"She was attacked? That's all you know?" my father asked me.

I was slowly figuring things out. "Wait, I'll try thought trading."

"You'll try what?"

I explained it to him and he said, "Okay, go ahead."

Goldberry, what happened?

I got an impression of hysterical sobbing.

"She's not really able to answer," I told my father. "But it was bad. When I find out who did it…" But I couldn't finish the threat. It suddenly sounded foolish. I would do anything I could to get to the people who had attacked her.

My father put on his hands-free cell phone headset. "Call Clive." He got a quick answer. "What happened?" he said into the phone. "Yes, we're on the way." Listening. "Why, what does he have to do with it? … *Oh God!*"

Fortunately we found street parking. We headed up to the 14th floor and Clive Tinker met us at his door. "What happened?" I asked, trying to be calm. "Where is she?"

"With her mother. Look, Moore, I'm not saying your boy was to blame, but…"

"How was I to blame?" I asked. "I would die to protect her."

"Not you," my father said. "Peter. Their date was tonight."

"And?" I turned to Mr Tinker. He said, "So far as I can tell, the date went fine. The boy was well-behaved. But as they left the restaurant, he became very different. And when they got into his car, two others were already there. And then your son wasn't your son at all. I don't know what they did but she was in pain."

"It was Gott im Himmel," I said. "Let me see her."

"She's with her mother. What are you going to do?"

"Why did you call me here, then?"

I decided to press him. "I want her to know that I came for her.

You'd do that for your partner. Anyway, I hope you would have."

He was red-faced already, and now his breathing quickened. He must have found out that I'd researched his history at the school. "That's not your business."

"I've made it my business. I'm a sorcerer now, Mr Tinker, and my instinct is that I need to know."

"Know what?" my father asked.

"About my past," said Mr Tinker. "But his every word smacks of Solomon Archer. Those are Archer's tricks."

"Well, if you want to teach me some different tricks, do it! I have to beg or bargain to get something out of you. And you have taught Goldberry nothing too."

"I'm upset tonight, Simon," Clive Tinker said. "It's a bad idea to challenge me."

"I'm not challenging you," I told him, backing off, forcing myself to calm down. "I came here to help you. I'm just trying to say you could do something to teach us, for next time, instead of just getting angry."

Mr Tinker said. "Moore, rein in your boy."

"Fine," my father said, pressing on my shoulder to make me sit. "But I understand why Leicester wants to see Goldberry. How about it?"

"It's a warded room. Family only."

"I'm family," I said.

He gave me a dark stare.

"Adopt me," I said gently. Not a command, but a plea.

Clive Tinker thought about it. Finally he gestured to the secret hallway I had been steered away from during my tour of the house. "Go on."

Disturbing Details

When I knocked, Rosemary Tinker came out of the bedroom. She wore a long-sleeved dress. "Come in," she said.

Inside the secret room there was only light from a candle. I found my partner lying on a divan in the center. The candle was on a table next to it. There were two folding chairs, one on either side. Goldberry was wrapped in a large sheepskin blanket. She wasn't moving. Her face was shiny and wet. Blood? No, tears. Taking a chair, I found her left hand emerging from under the blanket and held it. She was wearing the ring.

"Goldberry. Partner."

She opened her eyes.

"Do you want to talk?" I asked.

"What they did," she whispered. "I can only remember pain. It hurt."

"Who?"

"Kaiser Petrus was there. I heard the name."

"Did you see…?"

Goldberry squeezed my hand tightly. Her nails cut into my palm. "No faces. Just your brother, and a woman in a black veil. And another man with a beard. Your brother was possessed, sounded like an old German witch. He said, '*Ich esse ihre Gehirne und Herz.*' Mother, what is that?"

"Don't worry about it, Goldberry," said Rosemary Tinker,

"So it was Gott im Himmel," I said. "I think I understand what they did. They did something to Peter that night–when Hélène's gang beat him up in my house so they could track him down later and possess him. Those four were there to find someone non-magical to attack first. Maybe they were expendable, and their masters didn't know I'd be alone when they attacked."

"You may be right," she said weakly. "What is *ich esse*? I eat? I eat what?"

"Oh, not now, Goldberry," said Mrs Tinker.

"Why didn't they kill me?" she asked.

"Thank God they didn't," her mother answered. "But what surprises me more is that I didn't sense this coming. I should have gotten ill. These people…"

"They hid it from you?" I asked. Normally Mrs Tinker, a skilled diviner and fortune-teller, became sick when she sensed possible future threat to her family members. "How could they hide it?"

"You can't hide the future," said Mrs Tinker. "So they must have aimed a spell directly at me, to dull my awareness. I was feeling quite well all day."

Letting go my hand with a slight pat, Goldberry sat up a little, but grimaced and slumped again. "How can they know us so well?"

"Well, that goes both ways," said Mrs Tinker. "Magicians can hide in their rat-holes, but these fools are in my territory tonight."

"Mine too," my partner said. She closed her eyes in a way I knew meant her mental tarot trick. This was a special technique she'd developed in school the year before that let her read tarot cards she visualized in her mind rather than cards she held in her hand. She used it to get immediate answers to minor questions and went on to more complex divinations later if needed. This time though it didn't work. Because we had recently thought-traded, we were still mentally connected a little, and I felt a heavy pain radiating outward from her. She couldn't focus or concentrate.

……………………………………………………………………………

"Not to worry, dear. Mummy will do it." Mrs Tinker took a tarot pack out of her pocket. Goldberry was good and in fact was doing important work for the school already, but she had inherited her ability from her mother.

"If you find them," I said, "I'll go and kill them."

"No, no," said Mrs Tinker. "Let my husband do that. You don't have to kill anyone tonight. Keep still dear." She laid down a spread of cards on the sheepskin.

A lot of people think tarot reading is fake. They think that for two reasons. One reason is that a lot of tarot readers, just like professional psychics, are fakes who do it for entertainment and prey on the nervous and weak-minded. The other reason is that tarot reading tends to produce general or vague answers, and you have to add to them a strong power of intuition to realize how to apply your results. I couldn't do it. I had tried many times but divination didn't work for me and all my magical information came from sudden cold flashes of understanding. They were usually there when I really needed them, but I couldn't control them, and I was commonly said to have "no talent for divination." Goldberry, however, was a prodigy. She could do any type of divination successfully, and she knew many that few people had heard of. Tarot and tea leaves were her naturals but she periodically tried other methods to fit the problems we faced. Mrs Tinker's deck was unfamiliar to me and I couldn't make sense of the cards. "Well there's your date, my dear. Jack of coins reversed. Not himself certainly. I wonder where he's gotten to. Yes, the Empress reversed–evil woman with worldly power–seems like more than one. A knight comes in, in the future. Swords. Is that you, Simon dear? It's not my Clive certainly: he is more the Emperor. But where are these miscreants? Nothing here signifies location. That's obvious. The cards are giving me general answers. What I want to know is hidden." She threw down new cards on top of the chariot and the four, but the new ones didn't satisfy her either. "I can't get the answer this way," she concluded. "I could try my crystal ball, but there's a malign influence this month."

She gathered up the cards and pocketed the deck. "Simon dear let her rest. I'll walk you out to your father."

"I'll stay," I said.

"Come along dear and don't be a bother," she said. "You can't help any more here. We'll see you tomorrow for lunch if you like."

"It's all right," Goldberry told her mother. "He can stay."

"No it's not. Go to sleep. Simon, let's go."

There was no point in arguing. We stepped out into the corridor.. "Did anyone call her boyfriend?" I wondered.

"Of course not," said Mrs Tinker. "She was out with another boy when it happened and from what I've seen, William is too sharp not to ferret out that particular detail. It will have to be attended to, but not tonight."

She was right. "What about the Dean and Dr Archer?"

"We've called the Dean. Your Dr Archer wouldn't be admitted here."

No he wouldn't. Clive Tinker hated him from when they were young men.

We came into the living room. My father was on his cell. "No, Kotone, I understand that. But..." He listened. "Okay, I will. I understand." He disconnected. "Peter hasn't come home," he said. "It's not unusual for him to stay out late so she isn't worried but I think we should try to find him."

"What did you tell her?" I asked him.

"I said his date had lost her cell phone. She had probably left it in his car?"

"That's lame."

"It is, Moore," Clive Tinker said, "but you are right, he should be found." He turned sharply and called down another hallway. "Belisarius!"

A small boy in a tuxedo appeared from the hallway. He had very large wet green eyes and pale skin, and his nose was somewhat pointed. He looked about him nervously, and finally started staring at me. I saw that the crystal around my neck was protruding partly from under my shirt and tucked it in.

"Have you got a picture?" Mr Tinker asked.

My father got one from his wallet. Mr Tinker gestured for him to give it to the boy.

"Belisarius, find this boy and bring him here. If he's guarded, come back and tell me where."

Belisarius nodded and went out the front door shutting it gently.

"Who was that?" my father asked. "You're sending a boy?"

"It's not a boy," Mr Tinker said. "I don't endanger children. That's Archer's job."

My father made a puzzled noise.

"It's a spirit servant," I said, cutting him off. The remark about Dr Archer bothered me, but I understood he was upset, and it wasn't a good time to argue that point.

Mrs Tinker left us. We sat looking at each other until she came back. "I've looked into the crystal ball but not much result as I had expected. The stars are aligned against crystal-gazing; I knew that since Monday and these people seem to have known as well. They had planned their attack accordingly. I did obtain a name, though I saw it written on a paper on a desk in a stone building. Probably the same building in Europe that Goldberry has been trying to view since last year. The name is H E Myra. Not familiar?"

"Initials?" Mr Tinker asked. "Spell it."

She spelled it out.

"I haven't heard it," I added. "I'll ask Dr Archer."

Thought trading would only work if he was awake.Dr Archer, have you heard of someone called H E Myra?

My cell phone rang.

....

"Simon, I believe you wished to talk to me?"

I didn't wonder at his being awake at four in the morning. Whenever I saw him, he looked as if he rarely slept.

"The name has something to do with Gott im Himmel. Does it mean anything to you?"

"I do not know it," he answered. "However, it has given me a strong feeling of dread. I must now resist my wish never to have heard that name."

"Could it be Kaiser Petrus, I mean, his real name?"

"There is proximity," Dr Archer said. "I cannot specify, Simon. This question has come at an odd time."

"Yes, but I can't talk more now. Can you call me tomorrow?"

"You may call me when you are ready." He hung up. I checked my caller-ID on the cell phone, expecting to see my own number, as had always been the case when he or the Dean called me in the past. But there was an actual number there, with a 212 area code–Dr Archer had given me his phone number.

"The name is important," I said, "but he doesn't know how."

"Of course not," replied Clive Tinker. "But someone is sure to be injured trying to find out for him."

We sat looking at each other.

"Is there anything else we can do for now?" my father asked. "If not, I'll take Leicester home, and we can talk in a few hours."

"Nothing else. Go home, Moore. Thank you for coming." The fathers shook hands.

"Call us with any news?" my father said.

"Anything on your missing son, I'll call you," he promised. "As for this one," he added looking at me, "I suggest keeping him indoors. He has blood on his mind, but whatever Archer thinks, he's not ready for these foes yet."

I wasn't sleepy as my father drove us home. I wanted to find

Kaiser Petrus and his allies to get revenge. I was quiet, and I thought my expression was blank, but at a deep level, where I could just feel it, a kind of itch began to develop. I had the urge to violence. It was like there was blood on my hands already.

More Aftermath

Here's what happened over the next few days. Belisarius found Peter sleeping in his car in a parking lot by Sheepshead Bay. He had no memory of anything after getting dressed for his date the night before. The Tinkers put him to sleep and had Belisarius drive him home.

Goldberry recovered well under her mother's ministrations. She called me the next day, but still couldn't describe what had happened or do any divination. Whenever she tried to use her mental tarot trick or use any standard divination like throwing the cards or reading tea leaves, she would get a sharp pain in her head and a feeling of overwhelming anxiety in the pit of her stomach. Meanwhile, her boyfriend William was calling her every day but she wasn't picking up his calls. Sharp as he was, he would have been able to get the story out of her that she was out with another young man–my brother–and that would have meant trouble for Peter, for me, and for Goldberry herself.

I called Dr Archer and told him the real details of the incident as I knew them. He acknowledged there was nothing he could do to help my partner while she was with her parents, and they were certainly better suited to help her. He told me that he regretted her being attacked, but that I should not worry about her or do anything rash out of a desire for vengeance.

"The enemy's strikes are bold and sudden," he said. "They tempt us to react without adequate planning. Instead, we shall plan, and then attack with swift precision."

"What happened to the prisoners, Dr Archer?"

"Clive Tinker did not tell you?"

"Nothing. I didn't ask him. I should have."

"Well," he said, "Yves le Maitre was of no help so we put him on a plane back to Paris. Delphine, however, the young girl from your basement is a minor so to hold her prisoner seemed to us unethical. We sought to identify her parents and found she had only a seriously ill mother. The Dean flew with Maestro Morgan and Delphine to Paris to see the mother who immediately requested our assistance caring for her child. Accordingly, the girl has been enrolled at School of the Ages. I believe we have saved her from a difficult life. She should prove an adroit learner of School of the Ages magic. I assign to you the task of welcoming and encouraging Delphine. She is a cheerful and pleasant child but deeply in need of positive role models."

"Okay, Dr Archer, I'll do that. Thank you, by the way, for giving me your phone number."

"Indeed, Simon, I am still your mentor, but we are now also fellow-soldiers in a bitter war."

❖ ❖ ❖

Each day after that, I called Peter's cell phone. He had refused to give me the number but I got it from my father. Peter never answered. I finally tried the home number. Again, there was no answer for a few days, but finally the phone was picked up by his mother, Kotone Murasaki, who had a light Japanese accent. I asked for Peter.

"Who is this?"

"Leicester Moore."

"I'm sorry?"

"Martin's other son."

She sighed. "Peter, talk to him."

A muffled sound indicated she was covering the receiver while she talked to her son.

"What do you want?"

"I'm checking to see how you are."

"What do you care?" Peter was very hostile.

"We're brothers."

"I was better off without a brother," Peter said. "You're nothing but trouble for me. Quit calling me."

I understood why he was angry. He could have hung up on me but he didn't, so I wasn't giving up yet.

"Peter, some time I'll try to get you to change your mind about me. But first I have to take care of the people who did this."

"As far as I'm concerned, you did it," Peter said. He cursed at me and hung up the phone.

Later that day we went to pick up the cats. They had been in shock but were recovered and showed no signs of injury as they resumed their normal life.

Busted

Robbie called me a few days later to invite me to go to Miami with him. His parents had bought a ticket to take Avery but her mother said she wouldn't be safe so far from home.

In Miami, we visited Miami-Dade Academy of Mystic Arts. It was a magic school run by LaDavid Kenyon–who was the nephew of School of the Ages' master summoner Mr Phillips. We also had café Cubano, a form of super-strong coffee that made me sick but had no effect on the Ravitzes.

After the trip to Miami, there were only a few days left before school started. I spent them making the magical objects Dr Archer had assigned me. I started with the protective amulet. To start there was a silver chain that had belonged to my mother's father, Saul. I took a scrap of stationery and copied out a nonsense poem.

I put this poem into a matchbox, covered it with tape to seal it, then punched a hole through the tape with a large nail and threaded the chain through that hole. Then I did a magical ritual using notes from Rabbi Horn's class.

Next I had to make an object for picking locks. It had to be metal. I had an antique British coin with a picture of Queen Victoria on it that was a gift from one of my uncles, Bertram Moore. Using a magnifier and a pen-knife I wrote some elemental earth signs and Hebrew letters on it where they would not be noticed, did a ritual as best I could, and put it into my wallet.

An object for protection against physical harm was next. Not another amulet, I thought; I already had two things to wear around my neck, including Leah's crystal, which I never took off except to hold it in my hands. I didn't want to wear a ring since my flesh still crawled at the thought of Yves Le Maitre, but... I thought of Helene and her scarf. I had scarves, but I took one of my father's from the attic with his permission. It was grey and very heavy. My markers and paint didn't write on it well, so I figured it should be embroidered, but I wouldn't be able to manage that. Rabbi Horn had taught us ways to work with cloth. I could sew a little since I used to help my mother when I was a child in Long Island. Using a sewing machine and silver thread, I managed to stitch some words and symbols along the edges of the scarf and practiced wearing it so that they didn't show.

That left me only with the hardest one–the weapon.

I couldn't decide about the weapon yet. I decided to get advice from my friends at school and let it go for the moment. That was where things stood on the first day of school. The bus came early to pick up my mother so she could be with the Dean before the students arrived. I considered going with her, avoiding the ride with the new kids but I had delayed my packing too long and wasn't ready yet.

When the bus picked me up, Robbie, Avery, Rocco, and Balaram were already there, but after giving them a smile, I sat by myself, looking out of the window. Goldberry was riding to school in her father's car as she was still recovering from the attack.

Some of my friends I haven't mentioned before in this book. Rocco was an athletic curly-haired boy from Manhattan who had been involved in a long-running battle with Yakov Mermelstein over a girl the previous school year. I'll talk about Yakov later. Rocco's specialties were sports and hiding in shadows. Balaram, an Indian boy from Yonkers was Robbie's study partner. He summoned spirits and sculpted in clay.

William Goodenough was on the bus, but he was on his cell phone enabling me to avoid saying hello.

Rocco's odd study partner, Corby Crow, was also on the bus, but as usual, he sat by himself in the very back row with his black cape over his face. Corby didn't live in the school, and he never hung out with anyone. He only studied with Rocco for tests. Usually we forgot he was around.

There were some new kids–two fair-haired thirteen year-olds in matching grey suits right by the bus door, and a stout kid in a blue coat who was reading, also a thin Indian girl. I ignored them all.

I had begun to stare grimly out of the window when the Indian girl came and sat by me. She was wearing a red dress under her fur-lined winter coat. Her hair was pinned back with a red clip. She had a round serious face with very deep, wise eyes. She had to be thirteen but her eyes looked older. There was something familiar about her, a little bulbous quality to her nose, a kind of nervous determination in her expression, which seemed very familiar to me. I could tell I wasn't going to be able to get rid of her easily.

"I think you are Simon Magus? Is that correct?"

I nodded.

"I am Miss Chatterjee." Her voice was soft. The Smoot Prep bus was taking it easy, going with the flow of traffic. "I have wished to meet you and your friends."

"You're related to Dr Chatterjee," I said.

"He is my father. Do you know my brothers?"

Dr Chatterjee's two sons had already graduated from School of the Ages. I had never met Chatterjee Major, who graduated before my time, but I had seen Chatterjee Minor, who was a senior during my first year there. Now this girl was the latest in the family to attend our school.

"Maybe you can explain to me," I tried, "why he looks identical to Mr Bannerjee."

"That is very complicated," she said. "I am ready to tell you, but we must be friends first. Will you agree to that?"

"I don't bargain with friendship. Tell me, why did you pick me to talk to?"

She looked down at her lap. I was left to continue the conversation. "What kind of magic are you interested in?"

"All kinds."

It was maddening. She wanted something but was leaving me to figure it out. I could just ask her directly but I didn't want to be rude to a younger kid. She was the daughter of our school mysticism expert and the sister of two reportedly very capable magicians, so I wouldn't want trouble with her, anyway. I decided to ask indirectly. "Can I do anything to help you get settled? Tell you about the teachers, introduce you to anyone, show you around the building?"

No response.

"Who is your advisor?"

"Dr Chatterjee."

"Your father is."

"Yes."

"Won't that be awkward?"

"I think he would be advising me anyway if I were assigned to someone else." Then she gave me more silence.

"Who's your study partner?"

"Miss Jonathan. She is seated in front with her brother."

"And your roommate?"

"Her name is Delphine. I am told she is very young. Do you know her?" asked Miss Chatterjee.

"No. But you can introduce me later."

Silence.

"Oh, you haven't met her either."

Silence.

"You guys have lunch with me and my partner sometime soon."

....

"We will." Miss Chatterjee rose and moved to an empty seat. So that was what she wanted.

Goldberry, I just had a weird conversation with Chatterjee's daughter.

She wasn't particularly interested.

We have to have lunch with her and Delphine.

Babysitting wasn't one of my partner's favourite pursuits I know, but she preferred it to the lecture from her father she was presently burdened with in the car.

I couldn't help smiling at the warm feeling of recognition this traded thought gave me. That feeling went away immediately, however, when the space next to me was occupied by someone who reeked of hair oil.

"Ladybug," he said. William Goodenough, my arch-enemy, tall, handsome, nattily dressed, a Manhattan old-money aristocrat. The image of him being serious about my partner disgusted me.

"Jack Good," I replied. "What's the matter? No chauffeur today?"

"I was rather hoping to meet Goldberry this morning. I thought she would be on the bus."

"Why don't you go look for her in the wheel wells?"

"Snippy, Ladybug. Snippy. But I think you know what I want to know, which is why she's avoiding my calls."

I knew why; she didn't want him to find out she had gone out with my brother Peter. "That's not my business, Goodenough. I'm not dating her. You are."

He sighed. "Look, Simon, I don't care for you, but I do care for her. That's common ground. Help me."

"I don't know anything."

"Of course you do."

"Well, I don't trade in knowledge and gossip like you do. She decides what to tell you. That's not my call. It's your relationship."

He nodded tensely. "I understand. Perhaps you can tell me something about yourself. Word is you were attacked."

"Yes, that's not a secret."

"Why didn't you call me? I could have helped."

This question surprised me and I couldn't hide it. "Why would I call you? What reason do I have to trust you?"

Goodenough put on a shocked expression. "Personal rivalry aside, we stand together when the school is threatened."

"Yes, but your problem is that you want to be trustworthy sometimes and obnoxious other times. I know you were there with us on 9/11, and I know we fought together in Paris, but my friends are people I can trust all the time."

"Oh?" he said. "And what makes you so trustworthy, little man? You have your games to play. You've tried to keep me away from Goldberry."

"I never did. She knows that you and I have issues, but she keeps that separate. I wish she had a better boyfriend than you, but it's been two years now, so what can I say?"

"I know you're involved, Simon."

"Don't blame me for your problems."

"Then help me now and tell me why she won't talk to me."

He wasn't just talking; he was using focused will, applying this pressure with magic in a way I didn't understand. It was very difficult to resist his magic and usually he got something out of me. Today the force he was applying was stronger than usual so that I could hardly keep track of my own thoughts. I had to make some kind of concession.

"What if I promise to tell her that she needs to talk to you as soon as possible? I'll do that, if..."

"If what, little man? Guilty conscience weighing you down?"

A small part of me–that part of my mind not engaged in battling his psychological control, told me to attack him, to put him on his knees, to sting his eyes. I couldn't do it, though. I couldn't muster the concentration.

"If you keep away from Ms Gale," I managed.

"Why, little man? Why is the well-being of the Dean's charming henchwoman so important to you?"

I was caught in his trap. To stop telling Goldberry's secret, I had had to shift his attention to one of my own. And now he was onto something he had wanted to know for over a year. But as he smiled, I actually became light-headed from the way he was messing with my mind.

"Because the Dean asked me to..."

"You're lying, Ladybug. Out with it. Got a little crush on her?"

"No, she..." Why couldn't I resist him as well as usual? Had he been preparing this attack for a long time, or was it reinforced with magical objects? I looked around desperately and then I saw the two kids at the front of the bus, the ones in the grey suits, leaning over the back of their seat looking directly at me. They were helping Goodenough! I had to put them out of action.

Closing my eyes, I visualized them—a pair of cobras dancing, heads bobbing on the other side of the leather seat back. What controls cobras? The *fakirs* in India used baskets. So I visualized two straw baskets and dropped them over their heads. I opened my eyes. Goodenough was still leaning towards me.

I checked the two kids. They had dropped out of sight. I hoped they had bad headaches, the rats.

"Playtime is over, Jack Good. Your henchmen are out of the picture for the moment." His smile faded. He looked over his shoulder.

"Robbie! Rocco! Avery!" I called. My friends' heads bobbed up. They saw me trapped in my seat by Goodenough. All three stood up. The two kids in the front got up again.

There was a sharp jerk. The bus had pulled over onto a tiny grassy margin of the Jackie Robinson Parkway, an impossibly small space. Mr Saluto, the driver, stood in the aisle. "You kids sit down and cut it out," he called.

Goodenough slid out of the seat. "We're not finished," he told me.

He looked at my friends.

My friends volunteered to back me up in a battle against him and his cronies. I told them I wanted to cool things off and see if I could meet the cronies–Miss Jonathan and her brother–privately to smooth over any hurt feelings, or at least take their measure. They were only thirteen, but even novice magicians should never be disregarded. After I told Robbie and the others about meeting Miss Chatterjee, they all went and introduced themselves.

Rocco sat by me a little while later and told me that intramurals were going to be hot that year, and he needed me to help out.

"The Cabala school team has this kid Lowenthal who's like six feet six at age thirteen," he explained. "And Finkel's little brother, Yonah, is supposed to be really good at hockey. And they still have Shifrin, he's a senior. Haim Fox called me up last week and said they were going to kick our asses." "I'm not good at hockey," I said. "What can I do?"

"You're good at hexing," he said. "They're allowing sideline magic starting this year, so long as the person doing it is out in the open. I'll take care of the action on the court, but King's the best hexer I have and he's playing."

"What about Corby?" I asked, looking back at his study partner. "Can he hex?"

"Who the hell knows?" Rocco said shrugging. "He hardly even comes to class."

"But he's a Russian, isn't he? He might be a hockey fan."

"He might be. He never tells me anything."

I didn't know what to make of this information. "Okay, I'll back you up," I told him, "but just use me if you have to."

"Fox is a senior, and he wants to win," Rocco warned me. "I'm pretty sure I will need you."

Goldberry's Dismay

Robbie and I dumped our stuff in our room and went to the girls' room. There we found Clive Tinker still making a lot of grim remarks, while Rosemary was sitting with Avery on her bed showing her a small pocket crystal ball. She greeted me with a peck on the cheek. "I think you got through to my husband that night," she told me. "Clive," she called. "Do you have something to talk to Simon about?"

He rose. "Yes," he said. "Come here."

I looked at Goldberry. She shrugged.

I pulled up a chair and sat by Mr Tinker.

"From talking to my daughter, I know that even in your first year, you were all able to take advantage of probability somewhat, especially on 9/11. Am I right?"

I didn't like to think about 9/11, but he was right. In the intense atmosphere of that day, I had done a few spells including making face masks appear in a store drawer where the clerk had said there were none. It's not possible to create objects with magic, but you can make them appear from elsewhere, if you have a proper technique. Adjusting probability was a good way to explain what I had done that day. They might have been there or not; no one knew. I decided they were there and since the chances were reasonable either way, I got what I wanted.

"I haven't done that magic much since first year," I admitted. "Goldberry is better at it."

"It's useful for finding things. That's only simple visualization. Any magician can do that if it's a mundane object. Need a pencil? Should be one in that drawer. Look, there is. Was there one there before? Who cares? The universe moves on. But probability magic is more useful than just that. See both possibilities clearly in your mind, side by side, and then pick the one you want and have it push aside the one you don't want. Then there is only one option."

"Easy enough," Goldberry said. "Mother put a thousand dollars cash in my wallet when I was sleeping," she added thoughtfully. "Didn't you?" Opening her chic handbag, she extracted her wallet, opened it, and found a stack of hundreds.

"Your mother won't recall doing that," said Mr Tinker, "but she did."

"Then she gave me a thousand dollars too," Avery said, but she was joking; she didn't check her wallet.

"There needs to be some level of probability, dear," Mrs Tinker said. "I haven't had a chance to hide anything in your bag. But I do have a gift for you."

While Avery tried on her new earrings, Mr Tinker told us more. "This magic works in battle. You have to have strong concentration, but with it, you can be very hard to hit. I tried to use it when I was playing rugby, but I couldn't focus well enough coming out of the scrum."

"How does that work?" Goldberry asked.

"Try to hit me, Radish," Mr Tinker told Robbie. "I'll close my eyes. Just hit me right in the face."

"You're kidding, right?" Robbie said. "I wouldn't mess with you without a really good reason."

"If you don't I'll drag you outside and pin you to the wall above the entrance doors." He closed his eyes.

Robbie cocked a fist but he looked nervously at Goldberry. She shrugged, "Go on."

Robbie swung clumsily at his face.

"You swung too far left," he said.

Robbie missed again.

"Keep trying. I'm only a foot away. You can't miss me."

Robbie got into a boxing stance–he looked silly–and threw a succession of punches. Although Mr Tinker's eyes were still closed, he swiftly countered each one with probability magic.

"Twinge in your side–you missed. Stance was wrong, swung wide. You pulled back at the last minute. Whoops, tripped."

Robbie stumbled but caught himself on the desk.

"Dude, that was nasty," he said. "My dad taught me a little boxing when I was a kid but I couldn't do anything right just now."

"Suppose he had hit something," said Mr Tinker. "I could have controlled the strength and angle of the blow."

Goldberry nodded. "Does it work on larger problems?"

"Can you make Kaiser Petrus accidentally fall from a rooftop to his death? Or change the outcome of a presidential election? Not with such a simple magic; you will need to do a whole sequence of strongly opposed actions. This magic is instantaneous. Do you understand it, Simon?"

"I understand," I said. I wasn't suited to this type of magic but Goldberry was.

Mrs Tinker gave me and Robbie our gifts for the first day of school, Montblanc pens and bars of fine Swiss chocolate. Then it was time for the Tinkers to leave. "Take care dear," Mrs Tinker said, kissing her daughter goodbye, and then the rest of us. "Oh," she added as she stepped into the hall. "William, how are you?"

Goodenough barged in, smelling fresh and looking good. He shook hands with Mr Tinker and pulled up a chair by Goldberry's side.

"So long," Mr Tinker said as they left.

"Would you all mind leaving?" Goodenough said.

"Yeah," Avery said. "I live here too, and they're visiting me." I could tell from her expression that she wanted to protect her roommate.

"I'd go," I told him, "but there's not much point. I'm going to hear about it later anyway."

"Oh leave off, William," Goldberry said. "Let's just talk. There's no privacy in this building anyway."

"Well, I'm worried," he said, giving me a vengeful look over his shoulder. "You haven't been taking my calls. Are you angry with me?"

"No," she said. "William, I was attacked. I've been recovering."

He whirled on me. "You didn't tell me this." Who attacked you, Goldberry? I'll kill him."

"It was three Gott im Himmel magicians."

"Three… What, those French cretins?"

"No. Adult magicians. Cabal members. We don't know who they were exactly, but Kaiser Petrus was there himself."

He turned back to Goldberry. "It doesn't fit. If you were attacked, you still should have taken my calls. That's not the reason."

"William, try to understand. I really shouldn't even be here but I don't want to miss classes and get behind on school work. When they attacked me, they did something to me that stops me from doing divination. When I'm in proper form, it's like the world around me has a kind of a hum in the background, like singing on a radio that's turned down really low, and I can just reach out with whatever the technique is and turn up the volume. You know? But I can't hear that singing anymore. When I try to turn it up, I get dizzy, I get headaches."

"Oh my God," Robbie said. "That sucks. Uh, you'll recover from it, right?"

"My mother says so, but we don't know how long that will take."

"Can you do other magic?" Avery asked.

"Yes, anything except divination. It seems like they attacked me just to get rid of the ability I was using against them. I don't know why they didn't just kill me."

"We can figure it out together, Goldberry," Goodenough said

soothingly. "We'll make it better." He took her hands in his, holding them gently, calm now, just wanting to care for her showing more tenderness than I had ever seen from him. But then, as I watched, his eyes narrowed. "You're hiding something." He lifted her hand till he could see the diamond ring on her finger. "What is this? A diamond solitaire? Looks like an engagement ring." All tenderness was gone; rage was simmering at the corners of his eyes.

"Don't, William," Goldberry said, but without force. Having dated him for two years, she was very emotionally connected. She didn't stop him from pulling the ring off her finger.

"Who would give you an engagement ring before I could?" he said aloud as he bent his head over the ring in his cupped hand. I realized he was testing it with psychometry, the ability to read mental impressions from objects. After a moment he looked up. "This ring was given to you by Ms. Gale, the Dean's assistant? That makes no sense, unless…" Lashing out, he caught me by the wrist. I quickly pulled free, but the moment of contact had helped his magic, and he had figured it out.

"She's your mother," he said to me.

"Goldberry isn't my mother," I said weakly.

"Shut up idiot. I know your secret now. Why did Simon's mother give you an engagement ring, Goldberry?"

"She said she was taking me as a daughter, William. And as her partner. It was so lovely of her, I couldn't say no. I was going to tell you. Simon and I aren't that way."

He nodded. "Oh, I know. Ladybug here hasn't the guts to go for a real girl." Remembering Leah, I wanted to smash him for that but it was the wrong time for a fight; it was my partner's moment.

"But then," Goodenough continued, "I still don't know why you wouldn't take my calls."

"I'll explain, William, but you have to stop being angry."

"Yeah, chill out," Avery said. "You're giving me bad vibes over here."

"Go on, then," he said. "Explain."

"When Simon was attacked his brother was there and he was beaten rather badly. He's not a magician. And when I was attacked, I was out with him. I didn't want to be, but…"

"You went out with Ladybug's brother? Why? After two years with me, you suddenly wanted a change?"

"No, it wasn't that. It was a bargain I made with him so he wouldn't tell his mother how he got beaten. I demanded an expensive date hoping he would back off but he got the money somehow. I didn't think he would. And the Gott im Himmel magicians, they possessed him during the date."

"That's why none of us were with her when they attacked," Robbie said. Perfect timing.

"You don't trust me anymore after I told you I loved you?"

"Of course I trust you," Goldberry said wearily. "But William, I wish you hadn't said it. I'm not ready for all that."

"After two years, not ready for a guy to say he loves you?" Goodenough was livid. "You really are a baby, Goldberry. It's a shame."

"I'm sorry, William," she said. "It doesn't make sense, but I just started feeling nervous when you said it."

He settled back in his chair. "You don't mean we're done?"

"Think so. Sorry."

"Nothing?"

"We can still talk."

"About what, Goldberry? About how you didn't have the courage to love? Or," pointing at me, "about how he got in the way?"

"I'm not in the way. I told her to go ahead and get serious with you if she wanted to."

"That's a lie," he said to me. "You wanted her to break up with me. Why?"

"I didn't do anything, Goodenough."

"Still lying," he said.

"It's not his fault," Avery said.

"We'll see," said Goodenough going to the door. "We'll see what condition you are all in when I am done."

"William, don't be like that…" Goldberry tried, but he was up and out of the room.

"Uh… Sorry," said Robbie.

"Get out of here, you prats," she ordered as she began to cry.

It was time to leave for Amsterdam Auditorium anyway. We shut the door behind us.

Orientation

The school assembled in the Auditorium for the Dean's first-day orientation speech. It was a gigantic room with a high ceiling. Given the school's lack of electricity, lighting was always unsatisfactory in this room, but collections of battery-powered lanterns, a gigantic overhead chandelier with many candles, and additional candelabra on small side tables did the job adequately. Usually all the students and only a few faculty attended this event, where we met each other after the winter vacation, sized up and were sized up by the new kids, and took care of pending business, educational, romantic, or confrontational. I had missed the speech last year when I was called out to talk to my mother in the Dean's office. This time it was my partner Goldberry who was missing, shaky because she was still recovering from being assaulted and because of the stress of her breakup. I had already met most of my friends, so I had only a few to catch up with.

As usual, I wanted to avoid any major issues with the aggressive personalities that surrounded me. One sure way to discourage Goodenough, the Jonathans, and other pests was to sit with Yakov Mermelstein.

Yakov was a big Chasidic Jew, now fifteen years old, with a long earlock and beard. He was six feet tall, stocky, wearing as always a black suit. He was a fierce fighter with a short temper. In the first year we had been enemies; in the second year we kept a respectful distance, and then finished on good terms. People saw us as natural rivals because we had fought in the past but come out even. Among Cabala students, he was the most dominant personality to have entered the school in the last few years. Most of the kids in the *yeshiva* weren't known very well in the non-religious part of the school, but everyone in the building knew Yakov Mermelstein, and believed correctly, that he was a dangerous enemy.

With him was his roommate and friend Meir Kupferberg, very much his opposite in most ways. Also Chasidic, Meir had a light frame, a youthful face and a friendly personality, so he was always smoothing over Yakov's messes, calming down both sides. Most kids who needed something from Yakov would talk to Meir, but as for me, I was fine with both of them.

They both nodded to me as I sat by them. "I saw that huge kid Lowenthal," I told them. "He was on the bus. You met him yet?'

"He lives around the corner from me," Mermelstein said. "My father did his *bar mitzvah* last summer."

"You should see his mother, not even five feet tall," Meir added. Then he looked up. A very young girl with blond hair, wearing a blue beret, jeans and t-shirt, was approaching us. She was dressed much as I had last seen her and clearly needed new clothes.

I said, "Delphine, right?"

"Yes. Yes, of course, you know me," she said in an adorable French accent. "I know, I know, I broke into your house and ate all your cookies." She handed me a folded napkin. "Here are some cookies to pay you back."

I put the cookies in my sweatshirt pocket. "Welcome to School of the Ages. I met your roommate, Miss Chatterjee, on the bus. You guys can come to us for homework help and stuff like that."

"Oh! Of course we will. Everyone is very nice here," she added.

"Not really, but my friends are, anyway."

"But," she continued, "maybe you can explain why all these boys are dressed so strangely. Almost half the boys in the room. Is it a club?"

"We're Jews," Meir said. "Ever heard of us?"

"Oh! The Teacher told me to hate Jews. I never understood why. I never met any Jews before and I don't like hating people."

"Who is this Teacher?" Meir asked.

"He lives in Paris," she said. "He is not a nice man. He didn't feed me every day and was always making me clean up. I think maybe he is an evil man. Maestro Morgan said to me, just the day I got here, that evil men have, lost their way to connect to the music of the universe. You think so?"

"That's a little too nice," said Mermelstein. "Anti-Semites like your teacher should have their heads crushed."

"Maybe," said Delphine. "I never liked the Teacher, but he did show me a little magic a few times. But I was always hungry! Look how thin I am. Say you two, are you nice? If you're nice, then I think I will decide the Teacher was wrong about Jews."

"I'm nice," said Meir. "Trust me, he was wrong. We have the best food. You should try the *holishkes* my mother makes.."

"I'm not nice," Mermelstein said. "But I don't eat babies, either. So here's a bargain for you. Your end is just to believe Jews aren't bad. My end is, if anyone ever bothers you that you can't handle, you tell them Yakov Mermelstein is your big brother."

"Oh! Thank you! I accept your bargain–but I think I can handle anyone." She laughed, looked around suddenly and ran off.

Meir turned to me. "Why did she break into your house?"

As I was filling them in on what had happened, I took note of who was in the room. As usual, the Rambal wasn't there; only his deputy, Rabbi Shulman, who was gaining weight and going gray, and the younger Rabbi Zylberberg, who always had a frantic, haunted look. There were a lot of new faces, mostly younger kids. The Jonathans saw me looking at them and gave me, angry stares. They were holding a grudge for the events on the bus. I would deal with it later assuming they cooled off enough to reason with.

The Dean finally arrived, accompanied by his two assistants, my mother carrying a stack of floor plans and other documents, and the registrar, Ms Roosevelt-Wilson, with our programs. There was some delay while everything was handed out. Then the registrar took the podium. A petite woman with a grey pixie haircut, she was always businesslike around students.

"Beginning this year, your floor plan maps are clearly marked," she explained. "If an area of the map is darkened, you cannot enter it. We are not relying on you to respect our ruling. Some of you insist upon opening unfamiliar rooms, correct, Radish?"

"I hate that hat," Robbie called.

"Instead," she continued, "you simply will not be able to locate any entrances to places not coded for your year. As always, there is bound to be a way around the prohibition, but don't expect it to be easy. We have reorganized our library holdings so that younger students may see some books. Third-years, you may now access the elementary *grimoire* library, located on the sixth floor. It is marked 'Refectory' on your map, and is modelled on the refectory of Santa Maria delle Grazie in Milan, although slightly smaller. The advanced *grimoires*, located in the Heptagon on the third floor, are only for seniors."

The Dean came to the podium. "We are pleased to welcome our new math teacher, Mr Súanpàn. Would you stand, Mr Súanpàn? He is joining us from the Hong Kong branch of British Wizardry Ltd."

That was a step up in the man's career, I knew. Goldberry had told me BritWiz was a second-rate school even in its main campus in Manchester. The teacher stood, a short Chinese man with plastic eyeglass frames. I was done with numerology and was returning to traditional high school maths, so he would be teaching me.

"Rabbi Dovid Kraus will be joining American Academy of

Cabala for one year," the Dean continued. "He is arriving next week. Additionally, I'm pleased to announce that soon, we will have a special public forum with retired School of the Ages faculty. The former teachers who have been invited are those who instructed many of the school's current faculty, such as Dr Archer, Dr Chatterjee, and your Dean. They are all quite elderly, so we insist that you do not attack them. You will be able to confer with them but do not tax them beyond their limits.

"Now to the main business. We would like to welcome the new students—seven new pupils and five transfer students. You should know that we declined a dozen more applicants. As usual in times of political uncertainty, interest in magic increases. "Welcome, all of you. As you are new to School of the Ages, I shall review the fundamentals.

"First principle is a regimen of daily meditation. Maestro Morgan supervises this event each morning, with an elaborate program of geometric visualization. All students must gather at 7 A.M. in the Great Hall, just around the corner from this auditorium. No exceptions. No sleeping late, and no being delayed in the bathroom."

"Too early, Dean," one of the Orthodox boys said. "What about *tefillah*?"

"*Tefillah* is at 6 A.M. Rabbi Mendy is always prompt, and *davening* is completed prior to meditation, so there is no conflict. If you are particularly hungry in between Finkel, we will have some bagels and cream cheese available each day at 6:45."

"Thank you, rebbe," Finkel called sarcastically.

"Through meditation," the Dean resumed, "you will develop advanced capabilities in the realm of mental focus. Again, it is not concentration or clenching of the will that we seek but a kind of relaxation which attunes the mind. You will attain via meditation a universal connection that enables what in business jargon is called multitasking. And what is that good for..." He gave me a split-second's warning with his eyes before calling on me. "Simon Magus?"

"We can keep multiple magic spells active at the same time," I answered. "It's like your brain has a bunch of compartments open and working at the same time, and they keep going when your main attention isn't on them."

"Like a computer running Windows inside your mind," Goodenough interrupted. "That's how I explain it on my website, which by the way I can update from here while my computer is plugged in at home. That's how magic is supposed to be done, Ladybug."

He had just put out the obnoxious nickname for the whole school to hear. Kids who knew us knew the score, but new kids might start using the nickname and so he'd just given me a respect issue to deal with. As angry as he had been less than an hour before, I knew there was more to come. As for his claim, if he was operating a computer remotely, it was impressive. That computer would have to be specially prepared, like all magical tools, with a construction ritual, but Goodenough was a year ahead of me and very talented.

"Moving along," the Dean continued, "there is next the principle of Universal Language. Those versed in spirit lore know that spirits are able to converse with anyone, disregarding concerns of language. Using a technique developed at School of the Ages, our students are able to activate their spirits in order to speak with any person in any time. There are limitations. Universal language does operate when watching a film or television, but most users cannot translate musical lyrics when they are sung. Also, the principle has no effect upon written language."

"Why do people still sound like they have accents?" Balaram asked.

"There is no need for the technical explanation here," the Dean continued. "In practical terms, you should be able, by your third year, to move about in a foreign country and speak to everyone you meet. Like an electric light, you switch on universal language, and it remains on for your use without your having to hold open the switch.

"On now to the third principle, which is concealment. Concealment is the ability to go unnoticed by ordinary people. Using concealment, you may move past rank-and-file individuals, enabling you to perform such feats as passing through a dangerous neighborhood unmolested or entering public transportation unpaid. You will not be able to avoid the notice of anyone who is actively seeking you; nor can you hide from those who know you. Alert guardians can spot you, as can any normally attentive person who possesses a higher degree of magical skill or talent. For all of those situations, there are of course more advanced strategies. Note that we do not encourage you to use concealment in support of theft or any other kind of criminal activity. Criminal behavior tends to cause anxiety and anxiety tends to cause concealment to fall away."

The Dean continued. "The final of our four principles is continuous defense. Continuous defense is a kind of distortion of your time perception which enables you to recognize and react to an attack. Under continuous defense, an attack, physical or magical, will be known to you prior to its impact, and you should have an opportunity to analyze that attack and prepare a response. While continuous defense gives you a significant edge in battle, the quality of your response is a key element that you must develop in order to enhance your chances of escaping, surviving, or winning a battle.

"Magic is not necessarily an answer to every situation. As you know, it is unlikely to work when you are in the presence of individuals who are observing in disbelief. Subtlety is essential to create significant effects and the best magic is not seen at all. You will become accustomed to success here on the school grounds, but in the field, you are still advised to avoid danger as you would if you possessed only typical resources of intelligence and athleticism. Yes, Mr Jonathan?"

Still in his grey suit, the boy rose. "Sir, is it true that there is a discipline called continuous attack?"

The Dean regarded him with curiosity, awaiting an explanation.

"A discipline where anyone who approaches you gets attacked with the same power."

"Such as?" said the Dean carefully.

"Such as everyone who approaches you collapses with stomach cramps, or gets his hair lit on fire."

The Dean cleared his throat. "I believe this is a new question for student orientation. Mr Bannerjee will be the primary teacher in your Magic Theory I class so I will ask him to respond."

Mr Bannerjee, who resembled Dr Chatterjee exactly in face and build but dressed more like a sports coach, stood. "Aggression without subtlety not being encouraged," he said. "There is a tendency of such efforts rebounding, yes? What purpose serves this continuous attack?"

Jonathan looked at him with puzzlement. "Why do you talk that way?" he asked. "Are you sick?"

Mr Bannerjee did not back down from kids. "All words are in your vocabulary, everything you are comprehending. Back to you, same question. Why continuous attack? For what use?"

"You should know why," Jonathan said. "To impress and intimidate people so no one gets in your way."

"He could start by just being taller," Meir joked to Yakov and me.

"You have something to say, Simon Magus?" Jonathan shouted. I was seated nearby so I got the blame.

"Just joking," Meir said.

"Tell me your joke, I want to laugh." Jonathan was still focused on me.

"Shut up," Mermelstein barked. "It's a dumb idea, kid. Drop it."

Jonathan sat down. He would have to be crazy to take on Mermelstein.

"Thank you, Yakov," said the Dean. "Now, on to our final business. Intramurals will again this year feature three five-member squads. The squads will compete in basketball and floor hockey. I think many of you already have your equipment, correct, Mr Lowenthal?"

The huge kid laughed.

"We are pleased to allow a designated sideline hexer this year. It is a characteristic of league play which we have previously avoided due to the likelihood of injury, because School of the Ages students are generally quite good at hexing. However, we are shifting our policy. We feel that with the international situation continuing to look dire, and the near-certainty of an invasion of Iraq in the next few months, it is more important than ever that we in the community of magicians interact and form bonds of friendship. My counterparts in these other institutions agree. There are presently five schools in North America of size equivalent to ours, which should make for lively competition. That begins next year; we shall practice the new format in intramurals for one year; we begin league basketball in March of 2004 with a three-game series in California against San Francisco Hospitallers. Any questions?"

"Can we go play in Israel?" asked Finkel.

Psychic Scars

At meditation, after working with the younger kids, Maestro Morgan introduced a new exercise for the third year and up.

"Schrodinger's cat," he said. "This should be easier for you than for others, Simon Magus."

"Thank you, Maestro."

"A cat is in a box. You do not know how long the cat has been there. It may be alive, or it may be dead. Since either may be true, philosophy suggests that both are true until the moment the box is opened. At that moment the two possibilities resolve into one reality, but prior to that, the chances, living cat and dead cat, are functionally equivalent. According to Schrodinger, the mathematician, who speaks of probability, this cat exists in limbo, neither live nor dead till you open the package to learn its fate. Therefore, you students will form a visual model of two cats inside a box. One is quite decidedly dead. Perhaps flies are buzzing on it. The other is quite alive, and it is gradually cleaning its fur with a barbed tongue."

We began to work on this. I started to visualize Leo, our cat. I remembered him fighting fiercely beside me and loved him all the more for it.

"A beloved pet is not advised, Simon," said the Maestro. "The dead version will tend to be under-visualized. Goldberry, that is a puppy not a cat."

....

"Right, I'll get it in a moment."

The Schrodinger's cats were a difficult visualization in a static position. When we began to rotate the box, looking at them from above, below, behind, and from diagonals, it became intense. Even when visualizing the French gang, I hadn't seen them fully, only the parts that I wanted to use hexes against. Meditation was going to make me mentally tired for weeks, I thought. But Maestro Morgan was right that cats were easy for me to visualize, given the five I knew at home, especially Cougar, who had taken up the habit of standing on my chest and mewing to calm me down when I was having nightmares.

I decided I liked Mr Súanpàn, who taught in Chinese, forcing us to use universal language to understand him. The rest of my schedule was predictable. After the first day of classes, Miss Chatterjee appeared at the dinner table where my friends and I usually ate. She sat by us, setting down a tray of vegetarian food, resting her huge backpack on the floor by her feet, and ate without speaking. Balaram tried several times to engage her in conversation, but she never gave more than a quick, polite reply. After dinner, she followed us back to my room and sat at my desk studying while Goldberry and I studied sitting on the bed. Twice she looked up, asking for homework help, which we gave her. After about two hours, she rose, said "Thank you," and started to go.

"Miss Chatterjee," I said finally, "you can come here any time, but what about Miss Jonathan? Isn't she your study partner?"

"Josephine is with Jonathan this evening."

"Josephine?"

"Yes. Miss Josephine Jonathan and Mr Jonathan."

"His name is Jonathan Jonathan."

"Race-horses have more sensible names," Goldberry commented. "What sort of family is that?"

"Your boyfriend never mentioned them?" I asked her.

"Not by name. He only said there were some kids he knew coming to school this year. I didn't mix with all the city's important magical families growing up the way William did. Remember, my father didn't want me to attend this school or to be a magician."

That was true; she had applied to School of the Ages behind her father's back.

"Well, I want to deal with it," I said. "Miss Chatterjee, do you know where they are?"

Miss Chatterjee led me around the corner to Jonathan's room and I knocked.

"Go away," two matched voices responded from inside.

"I want to talk," I announced.

"You are denied entrance to my territory, Simon Magus," Jonathan announced.

"You can't do that," I called through the door. "The whole school is shared territory for all of us; your room doesn't give you any advantage. Come on, let me open the door."

The door burst open. Josephine Jonathan was there, a short girl in black jeans and a black jacket, with fair hair and angry eyes. "Begone, enemy!"

"Excuse me," said Miss Chatterjee. "Simon Magus is not an enemy. I don't think so. He is assisting the defense of the school."

Miss Jonathan lowered her eyes. "Why would you take sides against me?"

She did not answer the question. "You must study with me."

"I have family business tonight. That's more important."

"Look," I said. "I am not your enemy or your brother's. I have bad blood with Goodenough, but that's not your fight. Why don't you guys shake hands with me and make peace?"

"He can't be trusted," Jonathan Jonathan announced from inside. "Ask anyone except Goodenough and you'll hear something different."

* * *

He crowded into the door beside his sister. He was also wearing black jeans and a black jacket. "You liar! You've hidden your secret connection to the Dean! You tried to conceal your sabotage of our cousin William's love affair!"

"I don't have a secret connection to the Dean. He helped us with an assignment last year but plenty of people knew about that."

"Ms. Gale is your mother! You hid that fact from your fellow students!"

"I can name plenty of fellow students who knew. Do you want to meet her? I'll take you up there tomorrow. You can see the Dean and make your own connection, okay?"

"I also know the Dean," said Miss Chatterjee. "He is my father's friend. Dempsey was at one time my baby-sitter."

"You shouldn't trust him," Josephine Jonathan said, meaning me. "How can we be partners when you have an evil ally like him?"

'I'm not evil," I protested. "That's stupid. I came here to make up with you guys. I want to help some of the new kids, like you and Miss Chatterjee and Delphine. That's it."

The Jonathans slammed the door in our faces.

"It is distressing," said Miss Chatterjee.

"I'm sorry. I didn't mean to cause any trouble between you and your partner."

"It has been the same since I first met her. She is not a friendly girl. You must stand with me, Simon Magus."

"Yes I will."

❖ ❖ ❖

It was after the first week of classes that I had the most horrible dream I had had in a while. I saw Hélène La Méduse dancing at the foot of the bed spinning and cackling as her hair wriggled and twisted like real serpents, and a cat leapt up on the headboard, a cat that looked ordinary but familiar, and was smiling. It said "Unlucky in love." I began to shake, and Hélène stopped dancing and tiptoed to the side and began to whisper in my ear words in French that I could not fully understand.

There was a loud cough from the other side, and she jumped back. A thin, pale man leaned and said in a heavy Scots accent, "Wake up, ye loon." To Hélène, "Shove off."

I awoke, sweating in the cold room. I knew who the coughing Scotsman was: Tusitala, Madame Farfalla's spirit guide. It was time for mediumship class, which was always held in the middle of the night. The students were Goldberry and me, William Goodenough, and his study partner Mina. Mina did her best to seem aloof and mysterious, but wasn't particularly good at it, and this annoyed Goodenough very much.

We met in a windowless sixth-floor chamber called the séance room, which had no furnishings except a small round table and various chairs. Only one candle at a time would be lit in the room, and other kinds of lights didn't work at all. When I arrived, meeting Goldberry in the hall, Madame Farfalla, a fat redhead in her fifties was leaning over a crystal ball illuminated by the dim taper candle she preferred. Mina and William Goodenough were already there.

"Look deeply children. Inside this globe the spirits waltz. Yes?"

"Yes," said Mina.

"What do you see, Goldberry?" Madame Farfalla asked.

"I can't, sorry," she said.

"Why not? Out of sorts?"

"No, that's not it at all. But…"

"She was attacked," Goodenough said, "while she was cheating on me."

"I was not cheating," Goldberry protested. "I told you…"

"Children!" Madame Farfalla cried out. "My extra-material allies told me of this quarrel between you. Do not voice it here! Such angry emotion attracts negative entities!"

They both shut up. Madame Farfalla had been a medium for many years, and she had presence.

"We shall look into the matter further," the teacher continued, "but first, as we are beginning this course, some reading and assignments are required." She gave us textbooks and a month of homework, mostly historical reading and vaguely defined essays about it. The previous year, we'd only had three classes, so there was no work, but this time, we were to leave the written assignments in this room for Tusitala to collect.

Madame Farfalla always lectured, in this case about etheric and astral bodies, and then finished the class with a demonstration of séance technique, bringing in spirits to talk to us. Madame Farfalla's own voice and personality disappeared, replaced by that of her spirit guides, who then introduced the other entities in the area, most of whom talked nonsense. In this case, however, something useful came towards the end.

Falling Water, a young Native American girl was one of the frequent visitors to the séances. She liked to tell stories about the cruelty of the original Dutch settlers. Tonight she had something different to say: "One of these is grossly wounded." Her light, sweet voice always seemed odd emerging from the gaudy, bulky face of our mediumship teacher. "I am studying her etheric field, and it is covered with dark patches."

"Obviously Falling Water means Goldberry," Goodenough said. "What can be done about it?"

"I will try to remove the damage," said Falling Water. "No, no, it is very bad. I will need help."

I touched the crystal and said in my thoughts, Leah, can you help?

To my surprise, her actual voice came from Madame Farfalla's lips. "I'll try to help."

Goldberry winced. "My head. Oh, God, what are you doing?"

"Take it easy," Tusitala interrupted.

"Stop interfering," Leah said. The three spirits went back and forth arguing, their voices and expressions rapidly supplanting each other on Madame Farfalla's pudgy face. Goldberry put her head down on the table and moaned.

"It is difficult," Falling Water said. "Healing must be natural. A recovery of memories will be necessary, and she is not ready."

"I think we should stop," Leah agreed.

Madame Farfalla tilted her head back limply. "What happened? Some other spirit was bullying my guide. My dear, what happened to you?"

Goldberry was wiping her cheeks of tears. "It bloody hurt. It's a long story." I explained to the teacher in greater detail what she had suffered: Goldberry had been psychically attacked by enemies of the school, and the spirits had just tried to help her by removing the long-term damage.

"If she hadn't been cheating on me, I would have been there to protect her," Goodenough said.

"Oh, shut up," said Goldberry. "Simon, walk me back."

Avery was asleep when we returned to my partner's room. The crystal lying against my skin had a slight heat, telling me Leah was still annoyed with the other spirits. I tucked Goldberry in and slept in the chair.

❖ ❖ ❖

Dr Archer set the second-years to develop their first-response powers. A first-response power was a personal magical ability that would be used in a tough situation when there wasn't a lot of time to react. After a lot of discussion, Avery decided to develop one called "find a friend." It was sending out a mystical call to the area to get someone to come and help out.

Chimes

Classes went smoothly for a while, but as we came into February, I was feeling that something was going to happen. As my ability as a high sorcerer developed, the body sensations grew stronger–physical reflections of a mystic knowledge, or if you prefer, a psychic connection to the energy of the universe. Human beings experience time in a line, one event after another, and for the most part can't change that way of experiencing time. We magicians, however, can get flashes of something else. The school time-travel trips are an example; the sorcerer's experience is a small one. When the sensation comes, it's like feeling your body expand, and pieces of the future enter it, and while you don't know what they are exactly, you know what kind of pieces they are.

The feelings were transitory, and came unpredictably, and I didn't have a sense that I understood what to do, or even how to influence it.

I went to see Dr Archer. "Something will happen tonight," I told him. "On the roof."

"Thank you for telling me that," he said. "I was aware of a pending event, which is a reaction to one of my initiatives, but which apparently tends more to your interest than mine. I must participate, however. I shall make arrangements."

I ate dinner with Goldberry and Avery. Robbie was studying with Rocco and Balaram in the summoning lab. After we finished, I said, "Let's go to the roof."

"Good God, why?" Goldberry said. "It's bloody cold up there. The sun's going down."

"No, he's right," Avery said. "Let's go."

"Wait a tick." Goldberry did her mental tarot trick, wincing at the throbbing pain divination still caused her. The effort of Leah, Falling Water, and Tusitala in mediumship class had restored to her a small amount of her former ability. "Hmm, the Hierophant - an interpreter of the greatest mysteries in life. All right, that's got me curious."

"Only one card?" Avery asked.

"Yes," my partner said bitterly. "One card is all I can manage."

We heard howling as we climbed the stairs to the roof. "Big wind blowing up," Avery said.

The door was propped open; someone was already up there. We stepped carefully forward, looking left and right. Who would be waiting for us? Immediately we saw three figures, side by side, but then I remembered they were the three stone gargoyles that always stood on the roof: Kalkas, the eyes covered with the hands; Humperdinck, ears similarly covered; and Ellen James, with a covered mouth.

"Let's wait there," I suggested. We stood by the gargoyles. No one else was visible to the eye on the roof at dusk, but while advanced concealment was a fourth-year lesson, we had recently learned how to see through it. Scanning each region of the roof, we visualized doors opening and big feet kicking people through them. Using this method, I was able to spot Mina hiding crouched by the southwest corner, recognizable by the violet scarf she had been wearing earlier in the day. Then I found three teachers. They were on the other side of the gargoyles from us, standing stiffly in the traditional hooded robes School of the Ages faculty used to greet new arrivals.

A strong wind came out of the trees below, shaking them with a rustle and a whoosh, and blew across the roof, fluttering the teachers' hoods and chilling all of us. The sun was going down. Avery left and finding a nail already driven into the doorframe, hung some tiny wind chimes, which tinkled. She rejoined us and together we watched the sky. As we waited, a small speck seemed to emerge from the clouds right where a spot of orange remained from the descending sun. At first I thought it was a plane but soon we could all see it was something smaller. The blurred speck became two small grey shapes. As they drew closer we saw that they were two upright men in trailing robes, moving toward us as if standing on a descending escalator.

The two men halted hovering just short of the roof's edge and shrugged off their robes. The bigger of the two was a strong-faced man with a long beard, white hair and brows. The other was pale, with a fierce aquiline nose and long black hair tied behind him. The two surveyed the entire roof. We were not hidden, so their eyes focused on us.

I looked at our teachers. One nodded to me to begin.

"You've come to School of the Ages," I shouted to them. "I am called Simon Magus. If you come as friends, give us names to call you and we will greet you by them."

"Can it be that I am not recognized?" said the icy-bearded man in a deep voice. "I have been here before."

"I know you," Avery said.

"Then I offer you return greetings Boris, North Wind."

"Call me Avery," she said.

"Aye, mistress."

"Mistress?" said the other man. His voice was like broken bells. "Have we no compact, that you turn from me to her with scarcely a word?"

"A compact was forged two thousand years ago with her forefathers," answered Boris. "I am a fierce wind, but I do love this child. If there be battle she must not be harmed but I shall crush any other foe you command."

I had a moment to take in the fact that the man was commanding the North Wind. I hadn't realized that was possible. It was best to keep the situation calm. "Boris," I said, "you are as old as the world and known to all its peoples. You are welcome to stand on our roof if you will promise not to bring snow today."

"No more snow this season," said Boris.

I called Avery over and whispered in her ear. She nodded and crossed the roof, standing by the door and holding her wind chimes in both hands.

Boris alighted on the roof.

"Keep me waiting, will you?" said the other man.

"I have given you a name for me," I said, "but I don't have yours. That comes first."

"Very well," he said. "I am called Jan Vorkin, Arch-Mage and defender of the city of Prague. Your teachers came into my territory uninvited and unannounced, and now I am returning the visit in similar fashion. I see them there behind the statues. Do they know how to speak?"

"You're still speaking with me," I said. "Now I know what you are called, and I greet you, Jan Vorkin. You still must tell me your intentions." I wasn't frightened, because I don't get frightened, but the title he had claimed, Arch-Mage, was unlikely to be an empty boast. The Arch-Mage is the acknowledged world expert in a type of magic. Whatever type of magic he did, he was the best.

'And what about you, girl?" asked Jan Vorkin. "Who are you, and will you welcome me, or delay me, knowing who I am?"

"I am called the Daughter of Rosemary. I will delay you and there is no king in Prague."

His lip twitched. "Very well stubborn children. I am here to learn why your teachers came into my territory uninvited. After that, if there is no quarrel, then I will be your guest for a short stay. I am not an enemy, unless provoked. It is Prague that I am concerned with and my own private affairs."

"Then step onto our roof," Goldberry said, "but no further until invited."

Vorkin now stepped down and onto the roof. "Now, with all these formalities done, will you at last bid your teachers to step forward so that I may settle my business with them."

The three teachers came out from behind the gargoyles and put their hoods down: the Dean, Dr Archer, Dr Chatterjee.

"Ah," said Vorkin. "The Pedagogue, the Worrier, and the Yogi. You, Yogi, I remember creeping along the Vltava bank peering through your glasses. You didn't see me, and then when you did, you ran. Explain yourself."

"The matter was nothing to do with you, sir," said Dr Chatterjee. "We did not expect to find you present"

"I apologize for the intrusion," he said.

Dr Archer stepped forward. "My colleague defers to me to speak on this point. I am charged with the defense of this school. A man called Kaiser Petrus, leader of the Gott im Himmel cabal, has pledged to destroy School of the Ages. We were there seeking him."

"And if you find him in Prague, what then?"

"I will kill him," said Dr Archer.

"And if I say no?"

"Kaiser Petrus and his allies have attacked many of my friends and fellow students," I added. "You should respect that."

"And I should care about what you say?" he challenged.

"I claim that you won't enter this school without my permission."

Vorkin's expression flattened. His chest heaved, his brows arched. He took a step closer. I didn't move. He stopped and looked me up and down, then grinned and nodded. "And how may I persuade you to grant that permission?"

"Say that you are the enemy of Kaiser Petrus."

Vorkin nodded, understanding. "You have an odd way of going about things," he said. "Magicians should have better fellow-feeling. It happens that I have no objection to the death of Kaiser Petrus, or anyone else in that gang of trouble-makers and assassins. Now child will you permit me to visit your school?"

"Friend, or enemy?"

"Friend," he said.

"Then you have my permission to visit."

The Dean stepped forward and offered a handclasp. "School of the Ages is prepared to create a friendship with you, Jan Vorkin. To begin, freedom of operation, you in our territory, and we in yours."

"Done," said Vorkin. "I came here for exactly that reason. To be candid, you have a number of pupils that I want to meet. Here are three of them." He looked at Goldberry. "You are a lovely girl, Daughter of Rosemary, and clearly powerful enough to enter my circle."

"Not sure what that means," Goldberry answered, unease in her voice.

"Surprising. What of you, little breeze?"

"Maybe you know my friend," Avery said. She looked over her shoulder.

Mr N. Otis, the school's northeast regional recruiter, with his overcoat, hat, and briefcase, was striding across the rooftop, puffing a little so that we could see his breaths in the icy air.

"Thanks for coming," Avery said.

"I know it took a while," he said, "but I wanted to create some rain over Atlanta before rush hour ended." He nodded to his brother. "Quite a party, eh, Boris?"

"You command the South Wind, Avery?" Vorkin asked.

"Nah, he works for the school," she answered. "I asked him to come, that's all."

"Greetings, Notus," said the North Wind. "I expect she has called you here to oppose me, in case my master bid me attack. Fortunately, all are now on good terms."

"Fine, fine," said Mr N. Otis. "How you doing, kids?" We nodded.

"I recall, Notus, when Arch-Mage Aeolus used to pit us against one another for amusement," Boris said. "It was good to battle. What say you?"

"Yes, well, why not?" said Mr N. Otis. "Let's tussle. Anyone lightweight better get off the roof."

Wind War I

The teachers withdrew inviting Jan Vorkin to accompany them. "May I join you in a moment?" he asked. "I am curious to watch the winds fight."

"We shall await you in the Dean's office," said Dr Archer. "The students will show you the way."

A second later, Goldberry followed in the teachers' path, entering the door. I followed. We stood in the doorway.

That left only Avery.

Boris raised both hands and, like spreading tree roots, his fingers extended and branched and tangled up in the darkness. He took a deep breath, contracting so tightly that even his garments clung to him. Then he exhaled, bringing down his hands slowly, and as they descended, a violent gale came down also, its outer tendrils curling and twisting the dirt on the rooftop, flailing stinging bits of debris against our skins.

Soon I was able to perceive, even in the semi-darkness, that separate wind currents proceeded from each hand, and they lashed in turn across the tar roof, each driving wreckage before them.

The currents slapped and whacked at Notus, the debris clinging to his outline, fraying the edges of his form, causing him to buckle like wood twisted by great heat. His shape twisted, wobbled, flickered. Streaks extended behind the front of his image, almost as if he were being refracted by a prism.

Next to me, Goldberry shivered violently, but she continued to watch.

In the rush of grit and leaves, our friendly ally Mr N. Otis was spun and shaken too.

Boris' attack abated, and Mr N. Otis closed his mouth, smiled and shook himself, shedding dust in a massive cloud that then drifted backward and upward like smoke. Then he let go. Thunder crashed, and wild winds howled as he exhaled a blustering storm, and the leaves and roof junk scattered from the force of his breath.

Caught on the edge of this, Avery swayed backward. She let the wind chimes swing free in her hand, their previous soft tinkling replaced by a violent clinking.

When the assault struck Boris, he glowed. His robe shone glorious white and blue as it stretched out behind him. As the tempest battered him, his arms and legs stretched.

Mr N. Otis then became calm, and the two winds resumed their previous shapes and stood sizing each other up.

Mr N. Otis tossed his hat to Avery. She put it on. It looked cute on her. Then Boris let loose the winter storm. Winter gales struck and frost rebounded from the rooftop in great sprays like the crash of waterfalls against rocks. The bellowing of the storm was like the roaring of a thousand trucks in a tunnel. Chunks of hail, blocks of ice crashed around the South Wind and clung to him. I pulled Goldberry down and sheltered her with my body. My back was pummelled by gusts and the hailstones. It was painful, but it was beautiful too.

Setting down his briefcase, Notus brushed away the icy layers from his overcoat and passed it to Avery. Then, spreading his hands, he rose into the sky, and blue jagged flashes of lightning came from his eyes. He snapped his arms wider letting loose the lightning. Dozens of sparks and arcs and slashes were instantly between the two primeval beings, crash after deafening crash, till Notus and Boris appeared both as incandescent as the sun bursting through a grey cloud. Played out before us on the roof was a scene from the oldest days of the planet.

The battle done, both winds, walked towards each other, and shared a brotherly hug.

"A magnificent thing," said Jan Vorkin to us. "I believe they restrained themselves so as not to hurt us. Can you image what it would be for them to battle without limit? It would tear flesh from bones, strip branches from trees, and scatter rains of frogs and fish throughout distant continents. And we have shared this moment, the four of us."

"I knew something was going to happen tonight," I told him. "When I learned who you were, I thought that was it. But maybe it was this I knew about."

"I don't know the future," he said. "But sometimes I know what is good or right. I will talk to you all again soon, if you are willing."

The Arch-Mage's Proposition

The winds left. The teachers were meeting with Jan Vorkin. The rest of us went to the dining hall for a hot drink. I didn't see Mina leave the roof; she must have departed during the confusion of the battle. Nor did I see her the rest of that night as the three of us recounted what had happened to the other kids who came by to ask.

Dr Archer needed to see me in the Dean's office.

I went there. My mother had left hours ago, but my advisor and the Dean were there.

"I am pleased with your decisions on the roof," Dr Archer said. "You represented the school well. I must observe the irony that you were timid in your home when attacked by Helene's gang, four mere hooligans, and yet distinctly intrepid in the face of a man who could sweep away all of us with a wave of his hand. That intrepidity has doubtless improved our position."

"What happened in Prague?" I asked.

"Dr Chatterjee and I were investigating a Gott im Himmel magician. Late at night we were by the Rudolfinium concert hall and were engaged in divination when fires sprang up around us. These proved to be two elemental fire beings. Neither of us possessing elemental allies, we were unable to contend with them so we withdrew."

"Jan Vorkin has requested a private meeting with you," Dr Archer said. "While you have our complete confidence, we must be open with you about what is at stake. This man does not wish to be our enemy, and we must keep it that way. We believe you are perfectly safe with him. Recall only that his newly minted friendship with School of the Ages must be encouraged and maintained."

"Why does he want to meet with me?"

"I don't know," said the Dean.

"Nor do I," said Dr Archer.

Jan Vorkin was sitting in the conference room drinking coffee from a can when I arrived. He clapped me on the shoulder and smiled, guiding me to the chair at the head of the round table where the Dean usually sat. Now that he was out of his travelling robes and standing in front of me in a normal shirt and trousers, I realized that he was strikingly tall, and his long hair, tied behind him was both black and gray. His voice was more warm and pleasant now.

"Welcome, Simon Magus. Thank you for seeing me. I promise it will be to your advantage. A wonderful school you have here. So many talented youths are gathered together. I am much struck by it. I shall be questioning you, but I think it will not be too painful."

"I don't think it will be painful at all."

He settled into his seat sipping his coffee. Realizing I had nothing to drink, he took another can from his satchel and slid it across the table to me. The label was in a language I didn't recognize. I had some. It was unsweetened and bitter.

"I will start with your name. You could have chosen any name for yourself, yet you chose the name of a known deceiver and villain. Why?"

"At first, I just liked the sound. Later, I learned that the name tied me to events past. I think many people in ancient times called themselves Simon Magus, and now I'm one of them."

"But you are no deceiver?" "Maybe I am, and maybe I'm not," I said. "In our line, to use your words, we have to be deceptive and mysterious."

"Of course. Tell me, as you are a handsome boy, does your

handsomeness come from your father or your mother?"

"I look like my father. My mother is beautiful too." He might have met her, as she was the Dean's assistant, but I saw no reason to give him that information.

"Do you prefer fire or water?"

That was an odd question, but he was serious about it; his body was tilted across the table towards me, eagerly awaiting the answer.

"Arch-Mage," I told him, "I saw the attack on 9/11 from the ground. After seeing the towers burn, and walking in the smoke, I could never love fire."

"I have fire and water to dispose of. Now, tell me of your brothers and sisters." "Tell me about yours."

"In my case that is expensive knowledge."

"Then you see my problem," I said.

"You answer a complex question, and refuse a simple one," he said. "How did you come to be made that way?"

"I don't know. I know that I'm representing my school here, and I expected to be asked professional questions. I don't know why you're asking personal ones."

He nodded. Perhaps his eyes twinkled. "Do you dance?"

"No."

"Sing? Paint? Sculpt?"

"No"

"I thought not. Write?"

"I will someday when the story is ready. Why are you asking these questions, sir?"

"Imagine," said Vorkin, "that a great peril is approaching individuals near you whom you do not know. Perhaps you might help them, or perhaps you would perish trying. In the meantime, you are begged by loved ones to remain at home to solve an urgent family problem. What action do you take?"

....

This I had to think about for a while. Finally I said, "If it's loved ones, I put them before myself, and if it's strangers, I've tried to help before, and I would again." "How would you decide what to do?"

"I think being a magician isn't about being able to do things as much as it is knowing when you should." Dr Archer had taught me that. "If it were a real situation I'd probably have a feeling about what to do."

"You speak well," he answered when I had finished. "What is your goal, your plan of action?"

"I want to destroy Gott im Himmel."

"And then?"

"And then finish school and go to college."

"And then?"

"I don't know. My father expects me to take over his business. I don't know what I want to do yet. I'll decide in college, I guess."

Vorkin smiled. "Now you are more open. Good. Tell me, do you fear me?"

"No."

"Why not?"

"I don't really know what fear feels like."

"Why not? Don't you worry you will die?"

"I know it sounds strange, but anything that threatens me is just a problem to solve." He nodded. "Good. Your answers please me, and so I am ready to offer you a proposition. In two weeks' time you will come to Prague to meet one of my daughters. I would like you to marry her."

The 'newly minted friendship' between him and the school had to be preserved. I couldn't flat out refuse him.

"Well, I could meet her, I guess."

"That," with a friendly smile, "is guarantee enough for me."

Getting Ready for Europe

I told Goldberry about my meeting with Jan Vorkin. "So he's got marriage on his mind," she said. "Well, I refused to meet with him, but Avery was supposed to, sometime after you."

The following afternoon, Avery wasn't with us during lunch. While we were studying the Seventh Book of Moses for arcane literature class–amazingly, frantically dull reading–we heard her and Robbie shouting in the hall. Then they smashed into the room and continued their fight.

"I can't believe you're thinking about this," my roommate shouted. "Why didn't you just say no?"

"Just trying to be polite, like my mom taught me. You never know when a guy like that comes in useful."

"No, I know what it's about. You don't think I'm good enough to protect you from…"

"Shut up!"

The door was gently wavering between open and shut. Goldberry flicked her finger at it. It shut. The probability magic her father had taught was unreliable, but she had her moments. "We were studying, you know," she observed.

"Sorry," Robbie said. "We'll be done in a minute. Avery, you don't need any arch-mage's son. If he shows up, I'll handle it."

"If who shows up?" I asked.

"An old enemy of mine," Avery said quickly, cutting off whatever explanation Robbie was planning.

"So the Arch-Mage offered you a match with one of his sons," Goldberry said. "He offered Simon one of his daughters. Are you going to Prague?"

"Nah, I just told him I'd think about it."

"You should have told him no, flat out," Robbie complained. "Come on, haven't I always been there for you?"

"Just being polite, stringing him along," Avery answered. "You know."

"I don't know. That's not like you. Why couldn't you just say no?"

"I will. I'll say no sometime. Just not right away."

"You're scared. That's what it is. You don't think I can handle…"

"Shut up!"

They stood glaring at each other. I decided Robbie was right: Avery was scared of this old enemy. It wasn't like her to be scared, and as she was learning magic fast it was hard to imagine an enemy she would never be able to overcome.

"Then maybe you don't want to be with me anymore." It must have cost Robbie a lot to say this; I knew he was totally into Avery.

"No! No, I do! I just don't want you to get hurt, dumbass."

"I won't get hurt! I promise."

Avery shook her head and turned to me. "Simon, did you turn him down?"

"No, I'm going to Prague. But I don't want anything to do with his daughter."

"Why not?" Robbie asked. "You don't have a girlfriend."

"I don't want one. I promised Leah."

Goldberry said. "Jan Vorkin would make a creepy father-in-law though. I can imagine what his daughters must be like, all six feet tall."

"Maybe," I said. "I'll be polite, and then just say it doesn't feel right and back out."

Dr Archer wanted to see me.

At the same time I received a thought-trade from my advisor. Goldberry got it too. We went together, finding him in a classroom where he was teaching Magic Theory V to a group of older kids.

"Jan Vorkin has left the school," Dr Archer told us. "I am informed he will be expecting Simon in two weeks. Why?"

"To meet his daughter." I explained.

"I thought as much," said Dr Archer. "The meeting with him was of more significance to you, Simon, than to me. You must inform your mother."

"Why?" I asked. "I'm not taking it seriously. Maybe she'll want to come along and then it will be much harder to blow off the girl."

"Your mother's presence would not be advisable. I shall need you for a combat mission which can be incorporated into the same trip. Goldberry, you must come with us as well."

"Right. I'm up for some combat. What's it about?"

"You both have met Delphine. We have been working to clarify her information regarding a cabal member in Paris. We are convinced of the authenticity of the information, and an astrologically suitable time to act is approaching. Simon and I will thus confront this Gott im Himmel magician in his lair."

"What about Citadel d'If?" Goldberry asked. "They were happy enough to see our backs, last year."

"It will be necessary to persuade them to allow our operation," said Dr Archer. "That is why you are coming along. We shall leave in two weeks time."

Family Quarrel

It would have been nice to be back in Paris, if we hadn't to go to war. We were met at Charles de Gaulle Airport by a large contingent from Citadel d'If, calculated to keep us in check, I thought. Goldberry and I had previously met both the teachers in the group.

Leading the contingent was Madame Leveque, a short, trim woman in her late sixties, with her hair in a bun, wearing a dark skirt and sweater, with her glasses on a cord around her neck. She was the Paris school's deputy headmistress and had the same role at Citadel, defense, which Dr Archer handled at School of the Ages.

Beside her was Lescrot, a scrawny man with a ratlike face with an unlit cigarette between chapped lips. Then there were six students, three boys and three girls of various ages, all in overcoats and black berets.

"Oh look! It's an honour guard," Goldberry said distinctly.

After various greetings, the group piled into a black van. Everyone spoke French, so I used universal language. (Goldberry didn't need to as she had gone to French middle school in Manhattan and was fully fluent). I don't remember all the kids' names, except for two of the boys and one of the girls. This girl Angelique who was my age and chubby, attached herself to me quickly, sitting by me and looking me over. "Is it true you fought Hélène's gang alone?"

"Sort of," I said carefully. How had she heard that? Was she assigned to spy on me?

"And you beat them all? I don't believe it." She turned up her nose.

"Believe what you want," I said. There was no need to tell her any details. "I'm here as your guest, not to boast or make trouble."

Once we were all in the van, Lescrot lit his cigarette and drove. He steered the van aggressively, using the horn and shouting out of the window. Madame Leveque talked to Goldberry about her past visits to Paris. Dr Archer, preoccupied, said nothing for a while.

I said, "Madame Leveque, have you heard from your daughter?"

She gave me a look of astonishment, and then gave Dr Archer a look of pain and annoyance.

"My protégés are well-versed in the relevant history," he said frankly.

"And you have nothing to do with it," she said. "Of course you do not."

"I did not speak of it with them," he said.

"Ah well," said Madame Leveque. "Simon, I will answer you later. The children, you know."

Lescrot put his head out of the window shouting at a car in the adjacent lane to watch where he was turning. Eventually the van rumbled down a very narrow alley and stopped by a loading dock. He leapt out and ran into the building. The rest of us followed at a slower pace. The six students showed us to our rooms. My room was tiny and had a window close to the ceiling, a tiny bed, and a toilet and sink in a closet. Angelique smoothed the sheets and looked at me expectantly.

"Yes?" I said.

"I did not like Hélène and her gang," she replied. "All bullies. If you really fought them and beat them, then we have something to talk about. I think there should be a reward for you."

"I don't think I earned the reward," I told her. "I only beat two of them."

"Which ones?"

"Arnaud the Vampire, but he was very tough. And Master Yves.

He was easy to beat once I blocked the count."

"You blocked the count?" said Angelique. "No one can do that. Now I know you are lying. What sort of friend are you?"

She was being rude. "We aren't friends," I reminded her.

"You are rude." She turned quickly and left the room.

❖ ❖ ❖

After resting, we gathered for a short tour of the school, given by Madame Leveque. It was made up of a lot of the standard Parisian five-story houses, all connected by damp underground tunnels. The school halls aboveground passed through some very ordinary shops, the proprietors and patrons of which took no notice of us beyond nodding. The classrooms were small and had only a few kids in each. Citadel students all wore uniforms, although they appeared to have a number of fairly stylish options in several colours. Numerous teachers and students were smoking, so was the Headmaster, Duparc, when we stopped by his office. He was tied up with paperwork, and only shook our hands and whispered in Dr Archer's ear.

We finally settled in what seemed to be a parlour, with stuffed armchairs and students operating an espresso machine. Madame Leveque motioned us to chairs and signalled to the students to bring us all coffee. After the coffee, we got down to business.

"The students should go," Dr Archer said.

Madame Leveque waved him off. "They'll learn about it anyway. Ignore them."

"Very well," he said. He had to give in; we were in her territory. "The matter at hand is that we have an address for a member of the cabal of Gott im Himmel, here in Paris."

"Where?" asked Madame Leveque.

"In the Latin Quarter, on the Rue Gay Lussac," he answered.

"So near the Sorbonne! And how did you learn this?"

"We have enrolled one of his former pupils in our school. He sent her, along with your former students, to…" He looked at me.

"To attack me in my home in New York," I finished. "And that's not the only attack."

"My students?" she was shocked. "Who would do that?"

"Hélène the Medusa, Malevolent Gautier, Master Yves, and Arnaud the Vampire. With all due respect, Madame Leveque, you know this already. Angelique was asking me about it earlier today."

"Ah, you know, I am a busy person. There is never time to hear the student gossip. But I am interested that there is another pupil you have enrolled. Is she French? Perhaps we know of her."

"I don't believe so," said Dr Archer.

Rebuffed by this curt answer, she tried another tactic. "I am shocked that these four you name may be members of Gott im Himmel. Do you think they are?"

"They were working for a cabal member," Dr Archer said. "Members themselves? I doubt that."

"Were you badly hurt?" she asked me.

"I'm glad you've invited us here, Madame, but I think my injuries are private. You're not my teacher or my friend, and we're here for business."

We locked eyes. At last she gave me a dismissive look and turned to Goldberry. "Any comment, my dear?"

"I was attacked also," Goldberry said. "Three cabal members trapped me and hurt me."

"My God! How wretched of them! It is fortunate you are here to talk about it. What do you remember?"

"Kaiser Petrus himself was there, and a woman in a veil, and another woman whose voice sounded like a possessed man."

"Their names? Did you hear any names? Any clues to their identities?"

"I don't remember anything else. But I will tell you that I am now convinced that it's them or us, and I'm every bit as determined to fight as these two. If I might say something else, on behalf of my father, we can't help wondering how your school isn't aware of the movements of that gang of thugs. Why indeed would you teach magic to such bad people?"

"All young people deserve a chance," she answered lightly, "and even a mean dog may love its owner, isn't it so?"

"Let us move to the primary issue," said Dr Archer. "We are here to negotiate permission to act within your territory. We intend to enter the home of the magician we know only as the Teacher. Simon Magus is here to participate as an injured party, and Goldberry will coordinate our action from here."

"I absolutely will not," Goldberry blurted. "I want to fight."

"No," said Dr Archer.

"What will you do inside that magician's home?" Madame Leveque asked.

"Overcome and interrogate him, and then, whatever else is required. We may need to kill him."

"Hmm. And you want us to get out of the way?"

"To look the other way."

"It is a black game you play, Solomon." This does not fool me. My daughter was not a good enough replacement for that Ada of yours?"

"Colette and I had a bad misunderstanding," he said stiffly. "I don't know why you mention this old history. Nothing is a game to me. I have a purpose, and I have stated it, and sentimentality does not drive me any longer. This cabal is attacking our students. Dempsey and Chatterjee Major are among our most able recent graduates, and these two I have brought, Simon and Goldberry, will one day be described in like terms. Were it your students who had been wounded, you would understand the seriousness of my intentions. You know there will be more attacks to come. I mean to make an end of Gott im Himmel.

Duparc is not entirely wrong to nurture vipers to bite his enemies, but that strategy does not fit this time of war. You must choose sides. Why try to distract me?"

"Because I do not like you."

I remembered at that moment how the Arch-Mage had said there should be more fellow-feeling between magicians. I didn't like the way she was talking to my teacher, and I was tired of her caginess. "We were attacked," I said, trying to imitate Dr Archer's usual poise. "We were hurt. My family was threatened. You can't expect us to do nothing."

"Yes, but that is because Solomon Archer put you onto the front line. You are children. It is wrong."

"He's teaching us how to be responsible and fight evil," Goldberry argued. "My father never taught me that!"

"And Solomon and his pet Dean told you that you were born to fight."

Dr Archer slammed his hand on the table. I had never seen him angry before. The table cracked slightly, and the kids by the espresso machine jumped and then warily lifted their hands into a chopping position.

"Back off," Goldberry snarled at them. "You really think *she* needs your help?"

Madame Leveque turned back to Dr Archer. "Solomon, I know I am being unkind. But you do not question yourself enough. You do not know yourself."

"I have studied my charts. Astrological influences clearly tell me…"

"Your charts do not tell! The heart tells! Not the stars! My God!"

Dr Archer was breathing rapidly, but already he had begun to calm himself.

"If the heart tells, then mine tells me to support Dr Archer," Goldberry said.

"Mine, too," I added. "And my heart also tells me that you're not bad, Madame Leveque. You're just worried."

Her expression softened, and she reached out to pat my hand. I decided to allow it, and found some warmth in her touch. She touched Goldberry's hand also, and then letting us go, reached for Dr Archer's hand, the one he had slammed on the table. He pulled it away.

"We wish to attack the magician in the morning," he said. "For the last time, will you consent or deny?"

She nodded, as if finally understanding something. "Oh! consent, of course. I will go with you. I want also to meet this man. Solomon, your children don't understand that you and I are family, and family argues. Tell them! Don't let them think badly of me."

"My students have keen perceptions of their own, and are able to assess your worth as well as I."

"Solomon," she said chidingly.

"I have known Madame Leveque since my childhood, and she looks upon me as a son," he admitted. "For that reason, I am certain she will not betray us."

"To answer your question," Madame Leveque said to me, "I have not heard from Colette in many years. I would like to find her, but she is very good at hiding. I fear for her. It is not good to be sad and alone."

Proteges

We ate that night at a café on the Seine. It was too cold to sit outside so we were on the second floor, by a window overlooking the dark water and a large footbridge. I had *coq au vin,* Dr Archer *quiche*, and Goldberry *escargot* in butter sauce.

"It is possible," said Dr Archer, "to have a conversation that no one without universal language can understand. I will teach you the technique." He sipped his wine. "Visualize a book with blank pages."

We did that.

"Now visualize an alphabet upon the pages–not one you know–an imaginary alphabet."

This was difficult, but we did it.

"Now we must each move our books together onto a visualized shelf. Line them up vertically, spine first. Do you see my book?"

"It's green," Goldberry said.

"It is. Good. Now while the books remain shelved, we have a private language in which we have already begun conversing. To others it will seem as if we are speaking in a tongue that sounds familiar but which they cannot understand."

"How do we talk to other people?" I asked.

"Take your book off the shelf. Replace it to rejoin our conversation."

I slipped the visualized book on and off the visualized shelf. Easy.

"Now," said Dr Archer, "we shall make our final plans."

"Can spirits understand us?" Goldberry asked.

"They can, but if we were being overheard by anyone who could understand, additional books would appear on the shelf. It is not a concern now. Tomorrow's action is our topic."

"Then I think you should explain why you're stranding me at Citadel," my partner challenged. "Why bring me all the way here if I don't get to fight?"

"As an injured party, you have helped me to make my case. I cannot bring you into combat, much as you may wish it, for numerous reasons, the primary one being the fact that we are not certain what psychological damage was done to you by the previous attack. Additionally, though it may seem otherwise, I do respect your father's wishes. I am acting as an agent of School of the Ages here, and his guidance and support are extremely valuable to the school. Finally, I am not sure what will come to pass tomorrow morning or after and you may yet have a role. No battle is won without intelligence. You understand this, I trust?"

"Intelligence, as in information?"

"Of course."

"But my divination ability is still crippled. You should have brought someone else."

Dr Archer looked at her. "You have still a divinatory role to play, I believe. Perhaps it will comfort you to know that we are in little danger tomorrow. As Madame Leveque will be with us, the only potential defeat that concerns me is our enemy's escape."

"He won't get away," I said. "I don't think he's planning to run. He has some other kind of strategy in mind." "You sense that?" Dr Archer asked. "I have no sense of the matter. As we are collaborating on this project and you are my protégés, a part of my capability is being transferred to the two of you." "Don't do that," I said. "You need everything you have."

"Such a transfer is inevitable," he said, "and I would not prevent it if I could." Goldberry was thoughtful for a moment, as if working through something in her mind, and then asked, "What about Donovan? Shouldn't your power go to him before us?"

"Donovan has been my protégé since his birth. He is fully capable now, and is his own man."

"But I don't understand why he isn't with us, why he isn't helping you." Dr Archer removed and cleaned his glasses. "Donovan is aware of my reasons and that is sufficient."

"No it isn't, Dr Archer. My father says you're using and exploiting us. Madame Leveque said the same thing. I don't believe that, because I'm happy to help, but I think we deserve an answer to that question."

"I don't need the answer," I said. "I don't care. It needs to be done. I'm doing it." "I will answer," he said carefully. "A captain may love his soldiers, and yet he leads them to battle.

"We're not the only good kids in our own year, either," she added. "Robbie, Mermelstein, Rocco…"

"They are not my protégés, and their advisors have judged that the time for them to participate has not come. For this foe, Simon and I will be sufficient, and Madame Leveque will also be there."

"But he'll be in his home," I said. "He'll be stronger there, the way I was in my parents' house in Queens."

"True. However, Madame Leveque enjoys that advantage everywhere in Paris. The entire city is her personal territory."

"That's possible?"

"Only for her. In Paris, she has never been beaten." "Then why does she answer to Duparc? Why isn't she running Citadel d'If? Or is he even stronger?" "Perhaps you may ask her that," he said. "However, I do not believe you will receive an answer."

Wine

I woke to a firm knock on my door. A student was outside, sent by Madame Leveque to wake me. I put on a black School of the Ages sweatshirt and grey jeans. I touched the crystal around my neck and said hello to Leah, and she whispered hello back to me. I had my other magical tools with me also. I still hadn't built the weapon against spirits, but I put on the scarf and the matchbox amulet.

I followed the student to a lounge. Goldberry and I sat over coffee with the two male students wearing Citadel uniforms of black turtleneck, black pants and wool caps. They introduced themselves as Noah and Jules. They were a year older than us and wanted to visit New York.

Dr Archer and Madame Leveque arrived a few minutes apart and we headed out, using underground tunnels until we had reached the Latin Quarter. At the door of the shop where we exited, we were met by four seniors, three boys and a girl, in uniform and overcoats. They followed us. We had only walked a few blocks when a truck began following us. It was hovering close behind us, its engine roaring and revving. In the slow Paris traffic, it was able to force its way through lights to maintain its closeness.

"It's ridiculous," Madame Leveque said. "Are we to wait until they run us down? Christophe, Denis." She gestured, and two of the senior boys fell back. As I watched, they made the chopping motion. The truck's engine cut out, and it swerved to the left and thumped lightly into a parked Peugeot. Two men climbed out. The students again chopped and they collapsed. The boys fell behind; I saw them hauling the men around to the back of the truck.

"He knows we're coming," I said.

"Oh, he has probably known for longer than we have," said Madame Leveque.

A few blocks later as we were passing a café, a group of seven angry-looking men rushed out and made a bee-line for us. She wiggled her index finger, and the man closest to her, who was wielding a heavy baton gave a little jump and fell onto the sidewalk. She then gestured again to her students. The remaining boy and girl stepped into the path of the remaining six men. *Un-deux-troix*. Two men went down.

"Keep walking," she said. "Clara and Ahmed will make short work of such petty annoyances. We will save our strength for something more serious, you agree?"

A block later I saw something from the corner of my eye on a rooftop behind us. I turned but couldn't find it. After another block there were two things on the rooftops. I thought they were tigers.

"Do you see those things on the roof?" I asked my companions.

"Spies," said Madame Leveque. "He will not be surprised that we had no trouble with his more expendable servants. Now he has tried something more serious, as I expected. Get rid of them if you like."

I didn't know how to get rid of tigers on the rooftop so I just kept monitoring them. It was a mistake. Soon there were three, and then four, all just on the edge of my perception, fading when I craned my neck to see them. No one else on the street seemed aware of them at all, so they had to be visible only to magicians.

"There are more and more," I admitted.

"They are *tulpas*," said Dr Archer. "Thought-constructs, given reality by mental energy. It is a clever spell by our foe, targeted specifically against the School of the Ages approach to magic. Visualization of the tulpa increases its solidity, and in this instance triggers the creation of more *tulpas*. As we visualize objects and entities in order to affect them, our typical strategy will only worsen the situation. He knows our magic well it seems. If you continue to focus upon these entities you will come to feel entirely encircled by them resulting in madness. Best to ignore them instead."

"How do I get rid of them?"

"I can think of no ready method," he said. "An allied spirit might make the attempt."

I had an allied spirit–Leah–and she was with me, but I would never ask her to fight, especially against monsters. I considered the tools I had with me. If these four–no, six tigers were a mental trick, then it was like mind control. My weapon against mind control was nonsense, the recitation of a silly poem. Would focusing on this break the grip of the *tulpas* upon my awareness, or set them loose? I held the matchbox amulet and repeatedly recited the nonsense poem that was inside.

At the third recitation, one of the six or eight tigers flashed at the corner of my eye then blinked out of existence. I continued to recite, a little louder now, and there was another flash, and then another, then two at once. Three tigers remained. I turned and looked directly at them, freezing them with my words. Perched on the roof's edge, there were three Bengal tigers with black stripes on black fur, starkly outlined against the morning light, their green eyes blinking as they hung their paws over the edge. I recited again. One sprang to its feet and burst.

"You are mine," I told the other two aloud. "Go from here into the spirit plane and abide there as guardians till I need you again."

"Name us." They spoke in my head in soft purring voices.

"You are *Chokhmah*, and you are *Binah*," I commanded. "Now, be gone."

They were gone.

"Well done," said Dr Archer.

"*Très formidable*," said Madame Leveque. "Our adversary must be quaking with fear." I wasn't sure if she was mocking me. "Simon Magus has an unusual kind of command over spirits. Even in Tibet I did not see *tulpas* handled so. But perhaps I have inspired him, hm?"

We continued walking. Turning a corner, we passed into a narrower street. The sign read *Rue Gay Lussac*. Like many Paris streets, it was made of attractive five-storey row houses. Half a block from the corner there was a house painted blue with a black wrought-iron gate enclosing a small flower garden. Net curtains showed in all windows. Steps ascended to a white door with carved panels.

Madame Leveque opened the gate and walked up the path. Dr Archer paused for a moment; then we followed. Unconcernedly she climbed the steps. The white door was firmly shut. The panels showed crude carvings of devils.

"Horrible," she said. She rang the doorbell. There was no reply.

"I do not mean to wait," said Dr Archer. He took out a coin from his pocket and pressed it against the knob. The door clicked open and he put the coin away. He struck the door with his open palm; it swung wide open with a creak. Briefly he observed the entrance, both with eyes open and shut, then stepped over the threshold.

"I am called Solomon Archer," he announced. "I am here as an enemy. Come out and face me."

There was no answer. I followed him inside. Madame Leveque came last and shut the door. We were in a tastefully decorated foyer, with finely crafted end tables and a painting of a woman on a sofa being watched by a dark-skinned slave.

"A long-lost *Ingres*," said Madame Leveque, examining the painting. "Stolen from Bertin's collection in 1840."

Further down the hallway was a set of doors. I felt butterflies in my stomach as I looked at them. "He's there," I said.

Dr Archer nodded and walked to the doors. He closed his eyes, meditating, holding one hand palm-forward at chest level. I decided to visualize the doors also and saw that there were six layers of hostile intent–or, if you prefer, magical traps covering them. As I watched, these layers peeled away. With them gone, Dr Archer pushed open the doors and crossed the threshold into a room with a strong smoky smell. I followed.

It was an elegant parlour, with an antique sofa and matching chairs, many shelves of leather-bound books, a desk with wines and goblets against one wall.

A man stood by the sofa. He stubbed out his cigarette and smiled. He was in his fifties, with a square jaw and a ridiculous pony tail. He wore a dark blue suit and a pink cravat. His mouth had a cruel twist at one corner.

"*Bonjour*," he said, then continued in English. "Madame Leveque, Solomon Archer, Simon Magus. And where is Goldberry Tinker? I hoped to meet her since learning she is in our fair city. I hear she is a beauty, *non*?"

Rage swelled in me. "You'll never hurt her again. You'll die first."

"Oh look, the angry boy. I was not there that night. I have not hurt her, Simon Magus. It seems I have not even hurt you. That is what I get from sending idiots to do a real man's job"

"You know why we are here," Dr Archer said calmly. "You may be in your home, but any of us is capable of defeating you. If you want to live you will do as you are instructed."

"Ah," the French magician replied. "Then you think I am the kind who surrenders. Not so. But I must congratulate you. After a long search you at last locate a member of my group. It has been hard for you. I am hard to catch but you are like a dog on the scent. Sniff, sniff. Eh?"

"Yes," said Dr Archer. "Now, I would like to know where to find Kaiser Petrus, please. I must have this information, but you do not have to die."

"I am Kaiser Petrus," said the Frenchman.

"No, you are not," said Madame Leveque.

"Worth trying, eh? Yes, you are right. I am Bayard Dupont, called the Connoisseur. An expert in wines and home decorating. You like my house, I hope? Come, let us be civilized. I have *Haut Brion* 1961. Have some." He took a few steps to his sideboard, uncorked a new bottle with a light caress of his finger and poured four glasses. Quickly he sipped one, handing another to Madame Leveque, who also drank, then threw her glass into the smouldering fireplace. Dr Archer and I did not touch our glasses.

"Now don't be unfriendly, Simon Magus," he chided me. "There is much I can teach you about wines, about art, and about magic. This Jew who teaches you knows no such fine things."

"I have a clear conscience and a defined purpose," said Dr Archer. "Superficial taste without a moral center is not a mark of quality. The location of Kaiser Petrus, please. Now."

"And then after I tell you what? You will kill me more mercifully?"

"Not necessarily," said Madame Leveque. "If you come to Citadel and make proper overtures to Duparc we will spare your life. You owe nothing to the cabal."

I said coldly, "what kind of ally will he be?"

He turned away from me to Dr Archer. "Kaiser Petrus will kill this boy and all your students once you are out of the way."

"Go ahead and kill me now," I said. "I'm waiting. Take your best shot."

He waved his hand dismissively. "I am outnumbered."

"So was I when you sent Hélène La Méduse and her gang to my house. That was four to one. This is only three to one."

He took a silver cigarette case from his jacket pocket, extracted one, and began smoking without lighting it. The smoke cloud framed his face, but I could see him scheming, calculating, planning his next tactic.

"Please, this is tiresome," said Dr Archer. "I don't want to go through the wearying exercise of threatening you. Whatever threat you can imagine I can do far worse. Now consider instead what is to your advantage. Kaiser Petrus has not earned your personal loyalty. Only shared ideology and mutual defense can motivate your connection. One is obsolete and the other now clearly ineffective. No one is rushing to your defense."

"Come and see Duparc," said Madame Leveque.

"I'm not listening to you, old woman."

"Then give up Kaiser Petrus, at least," said Dr Archer.

"Forget it, Jew."

Dr Archer turned to Madame Leveque. "Simon and I will have to kill him unfortunately. I did warn you."

She nodded. "We shall take the house, and first pick of his possessions. Acceptable?"

"Yes," he said.

I watched Dupont. I saw the fear in his eyes and something else too–they were beginning to glaze over. His breaths were quickening and his face was turning red. He was afraid? Good. He had it coming. I would make it worse.

"He attacked me in my home," I said. "I should have first pick."

"I am not dead yet," he said between gasps. "Perhaps you should argue this after you kill me if you can..."

"On your knees!" I shouted.

He dropped his wine glass soundlessly on the carpet and plummeted.

Dr Archer walked over to him. He was not moving. He checked the pulse at his neck. "Dead," he said.

"How?" I asked. "I didn't do anything serious to him." Had I killed the man?

"We will work out the details later. Let us now search the house for clues and objects of value. We must place highest priority upon his book of shadows–his diary."

The magician's dead, Goldberry. I think I killed him.

That was what I had meant to do, wasn't it?

No, I was angry enough to kill him, but I didn't mean to.

She didn't think any the less of me for it.

Dr Archer, Madame Leveque, and I searched the room, then the other rooms in the house. There was cash, approximately ten thousand euros, which we split three ways. I had never carried so much money before. He had a locked laboratory containing magic books and equipment. After proper precautions to remove traps, we unlocked, entered and searched it. His book of shadows, if he had one, was not there, but he had many other things of value. Most of these, it was agreed, would go to Citadel d'If, but we kept a few. Sitting on a silver salver, on a desk, was a large gold ring with rubies and emeralds set in it. As soon as I saw it, I intuited that it was for me. Quickly I picked it up and showed it to the two teachers. "I'm claiming this."

Dr Archer examined it, touching it as I held it. "This is a powerful object which causes me to wonder why he was not carrying it on his person. Still, I do not sense a harmful consequence. Madame?"

"Let him have it."

The ring was too big for my ring finger, so I put it on my middle finger instead.

We continued searching. In a drawer, Dr Archer found a large crystal prism. "This I will claim for Goldberry," he said.

Leveque nodded. "That is a fine piece. I had heard there was one such in Paris, and I shall be sorry to see it go. Still, she is a fiery young lady and should not be denied; we have other means."

Goldberry, Dr Archer got something pretty cool for you.

She thought urgently that I should go upstairs.

"I'm going upstairs," I announced.

I went back up the stairs, now sensing that I was facing some danger, but I thought to myself that the Connoisseur was dead. But still I could sense there was more threat now than there had been at any other time since our arrival in Paris. However, I also felt stronger and more capable than I had ever felt before. Ever. I went to the parlour and I smelled fresh smoke, and saw the smoke drifting as if carried on the sunlight that came through the curtains.

The Connoisseur or Dupont was seated, smoking, with his feet extended, resting on the right shoulder of his corpse.

"You're dead," I said.

"Yes, I am," he replied. "Bayard Dupont has breathed his last. Dead I may be, but I intend to haunt this house for a while, at least till my liquor is finished. I have Scotch whiskies from before the Second World War–magnificent. You don't mind?"

"Not if you stay out of my business." I knew better than anyone how dangerous a malevolent, powerful ghost could be, since I had been haunted and all but possessed by one during my first year at School of the Ages. It was best for me to keep my defenses up in the presence of this one, and I bitterly regretted not having prepared the weapon against spirits that Dr Archer had told me to construct.

"Well, why did you come back upstairs, Simon Magus? You knew I was here?"

"I had an intuition. *Chokhmah.*"

"Chockmah. Ah, that Hebrew nonsense."

He was in a cabal; the word 'cabal' was from Cabala, the essence of Jewish magic; and he referred to that magic as nonsense. What an idiot!

"I wish I had taught you, Simon Magus, instead of Archer and all those Jews." He got up, crossed the room, and poured another glass of wine from the bottle of Bordeaux. "Have a glass?"

"No."

"It is all right. There is no drinking age in France."

I looked at the corpse. "The wine is poisoned," I said. "That's why you died. I didn't kill you."

"Yes. A suicide, you see. My cabal-mate, Dr Beam of London, visited me last month. He cannot help but poison everyone he meets. How he gets poison into a sealed bottle–this is his art. I realized, of course, and saved the bottle for your visit. If I could catch Archer, or you, it would be a good trade for my life. I was a sorcerer, you know, like your teacher. We know when we are going to die, at least, roughly so. There are disturbed emanations for weeks or months, followed by the flat peacefulness of anticipating the end of earthly struggle. I was ready to die, and I chose the way. So demeaning it would be, to be killed by a Jew."

I paid scant attention to his babble. Meanwhile, I recalled that Madame Leveque had drunk the wine. While it killed the Connoisseur in only minutes, she had showed no ill-effects even after an hour.

"Why didn't the wine kill Madame Leveque?" I asked.

"Well, you know -- nothing can kill her. You ask her later and she will tell you. So now, Simon Magus, since I am unable to kill you, I will try to help you instead. What would you ask of this dead soul?"

I showed him the ring that I had taken from his room. "Tell me how to use this."

"Ah, it was *you* who took possession of that very powerful bauble."

"Why weren't you wearing it?"

The Connoisseur's ghost smiled. "I do not like the craftsmanship. Gaudy thing."

"Is it cursed?"

"*Non, non.* I would not keep cursed things in my house. I have many admirers to hold them for me."

"Then what powers does it have?"

"It is a consulting tool. The use is simple enough. When you lie down to sleep, wear it, and say the names of those you want to speak to, living or dead. Even me–I am glad to consult with you any time.

The ones you call will speak to you in your dreams. Of course, there is a risk. Once you consult, you may be consulted as well."

"Where is Kaiser Petrus?" I knew he had given me a clue, naming a magician called Dr Beam in London, but I decided to push for more.

"This I will not say. Kaiser Petrus is much stronger than you, Simon Magus, and you could not protect me from the retaliation if I spoke."

"Who is H.E. Myra?"

The ghost's eyes widened. "Penetrating question. Yet I fear to answer that as well. You shall learn if you ever meet Kaiser Petrus. It is better if you do not know."

"Who attacked Goldberry Tinker in New York?"

"You do not need my help to learn that," he said. "Come, enough of the questions." He sipped the wine. "Take my cigarette case. It is not cursed. It is a fine thing."

"I don't smoke."

"Take it all the same."

"Why give it to me?"

"I do not want Lescrot to get it. And besides, while we are enemies, I do not dislike you, Simon Magus. Not your fault you fell into the hands of those Jews."

I saw no reason to tell him that I was a quarter Jewish. Spirits trade in information. "I like the Jews," I said.

"Yes, you are deluded," he said pleasantly. He gestured towards the corpse.

I took the cigarette case. It was perfect for what I wanted to do. In my mind's eye, I formed a silver cord that began at the case and extended toward the ghost. I had learned from Dr Chatterjee about the silver cord that attached the astral body to the physical form. I had asked whether silver cords could be made artificially, by will power. Dr Chatterjee said he didn't know. I was now going to find out.

"Don't do that," he said.

"Shut up."

"I have been more than friendly! It's not right."

I imagined the cord ending in a harpoon shape, like a whaling spear. As I looked at the Connoisseur's spirit, I could actually see the harpoon hooking into the ghost.

"Don't do that!" he shrieked.

"In the name of God Adonai I bind your spirit to this object!" I declared. "Henceforth you shall be ready at my hand to answer my questions truthfully."

"You can't do that!" he wailed. "You have performed no ritual."

"I don't need them. I am Simon Magus, seventh son of a seventh son."

"You are bound to the object in my hand. I own you. I rule you. You tried to poison and corrupt me? You sent your thugs to attack my family? Well, here is my revenge. Crawl on the floor."

He fell on his belly.

"Stand up."

He got up.

"Where is Dr Beam?"

"Notting Hill Nursing Home. That is all I know."

"Where is Kaiser Petrus?"

"I cannot tell you. I would like to I but simply I cannot."

I wasn't going to get that information, if Kaiser Petrus had stronger command of spirits than I did.

"Disappear till you are called forth again."

The Connoisseur blinked out of sight. I put the cigarette case in my pocket. From the crystal at my chest I felt an angry vibration. Leah did not like being close to this nasty spirit and I didn't blame her. I touched the crystal with my finger and promised her I would get rid of the case as soon as I could. I slipped the cigarette case into Dr Archer's coat pocket.

Dr Archer, I bound the Connoisseur's ghost to the case.

....

He would discuss that with me later.

"Madame Leveque," I told her, "you've been poisoned. He gave you poisoned wine."

"Yes, yes," she said. "Cyanide, I think, and something else as well. I knew it at once. I have already tended to that problem. Your concern is very nice, Simon Magus, but it is a misdirection; it means that you are hiding something."

"Gentle please with my student," Dr Archer interrupted.

"Very well, keep your secrets, young man. I think they will not harm me."

Eiffel Tower

I kept my hand with the jewelled ring hidden in my pocket as we walked back to Citadel, collecting the students along the way where they awaited us in the street. "You don't feel the poison?" I asked Madame Leveque.

"Young man, I studied the yogic arts for some years in the Himalayas. One aspect of this training is total control of the physical body. The process is difficult to explain, but you might think of it this way: at the first hint of discomfort, I am able to contain the poison wherever it lies in my body and expel it later, generally as sweat."

"Who taught you?"

"An ageless yoga master. There are a few such but you cannot find them; they call to you."

"Did you meet her master?" I asked Dr Archer. Donovan had told me his father had been in India also.

"Yes," said Dr Archer. Goldberry met us by the door.

The teachers went to meet with Duparc, leaving us alone.

"You may be too tired," my partner said, "but if not, wouldn't mind a bit of sightseeing."

"I'm not tired," I told her, although I was.

When we headed for the street, Noah and Jules followed us, a few paces behind. The escort was annoying, but it would be unwise for us to confront Citadel students in Paris again. "They're spying," I suggested.

"It's more that they fancy me," Goldberry said. "But I think I know a way to lose them." We took the Metro and got off by the Eiffel Tower. Defying the early-spring cold, lots of people were hanging around but we would never lose Noah and Jules that way. Instead, we went under the Tower itself, where queues of probably a thousand people were waiting for tickets or the elevator. The titanic steel framework loomed over us.

The principle of concealment, which we had learned in our first year, didn't help against people who were looking for us or following us, but it was perfect for avoiding ticket lines. We quickly got on the elevator without being noticed, while Noah and Jules were stopped by the operator's demand for tickets.

We got off at the first level Jules Verne restaurant. I casually counted a stack of Euros. We ordered lamb and pigeon from the exorbitantly priced menu. Then we put our books on the mental shelf and could talk freely.

"So it's to London tomorrow," my partner said, changing the subject. I had told her the basic story during our trip on the Metro. "To find this Dr Beam. You're leaving for Prague in the morning, right?"

"Yes. I guess that's important, but I wish I didn't have to go. It's just for the school, to make the Arch-Mage happy. I don't know how I can get rid of this thing with his daughter."

"Jan Vorkin didn't seem a fool to me. If you don't take his offer seriously he'll know. Anyway, why are you so sure you won't like the girl?"

"I won't," I said. "I can't. I promised Leah that I'll always love only her."

My partner looked at me long and hard but with a softness in her hazel eyes that I rarely saw. "Simon, Leah doesn't want that."

"I promised her." "Simon, she's dead, and you're only fifteen. You can't play at being a grieving widow. You'll want to be in love again."

"No I won't," I said, but I was lying to her.

But Goldberry was right. I was growing up. When this trip to

Prague was over, I would have to try much harder to keep my promise to the girl I had killed.

As we were eating, Noah and Jules entered the restaurant and found us. For the rest of the afternoon, as we toured Notre Dame, they lingered nearby.

Later that afternoon, we met Dr Archer back at Citadel . We examined and discussed the ring and the cigarette case memento. He showed Goldberry the prism.

"I hope that this will be of use," Dr Archer told her. "It is called an *Akashic* Prism. When natural light is filtered through it, it will show details regarding the origins of objects upon which the light shines. Only a skilled diviner will be able to employ it to effect."

Goldberry held the prism up to the sunlight coming through the hotel room window. Multicoloured shafts played on the table. The grain of the wood was clearer, and we could all see distinct shapes and images moving in the bands of colour.

"It is responsive to your handling," said Dr Archer. "Now let us try a document." He laid on the table one paper from a sheaf of papers seized from the Connoisseur's laboratory. As the light played upon it, distinct human forms appeared, although faces and background details were blurred. Clearly it was a man with a neatly trimmed beard, leaning over a desk.

"It is the author of the document," said Dr Archer. "Dr Beam, I believe. Good… I shall recognize him now."

"Feeling a bit of strain," Goldberry said. "Can't do this for long, sorry."

"We shall construct a stand in the school that you may use for prolonged viewing." "That will help certainly," she explained, "but it's not just holding it up that's difficult. This prism has a mind of its own. It's hard to hold onto myself, if you understand. It's like Simon's grandfather said to me last year. You spend too much time in Akashic records, you get absorbed into them." She set down the prism. "Not ready for that just yet. Right now, I can't resist as well as usual because of what the cabal did to me."

"Understood," said Dr Archer. "Still, let us keep this tool a secret from other students. I think it will not take kindly to multiple masters."

"I think you're right," said Goldberry. "In the morning, we shall go to Charles de Gaulle Airport together," he added. "Simon, you are bound for Prague. Goldberry, your father has arranged for your uncle, Hugh Parnell, to meet you at the airport."

"Oh, forget him, he's a stuffy bore," she replied. "I want to go with you. I want to help you fight Dr Beam."

"No."

"I want to do my bit. And what if you can't beat Dr Beam alone?"

"She's right," I said. "Let me go with you. The Arch-Mage can wait an extra day." "You must go to Prague," said Dr Archer. "I do not require your protection, nor yours, Goldberry. That less than two years ago, both of you asked me to teach you how to fight, and now you wish to do so on my behalf is a compliment to your maturation and dedication. However, I obtained my role at School of the Ages as its primary defender with the expectation of confronting rival magicians, and thus far, I have performed the task adequately." He looked at us.

"I will be confronting Dr Beam alone. I assure you I am at the peak of my abilities now and fully ready for the task at hand."

There was no point in arguing further and we knew it. I withdrew into my own thoughts. The newly-forged friendship between School of the Ages and Arch-Mage Jan Vorkin would be in my hands. I would be his house-guest, entirely at his mercy. If things didn't go well between me and his daughter, would I even be able to leave the city safely?

Nothing Between

On the plane, I tinkered with my defensive cylinder. Walking down the airport hall, I was surprised to realize my hands were shaking. It wasn't just that Prague was cold–Paris had been cold, too.

Goldberry, are you okay?

Since I was on an adventure and she was stuck with her tedious Uncle Hugh, she thought I should mind my own business.

Goldberry closed herself off after that–no more thought trading for a while.

I approached the cab stand only to find a black car parked there, and beside it a stocky woman holding a piece of cardboard with "Simon" written on it. She opened the door and gestured to me to climb in.

"Who sent you?" I asked.

"I drive," said the woman in a dull, thick voice.

"You don't talk?"

She shook her head. "I drive," she repeated.

The outskirts of Prague were dirty and ugly, as is true with most cities: all concrete and train tracks. However, as we neared the city center, I began to see the old buildings that gave the city its nickname of the most beautiful city in Europe. It was constructed on both sides of a dark river, the Vltava or Moldau. Across the river from the old city was a hill crowned by a castle and a gigantic TV tower. The car pulled off on a side street. The driver opened the door and gestured which way

I should walk–down a cobblestone sidewalk to a gap where I saw a large roadway. I proceeded as she pointed, my trolley wheels roaring on the cobblestones in the late-morning sun. There was a crosswalk. On the other side of that, I heard an accordion and followed its music past a big theater on my right, and some tourist shops on my left, towards a big brown stone arch. At the shaded entrance to the arch, I could see, the curve of a broad paved footbridge and the glint of golden statues. I went to the inner edge of the arch and looked up at the gentle rise of Prague's world-famous Charles Bridge, with its larger-than-life statues of saints in gold. As I waited, a door opened on my left in the stone of the arch. The few tourists nearly didn't notice it. Jan Vorkin himself emerged, wearing dark pants, a peasant shirt, a heavy gold chain around his neck and a cape. He squeezed my hand and put his arm around me.

"I hear you have been busy already in Paris," he whispered in my ear, "and that you distinguished yourself there. Exactly what I crave in a son-in-law. You must need refreshment so come into my underground lair. Enter on pledge of safety."

"You live underground?"

"From time to time. I have many houses but this one is quieter."

"I see. I want to know how long the pledge of safety will last. If your daughter and I don't like each other you might become angry."

His eyes narrowed, but then he smiled. "Are you afraid of me, Simon Magus? Then why come here?"

"I'm not afraid, but I have family and obligations I want to take care of."

"Then do not be troubled," Vorkin said. "I know that young people have their moods and feelings, and I am no tyrant to punish them." He squeezed my shoulder. "Banish your concerns and come in with me; the magic that is making us invisible is not infallible."

Downstairs, we entered a musty stone corridor lit by dim overhead bulbs. There were many doors, all shut except one that was opened by a heavy-faced woman. "Thank you," I said. The woman grunted in reply.

"Take his coat, hat and scarf. Take them and his bag to his room. Don't open the bag."

"Your servants don't talk very much," I noted.

"My servants are beneath your notice." He gestured and I entered the room first.

It was a small parlour with a few stuffed armchairs around a round table. A door opened, and a plain girl with an apron came in holding a tea-tray. I quickly sized her up as another of his servants–an elemental spirit, not a real person.

"Put the tray on the table," he ordered. "Don't pour! Now go and fetch my eldest daughter and say the boy is here."

She left, shutting the door behind her.

"Today you meet my daughter. Why don't you ask about her?" He thought a moment. "You are nervous. Don't want to seem too eager, is that it?"

"Really, I don't understand why you picked me."

"I have excellent sources of information. I have been working for a while to keep track of the best young magicians, in the schools and in private tutelage. I had quite a list at one time. At least half a dozen were in your school. When I arrived at the school, who was there to meet me? You and two others I wanted to see. I don't think your teachers planned that, am I right?"

"No. My friends and I didn't know that you were coming, but we knew something was going to happen and we wanted to be part of it."

"That means something to me," said Vorkin. "I am no mathematician, Simon Magus. I don't calculate and I trust first instinct and shrewdness. I think you are of the same kind?"

"Yes, I am. I follow two cabalistic principles that the Rambal taught me–*chokhmah* and *binah*, intuition and reasoning. With those, I often figure out what to do just when I need to."

....

The Arch-Mage lifted his head. "Ah, she is coming at last. She is difficult. Do what you must. I trust you completely."

The door opened, and she came in. My life ended…

And restarted, as a new life that had her in it.

It wasn't that she was beautiful, although she was. There are lots of beautiful girls, but there are some who strike you in a special way that you never forget. She was dark-haired, bright brown eyes, a button nose and full lips. She wore a peasant blouse and shirt. She smelled like fresh flowers. All these things I liked, but that wasn't it: it was her great energy. I could feel it rippling through the room. Hers was a mighty and complex soul, and I felt my quiet space, my defensive cylinder, simply snap. This was a girl who could shake the world.

I think I stood up. Vorkin was saying something but I was lost and couldn't listen. My universal language ability had fallen away, and there was nothing that was real to me except the girl in front of me.

Somehow I met her eyes. What did she see looking at me? I created a thin sliver of mental space. I put up my defensive cylinder although it was useless against the magic of her presence. I turned on universal language. Part of me hated the Arch-Mage for doing this to me; I was barely in control of myself.

She looked at me too but curiously. I decided to look at the tea-tray and listen to Vorkin.

"…I brought it from London."

He meant the tea.

"I'll pour," I said. Despite my hands shaking, I managed to pour three cups.

Just a girl, I told myself. Just a girl, stop it, stop it. But it was as if I had never met a girl before.

The Arch-Mage said gently, "We have not introduced ourselves."

I managed to offer her my hand. "I am called Simon Magus, from New York."

She nodded, gave me a distracted smile and looked at her father. "Papa, he is speaking Czech?" Voice a little husky, very lovely, a lively but thoughtful voice.

"No, but in his school, they teach a way to speak every language."

"You understand me?" she asked, looking at me curiously.

"Yes."

"And now, you understand this?" She had changed languages.

"I understand every language, but only spoken, not written."

"This is a good magic to know," she said.

"Have him teach you," said Vorkin, sipping his tea.

"New York, it is good?" she asked me.

"Yes, it's good, but I don't go into the city often. "

I said, "I don't know your name."

"I am Ana Vorkina."

"Ana," I said. I watched her. She looked thoughtful, and then turned to her father and said, "You think I will forget Eduard because there is another boy here."

"Forget? No. Change your mind–why not? You can talk to this boy. Top magic student from America. Handsome. Smart. You see anything wrong with him?"

I had come there intending to meet her, refuse her, and return to being alone. Now ironically, I knew that if she saw anything wrong with me, I wouldn't want to live.

"No," said Ana.

"I know you will not pick badly for me," she continued. "It is only that you have chosen the wrong time when I am with Eduard."

"If you have someone else, I can just do some business with your father and go in the morning. I wasn't really looking to get married so early."

"Damn it," said Vorkin, scolding, "Look, Ana, you have insulted him. Is it so difficult to talk to him without mentioning some other boy who is nothing?"

"I'm not insulted," I said.

"I think you are," Ana said. "I am sorry. Nothing against you. It is only my father's ways that I am talking about." She gave her father a furious glare. "If you want to talk to me, I will talk."

"I want to talk to you."

"I knew it!" said the Arch-Mage. "Take charge of her, boy. She's a pain, but she's worth it."

He leapt up, swirling his cape, and rushed out of the room.

Trying Not to Fall in Love

When the door shut, Ana put down her teacup and asked frankly, "You like me, or you just said that to please him?"

Her directness surprised me. There was no way I could say what I was feeling. I said, "I wasn't taking the idea seriously of meeting someone when I came here. Now I'm taking it very seriously. But I'm only fifteen. I'm not in a hurry."

"I am sixteen, but I think age is not so important. I will ask some questions."

"Go ahead."

"You are a strong magician?"

"I'm a magic student."

"He said you challenged him when he came to the school, and you were not afraid. What does that mean? It doesn't mean you are weak."

"I'm no match for your father, but I've faced adult magicians more than once. I wasn't afraid of your father, but he didn't really give me any reason to be."

"He was with Boris, and you weren't afraid?"

"Notus is a friend of mine."

She laughed. "Smart talk. You talk already like a strong magician. Another question for you. You know it is strange for my father to bring you to me when I have Eduard. Maybe you have someone also. Tell me that."

"There was a girl I loved. She died. I still think about her and miss her."

"How long ago?"

"Almost two years ago." Should I tell Ana about the crystal? I felt Leah with me, and Leah, feeling my thoughts turn to her, gave me a friendly vibration. She was always with me, so did she know what I was feeling? And did she feel betrayed?

This brought me back. I had caused Leah's death, and I had promised to be faithful to her always. How could I say it to Ana? Ana, I am fifteen going on sixteen and everything from the time of her death is just meaningless? Ana, you will change that forever for me, but it must not change!

"I am sorry to hear. Also in my life too many people have died. You saw my mother is not here. She is in her grave." "My mother works for the dean of my school. My father is a businessman. I have brothers, but I don't really know them."

"What sort of magic do your parents do?"

"They aren't magicians, but they fit in pretty well with people who are."

"What did they say about you coming to meet me?"

"They don't know, actually."

"Don't know? What way is that to do anything?"

"I thought I would tell them only if it was going to be really possible."

Ana tapped her foot for a moment. Finally she pronounced, "Americans are strange."

"I'm not arguing with that, but my father is actually not originally American. He's from India."

"You like India?"

"I was young when I went there the last time."

She looked around, deciding something. "This talk is not so good," she said. "Well, is your father listening to us?"

"I will take you to my room. No one can spy on us there." She set down her teacup firmly.

I was surprised she would do that so soon after we met. "You're sure you feel comfortable doing that?"

"Why not? You think I don't understand boys? With you I have something to worry about?"

She did. She had to worry that I had fallen in love and that she wouldn't be able to get rid of me.

Together we went down a stone hallway. There were four sturdy doors, each marked with elemental symbols that I recognized from my classes at school.

"My brothers and sister," she said, without explanation.

"How many do you have?"

"We are four. Two brothers, two sisters." She led me to the last door. Beyond was a large room, dominated by a gigantic aquarium in the center. Only some water plants and snails were in the tank, which was large enough for both of us to stand in. The rest of the room, lit by a chandelier, was a cluttered mess with books, magical paraphernalia and used dishes. Clothes were scattered everywhere.

"Sit anywhere," Ana said, waving her hand vaguely.

I pulled a wooden chair next to the fish tank. She studied me, with that puzzled furrowing of brow that I liked so much.

"Why such a large tank, and no fish?"

"My exercises kill fish." She approached, standing near me, resting her hand on the tank.

"You swim in there?"

"No, don't be stupid." I could smell her fragrance. She pressed her hand more firmly, and hummed. Gradually the water began to move inside. It formed a wave that rolled to one edge of the tank and back. The plants quivered. As I watched, the tiny wave rebounded from side to side and gradually a little white peak rose from the crest. Ana began to sweat and finally removed her hand. The water settled, and she leaned against the glass.

"I try to put the horses, like in the movie."

I knew just what she meant. In the movie and book *The Fellowship of the Ring*, the wizard Gandalf makes white horses dance on a raging river as it engulfs the evil Black Riders.

"It is very difficult. Water is disobedient."

I nodded, then put my hand on the cold glass of the tank. Closing my eyes, I visualized the water, and then the movement I had seen Ana create. I opened my eyes.

Nothing. Not a ripple.

"I am working a long time to get that motion," Ana said, eyes flashing. "What, you think you can walk in here and do it?"

I lowered my hand.

Ana shrugged. "Well, now you understand me. I am water. My elder brother Tomaš is earth, and my eldest brother František is air. Willa, my little sister, she is fire.

When she said this, I understood the Arch-Mage's questions, weeks before–did I prefer fire or water? That had determined which daughter he paired me with. He had paired me right. Ana was perfect for me. Did she realize that? Could I tell her? And having met her, how would I ever find the strength to keep my pledge to Leah?

No. There was a way out.

"Tell me about Eduard."

Ana looked surprised and blushed.

"He is in the military police. Often away."

"Military police? A high school boy?"

"No. He is twenty-six."

It was my turn to nod, understanding. "So your father brought me here because he doesn't want you to be with an older boy."

"Not that," Ana said. "I am old enough to choose. Eduard is very nice, but he has no magic. I am the kind that will make enemies. You will learn that about me soon. So Papa wants someone who can protect me. Eduard is just an ordinary man."

"Enemies?" I asked. "What kind of enemies?"

Ana took a long time to think about this answer. "I will tell you that," she said, "but first tell me what magic you can do. You understand languages. That is not all?"

"At School of the Ages we have the ability to walk around unnoticed by strangers, and if we prepare properly, we can't be attacked by surprise."

"Everyone in your school knows this?"

"We all learn it. Some are better than others. We also have specialties."

"Ah. Now I am hearing what I want. Tell me, what is your specialty?"

"I'm a sorcerer."

She didn't understand. "This word does not translate into my language. What does it mean?"

"It means that I have feelings about what's going to happen, and I tend to be in the right place at the right time, and I can figure out what to do and act fast. My teacher does the fighting for the school."

"And you? You do this also?"

"Yes, I do."

"You are good at fighting?"

"I don't enjoy it, but I do it when I have to."

Ana smiled and my heart melted. "This is very smart of Papa. He brings me a fighting expert, and doesn't even say that. Good." She took a deep breath. "I have an enemy for you to fight. It is a very bad man."

This request seemed odd for a first meeting, especially one that was supposed to be about getting married. What was she up to? Was she trying to get rid of me? Was I supposed to prove to her that I wasn't a coward? Or the opposite, to prove I was too wise to fight without a reason? I didn't understand her motive, and I had to question her.

"Why do you need me? What about Eduard and your father?"

"Eduard has tried to stop him, to arrest him. We went together once to his house, but we could not get in and we could not bring him out. Then Eduard looked and he saw cars coming. Pavel Rod's uncle is in the government. We had to run away. Eduard works for the government. He is military police and he must protect his career."

"What about your father?"

"He has his own ways. I cannot point him and shoot him like a gun, you understand? I have told him. He says he cannot fix every problem in the world and I also should not try."

"Why is this man, this Pavel Rod, so bad?"

"Children go into his house," Ana said, "and they do not come out. What he is doing, I cannot say, but it must be wrong. You must stop him."

"We need a bargain," I said.

"Why? You don't like me enough?" For the first time, she looked afraid, worried about my answer.

"I like you enough. But this isn't about you and me. It's magician's business, so we need a bargain. Teach me some magic. Teach me how to make the waves."

Ana rose and paced the room. "That knowledge, it is more like art, but very hard. I will teach something better: how to tell if water is safe to drink."

"No. I want to learn how to make the waves."

She kicked a book across the floor. "Why? You are a strange boy."

I waited.

"Stubborn boy! Why do you play this game with me?"

I waited.

"You ask me to teach you something that is very private." She dug her nails into her palms. "*Ty vole*, why did I show you that?"

"I don't know why you showed me but that's what I want you to teach me. You don't really need me to fight this enemy of yours. It's not life or death, is it? So if my price is too high, forget it."

"No! You fight him! I will give you money. Ten thousand euros, my entire savings, is that enough?"

"Well?" she said defiantly. "You like money, or not?"

"I don't care that much about money," I said. "Teach me how to make the waves."

She punched the sofa angrily. "Making the waves, it is very personal. You understand that?"

I understood her. I sat down on the sofa. "Your father didn't bring me here to take your money. He'd be angry with both of us."

"He will get over it, Simon."

"But your life savings? That's a lot of money, too."

"The difference between me and my father is not so much, Simon," she said. "He uses what he has to get what he wants, and I do the same."

"New bargain," I said. "I'll go and tackle this guy Pavel Rod. If I can stop him doing whatever he's doing, you have to come to School of the Ages for a visit."

"All right," said Ana.

❖ ❖ ❖

I just took a moment to grab my coat. She guided me along the corridor and out to the bridge and then we set off across town.

A ride on Prague's immaculate subway and another on a smoothly gliding tram brought us to a featureless residential neighbourhood of two-storey houses with small yards. We stood on the edge of a tiny park looking across the street at a house much like the others, except that its front door was at the top of a sideways flight of stairs.

"The house of Pavel Rod," Ana said in a low voice. "I do not know what is inside. I cannot get in. My elementals will not enter; they say it stinks inside. I know he finds children, homeless and runaways. Why they go with him, I don't know. They go into that house with him, and that is the last time they are seen."

"How did you find out about this?"

"I go to a Czech school. Not a magic school like yours—an ordinary school. The girls there tell stories. I have watched from here."

"How will I recognize him?"

"He is a young man. His cheek has a scar on it. If you are going there, I should go with you. I will fight beside you."

"That's not the bargain." I didn't want Ana to get hurt. "Stay here. Don't look at me or talk to me, or my power of concealment won't work, and someone might see me going into his house. Look at the trees or the sky."

"Take this." She pushed something into my hand. I saw that it was a small digital camera. "If he is not there..."

"I'll take pictures of any evidence I find that we can show the police." I nodded.

I turned on my power of concealment, watched the traffic carefully, and crossed. I passed a few pedestrians who didn't notice me and entered Pavel Rod's yard, circling around to the back. There might be an entrance there. Sure enough, I found one, a back door below street level. I went down the three concrete steps and tried the knob. The door was locked. I took out my antique British coin from my wallet, touched it to the lock as I had seen Dr Archer do in Paris and mentally recited some magic words. The lock clicked open. I paused, strengthening my cylinder of continuous defense. I wasn't a policeman or detective, and had never done this sort of investigation before, but one man operating alone, unless he surprised me should be no match for me. It would be serious if he had a gun but if I saw it I could probably disarm him before he could fire. With continuous defense operational, he wouldn't be able to surprise me. This would be over quickly. I hoped it would.

I wanted to crush Ana's enemies. I wanted her to love me instead of Eduard. In my mind, I apologized to Leah. Leah was agitated. Maybe she was disappointed.

The cellar was dark, so after shutting the door softly behind me I waited for my eyes to adjust. There was a terrible smell of chemicals that began to overwhelm my senses. This was the smell that had kept away Ana's elementals. I heard no sound from the room where I was or from any other part of the house. Distracted by the stench, I tried to visualize the house in order to find anyone inside, but couldn't form a useful picture. In the dim room I could see many oddly shaped shadowy objects but I didn't want to study them. There were no captive children here, and I wanted to head upstairs and get away from the smells.

Taking careful steps and feeling ahead of me with my hands, I crossed the basement and found a wooden staircase which I climbed slowly, hoping to control the creaking with slow steps since power of concealment didn't create silence. There was another door at the top. Pressing my ear against it, I still heard nothing. Leah was even more agitated, making the crystal pulse against my skin. The only sound I could make out was dripping water. No one talking, no one walking, no TV or radio. Gradually I opened the door. No creak.

Then I took stock of the situation. To my left were stairs to the second floor. The room to the right had some light. I walked carefully in that direction. I entered the kitchen, where I saw two boys sitting at a small table. I froze, waiting to see if they had spotted me; if they weren't alert, then power of concealment would still operate. Neither moved. Their arms were folded on the table. They were looking at each other, one with his head tilted. His eyes gleamed.

They weren't moving at all. I crept closer. What drug could make kids so rigid that their chests didn't even move with normal breathing?

It wasn't a drug. As I got closer, I saw that they weren't paralyzed. They weren't real. There was a smell like candle wax. They were wax figures; their eyes were glass. The crystal at my chest was practically stabbing me. What was Leah so upset about?

One of the wax figures was in a red t-shirt, the other in a blue shirt.

The bad smells of the house overcame me. I went on my knees, trying to shake off dizziness....

SIMON, LOOK OUT! Leah's voice in my ear was as clear as if she was standing beside me. I tried to turn, but his hand was over my face, a noxious-smelling cloth, and my knees gave and I fainted.

❖ ❖ ❖

I awoke with a splitting headache. I was sitting upright tied to a chair, my hands bound behind my back. My eyes were blurry. My head was wet, my hair dripping. He had revived me with cold water, and was speaking to me in Czech. A slim young man with a stubbly face, dark eyes, crooked teeth and a scar on his cheek. He looked so happy. Pavel Rod, my captor.

I wasn't fully alert or up to much physically. Could I do any magic? I turned on universal language.

"…and still you came. You are in good health. Someone will pay a lot to have you as a servant once I have weakened your mind enough."

Was I gagged? No, my tongue was thick, but I could talk if I wanted. Sitting back a little, he patted me on the cheek. His wet hand was like an icy fish.

"You ugly jerk," I said. "I'll kill you."

"Oh, I've heard that before," he said. "Many of them said it. But they didn't have nice things like you." He reached for my neck, pulled on the chains there, uncovered the crystal and the protective matchbox amulet, studied them and let them fall again. "Such a nice memento. I'll wear it once you don't need it anymore."

He could recognize a memento –then he was a magician himself! No wonder he had been able to carry on kidnapping children so long. Worse for me, I was in his home, where he was strongest. Could Ana possibly have known?

Ana, help!

There was no response; I hadn't made contact. She couldn't thought-trade. How long until she got worried and sent for help? How long had it been already?

Pavel Rod was squeezing my mouth.

"On your knees!" I commanded, desperately.

"Oh, that was good," he said, rising from his knees and getting back into his chair. "You'll have to teach me." My attack was supposed to sap the opponent's will as well as knock him down, but it hadn't done that. He was in control.

Dr Archer, help me!

I got an answering impression of blood and noise. Unable to formulate a response, he was engaged in battle himself. He had found Dr Beam.

"You are definitely magical," said Pavel, patting my cheek as he pulled his chair closer. "But … wait. I think I have heard of this magic called 'on your knees'. Can you be…"

Visualizing the scorpion's tail, the long scythe-like spike and the poison sac directly behind it. A strike between the eyes, all the way to the brain. That vulgar face was drawing closer as he studied me. Sting!

He rocked back slightly, feeling the pain, but it was momentary. "Not as good," he said. "Today you are facing a real master." Suddenly he lifted my jaw and squeezed hard I could feel blood in my mouth. "No more hexes, little magic boy. You will be in a lot of trouble if I tell them I am holding the one who killed our friend in Paris." He held up the camera Ana had given me. "Did you use this to make a record of his death to show your friends? Now I will use it to make a record of your humiliation and show that to mine."

He knew exactly who I was, and worse, he was himself a member of Gott im Himmel. I realized, too late, that it was also this encounter, and not only my meeting with Ana Vorkina, that had been making me sick and confused all day. They might not have learned about Pavel Rod specifically, but Dr Archer and Dr Chatterjee had been looking for a Gott im Himmel cabal member in Prague. They had found Jan Vorkin instead, but I had found the enemy they were seeking, and at precisely the wrong time, when I was unprepared for a magical adversary and distracted by falling in love.

Had Ana known the truth about this man? Was it a trap? Had she and her father set me up? I had to create a functioning mental space and get some help. Goldberry, I'm in trouble. What is Dr Archer doing?

He had gone to find Dr Beam in Notting Hill.

I need help badly.

She was very worried, but who could possibly save me from the Arch-Mage?

Not the Arch-Mage. He's not even here, I'm …

I broke off the thought-trade. I'd had an idea.

"Lost in his thoughts," Pavel said.

"Take me to Kaiser Petrus," I said. My mouth was dry. "That's why I came here in the first place. I thought you were him."

"You came alone to attack Kaiser Petrus?" said Pavel Rod. "I don't believe you."

"Not to attack. To join. I'm switching sides. Solomon Archer is a weakling. He needed me to beat the Connoisseur. I want to learn stronger magic."

Pavel thought about this rubbing the scar on his face. "Well, you're a nasty little liar." He got up, scraping his chair on the tile floor. "Wait here."

I heard him go up the stairs. He claimed not to believe me. Still, maybe he was bluffing, and wanted to check with Kaiser Petrus. If I could escape, the false information might confuse the cabal to our advantage. If I didn't escape, I could only hope for a chance to fight to the death before they extracted from me all the knowledge they needed to destroy School of the Ages.

I didn't have long to figure out a plan. My head was hurting, my focus was less than half what I needed it to be, and my allies were unreachable or far away. I had no planned magic to untie ropes. I tried to visualize them so I could improvise, but no good –all I could do now were things I had mastered with practice. Whatever chemical he had used to knock me out, chloroform or ether, had dulled my mind and weakened me also. I had only one resort. The crystal was still with me;

he hadn't yet taken it.

"Leah," I said very softly. "I need help."

Moments later, I felt warmth spread through my body. The misery of the room faded. Dry hands were working the ropes that held my hands together. Finally, I was free. I turned and saw the Rambal there. A bent, aged man in a black suit, with a long white beard, a black big-brimmed hat, and eyes that saw meanings no one else could guess about. He shook his head in disappointment.

"I don't know how you got into this mess," he scolded. "It's not often a boy is in so much trouble that I am required to fetch him out of it."

"Rambal," I said, wobbling on my feet. "Rabbi Lichtman. This house belongs to an evil man."

He looked around. "This I needed you to tell me?"

"I can't handle him. You must destroy him."

"Ah," said the Rambal. "Getting you out of those ropes, that wasn't easy. Now I am supposed to destroy a man. Well don't worry. All you need to do now is run away."

The Rambal vanished. Had he ever been present, I wondered? Unsteady on my feet, I stumbled for the front door. As I struggled with the lock, I heard Pavel running down the stairs.

"Stop, Simon Magus! Stop!"

But the door was open. I fell down the stairs, jumped and ran out. His footsteps were behind me, but when I crossed out of his yard into the street, he stopped. I dodged a few cars and fell on my face in the park. Rolling onto my back, I saw him enter his house and slam the door.

I tried to construct the cylinder of continuous defense. I couldn't do it. I pulled myself onto a bench, unable to go any further. My blood was full of chemicals and poison and my head was throbbing.

Ana wasn't there. She'd abandoned me. Not sure what to do next, I started a thought-trade with my partner.

Goldberry, I'm safe, but I have to get out of Prague.

She didn't understand how I could get into trouble if the Arch-Mage was on my side.

I'll explain when I can. Let me clear my head. I'll see you tomorrow.

I began to meditate. I should have run; Pavel Rod was still less than a block away. Yet I found myself hoping that Ana would come back, that she hadn't abandoned me after all.

I recognized a black car at the side of the road. The female driver was standing by the door. I got to my feet and started to stagger towards the car. I stumbled. A moment later, the Arch-Mage himself was standing next to me, putting his arm around me, helping me to walk to the car. He settled me into the back seat and climbed in beside me.

"Ana?" I asked him weakly.

"She has run off," he said, handing me a paper cup of hot coffee. "I did warn you that my daughter can be difficult. It will all sort out. What exactly happened?"

Sipping the coffee slowly, I told him that she had asked me to take on Pavel Rod; that he was kidnapping children and selling them into slavery; that he was a member of Gott im Himmel; that he had recognized me and poisoned me; that I had managed to escape somehow.

"I assure you of two things," said Jan Vorkin when I was done. "First, I assure you that I did not introduce you to my daughter in hope of this outcome. I was hoping to clear her mind of this nonsense of hunting and attacking criminals by giving her a sober and sensible boy to fall in love with. Second, I assure you that, out of respect for my new friendship with your school and because I like you, I will eliminate Pavel Rod. And I will punish my daughter for this nonsense."

I looked into his eyes and saw shame and regret. For the first time, I understood him fully. He wasn't going to punish her. He loved her too much, I knew that he was, very much as he claimed, a man who could be trusted.

The sun went down as we rode back into the old town. Vorkin

explained that when I didn't come out, she ran to him for help, and then ran away. He didn't know where she was.

"Tell her I'm sorry," I told him. "I wasn't good enough to beat Pavel Rod. Tell her it was nice to meet her."

"I came here to support the friendship between you and my school," I told him. "I hope that is still strong. I hope you aren't disappointed with me."

"I am not," he said.

"You came here expecting safe conduct, not a battle."

Ana didn't come home that night.

She was still not home in the morning. Vorkin was crestfallen, but he told me about the history of his city, and rode with me in the car to the airport.

I sat alone in the terminal.

Paralyzed and Captured

Dr Archer and Goldberry met me at Heathrow airport and we exchanged news. I wasn't in any mood to talk when I saw them, but what they had to say was a good distraction. Dr Archer had beaten Dr Beam. He had some clues to follow to find another cabal member elsewhere in Europe. There was a large bandage on his cheek, about which he would only say that it was a minor wound that would heal completely. Goldberry had been miserable with her uncle and had nearly persuaded him to bring her to Prague to find me.

I told them about my experiences in Prague:

Dr Archer said he would follow up on the situation with Pavel Rod personally and I should not worry about it any longer.

"You're hurt," I said. "I'll go back with you."

"You are returning to New York," he said. "You have done a great deal already, and you require a return to familiar surroundings. Goldberry, before you ask…"

"I'm not going to Prague," she said. "I don't want to hear any more marriage proposals or meet anyone else from that mad family. If I see that weasel Ana Vorkina, I won't leave her as pretty as I find her, and you don't want that, I promise."

"Ill-advised, indeed," said Dr Archer.

"I don't want that," I told my partner. "It means a lot that you want to protect me, but I just can't believe she was bad. The Arch-Mage did warn me to be careful with her, so it was my fault, too. I just assumed Pavel wasn't a magician and figured I could handle any ordinary man. I should have been more alert."

"Oh dear," said Goldberry. "He's smitten enough to make excuses for her. All right, Simon. I promise not to beat her up unless you tell me to."

I didn't talk much during the trans-Atlantic flight back to New York. Goldberry slept and I sat with my eyes closed, remembering Ana.

I was still in a fog when I returned to school. I avoided my mother except to wave hello in the halls. In class, I wrote down notes without trying to understand them. In maths, I didn't turn on universal language, and listened to Mr Súanpàn rattle on in Chinese without bothering to try to understand the problems. In my room, I drifted away in my thoughts while people went in and out, studying, chatting, tutoring Miss Chatterjee, and whatever else they were doing. Robbie complained to Avery about again failing to summon Lazar-El, Duke of Water, and I mumbled; Avery worked to develop the first-response power, "Find a Friend," and I was no help; Goldberry tested out her prism and I nodded, not caring; Balaram barged in to ask her out and she sneered at him. I looked at the wall. Delphine did her favorite moves from *Tecktonik*, not very well, in the space between beds, and I just shifted out of the way; Rocco reminded me of the big intramural game coming up, and I was indifferent.

Late at night, about a week after we got back, I went to the meditation hall to be alone. Although people sat in there to study or think, it was always quiet, and you could always feel private. I was there past ten, having ignored several thought-trades from Goldberry to come study, and another to forget it because she was going to bed and I could fail Arcane Literature if I wanted. Finally I got up and headed out, planning to go to the bathroom and then to bed, but as soon as the great doors of the hall shut behind me, I knew I was in trouble. My knees locked and I couldn't walk. My arms weren't working either. Then I lost my vision. Small hands pushed my back, and I fell forward into another pair of hands. I couldn't talk either; I could only feel and hear.

"Come along, Ladybug," said Jonathan St. John. He was dragging me, and the other hands, Josephine's, lifted my feet. They were carrying me.

Goldberry, I'm in trouble.

No response to the thought-trade. She was asleep, not that I blamed her. I was on my own. I tried to visualize the Jonathans, to strike at them, but whatever magic they had used on me had dulled my concentration. My only hope was for someone to come into view while they were carrying me.

The way to get out of trouble at School of the Ages when you were beaten was to surrender, but since I couldn't talk, I couldn't do that either. I was at their mercy.

No luck getting help. A door opened, the air changed, I was dumped on the stone floor. I cracked my head. It hurt. They spread out my arms and legs. I could feel the edges of blankets; I was in a private room, probably his, because Josephine was rooming with Delphine.

What were they going to do? They could stab me, burn me, put any kind of curse on me.

If they were like this at thirteen, what would they be like when they were much older?

I felt Josephine's breaths on my face. "This is nothing compared to what we could do if we wanted. No one crosses the Jonathan family without paying the penalty."

It's not about you, I thought. Just me and Goodenough.

"No, it isn't," she said. "Don't project your thoughts at me, you upstart cretin."

I didn't know I was in her head.

"Get out," she repeated. "I'll break your nose."

I could thought trade with her! And obviously she didn't know how to block that ability, which Goldberry and I had figured out how to do. Normally I used thought trading with friends, but how could I use it against an enemy?

You're angry because you don't have a boyfriend.

"Shut up!" she shouted.

"I will not, Jo," said Jonathan. "Why should I?"

"Not you! Him! He's talking in my head!"

Do you do your brother's laundry for him?

She kicked me in the head. "I said shut up!"

You missed my nose, silly girl.

I felt my eyelids pried open. Apparently I could see, but my eyelids were paralyzed shut. Jonathan St. John was squatting next to me. "Stop your tricks," he said calmly.

You're ugly and you dress funny, I sent to his head.

He stomped on my stomach. I coughed and choked. This must have been how Rocco felt getting beaten by Mermelstein the prior year.

Your feet smell bad, Jon-Jon.

"Stop!" he roared.

Seconds later, the door banged open. His yelling had apparently clued in whoever had noticed I was missing.

Detente

I heard a slap, and he fell across me. Pounding footsteps, scuffing noises. "How dare you?" he shouted, stepping on me as he got up. "This is my room."

"Back off, or I'll snuff you again, and her too," Avery barked. "Let's go, Simon." Her warm hands grasped mine, but she couldn't pull me up. "Get him. I'll watch them."

Stronger hands closed around my wrists and lifted me. I was across Robbie's shoulders. Carrying me, he knocked my head into the doorframe. I tried to groan, but could only breathe hard.

"Whoops. Sorry, roomie. Avery, he's totally paralyzed. How do we get him out of this?"

"They'll tell me," she said, "or I'll beat them both down."

"We're not telling you anything," Josephine said coldly. "and now you're ahead of him on our list."

"You don't scare me," Avery returned, and then Robbie had carried me clear, and I couldn't make out the voices anymore. I was deposited on my bed, and shortly after that the door was shut, and someone was wiping my face with a wet cloth. Blood, I figured.

"They're not talking," Avery said. "Let's figure it out ourselves."

"Right." Robbie stopped dabbing my face. I heard him riffling through a book. "Simon, can you move anything?"

I flexed my facial muscles a little.

"Okay, cool. Once for yes, two for no, okay?"

I flexed once: yes.

"Cool. Do you know what they did to you?"

Two flexes: no.

"Can you turn it off by yourself, now that we have got you clear?"

I didn't know if I could. I tried moving my eyes a little, trying to signal with them, but my eyelids were still stuck closed.

Avery left. Robbie continued to go through books. He was looking for a counter-spell. Finally Avery came back with Goldberry.

Sorry they woke you up, I thought-traded.

"You woke up when I was attacked," she reminded me. "Now what is it? Muscle paralysis?"

I think so, and my mind is affected, too. I can't visualize anything.

"They interfered with his concentration," Goldberry translated. "He can send me thoughts but he can't do anything else."

Robbie was still flipping through books. "I can't find anything in this one, either. Is the Refectory open?"

Goldberry must have closed her eyes. "I don't see anything in his aura, like chains or other bonds. I… Okay, there it is. It looks like a nail through his spine. Can you two visualize it?"

"Yeah, got it," Avery said.

"Uh… Okay, got it," Robbie added.

"Okay, visualize pliers. Let's pull it out."

I got a little feeling in my hands, and I could open my eyes, but the rest of me was still immobile.

"It's stubborn," my partner said. "They must have worked a long time on this spell. We'd better learn how to break it. It could be used on us some day."

"I think I got it," said Avery. I felt a little more relief. I could wiggle my toes, and now I thought I could talk.

"Duh," I said. My tongue wasn't cooperating. "Uhss nug ud."

"One more try," Goldberry said. They closed their eyes. This time all three of them accomplished nothing.

"Help me sit him up."

They manhandled me into an upright position, seated on the bed with my back against the wall. Then she took the crystal from around my neck and sat on a chair as she spoke to Leah. Finally she opened her eyes and spoke a magic phrase: "*Bakhi-a-rot'a.*"

"Nuf," I said.

"It didn't work," Goldberry said. "*Bakhi-a-rot'a. Bakhi-a-rot'a.* Come on, you two."

Robbie and Avery repeated it.

"Well, that hasn't helped much," said my partner. "Right, we'll go to the Refectory and check some books. Simon, want to take a nap?"

If you leave me alone, they might come back, I thought-traded.

"He thinks they may come back," she translated.

"They won't come looking for you," Avery told me. "They're after me now."

Left alone to sleep, I drifted off, waking up briefly to find Robbie dressing for bed himself. "We're going to see if it wears off overnight," he explained. "In the morning, we'll take you to meditation. Maestro Morgan might be able to tell us how to get rid of the spell." He looked sleepy. Soon he was snoring, and I was lying there. I fell asleep. When I woke up hours later, someone was sitting at my bedside leaning over me. "Ladybug," he said. He held a candle near my face.

"Ruh buh," I grunted.

Goodenough leaned back in his chair, looking over his shoulder at Robbie, who was still fast asleep.

"I expect you'd like to go back to normal," my enemy said. "You must be hungry. Wouldn't it be nice to chew or swallow?"

"Don't bother trying to argue. I have the upper hand now, and I'm getting what I want. I'm going to free you to speak, and when I hear what I want, I'll free the rest of you. If I don't hear what I want, I'll paralyze your mouth again. Understand?"

I made a noise. He smiled, and my tongue loosened.

"We don't have to be enemies, Goodenough. We can stop this thing between us."

"Spoken like a boy who's ready to surrender to a man."

"Is that what you want, for me to surrender?"

"No. Goldberry will never take me back if I humiliate you as you properly deserve. My cousins the Jonathans did this on their own anyway; I'm here to help you, not take the blame. I just want a bargain to remove the spell."

"You put this spell on me, Jack Good. Those two are still novices."

"I didn't put the spell on you. Why would I do that?" He smiled, and I saw hatred in his eyes.

"I'm not an idiot, Goodenough. You vowed revenge on me. This is part of your revenge. Goldberry will realize it, too, even if I promise not to tell her."

"Hmm." He actually seemed to be thinking about this.

"And I'll tell you something else. I'm helping the school to fight Gott im Himmel. I shouldn't be tied up fighting you and your insane cousins."

"That's true," he said. "In that case, let's accomplish a few of my goals. I'll free you, and I'll persuade the Jonathans not to beat you up again. In return, I want two things. First, you take charge of that silly puppy Miss Chatterjee. She's been bothering Josephine to study with her, and my cousins don't like her. Tell her to come to you instead. Second, next time Dr Archer is going to Europe, you tell him to leave you here and take me."

"Listen, Goodenough. First, the Dean assigned Josephine to study with Miss Chatterjee."

"I'll have to imagine that was done in order to set up this situation," said Goodenough. "The Dean and his staff can foresee patterns and relationships in a way you can't. You may not see all the connections, but they can, and so can I. Think how that adventure happened to you in your first year–everything just right. Even the worst part, the death of Leah Ritz, gave her a chance to do something that people could admire and talk about. No offense, Ladybug." He saw my face purpling with anger. "Say what you're thinking, and you'll regret it. Just calm down."

I choked back the curses I was thinking of. "Second point," I managed, "the trips to Europe are dangerous. Why do you want to take the risk instead of me?"

"That's not as complicated as you imagine," he said. "Reputation, increased power, and material reward. You came back with money and magical objects, didn't you?"

"I was nearly killed."

"I'm stronger than you."

"So were Dempsey and Chatterjee Major, and they were both badly hurt."

"Is it a bargain?"

"It's a bargain."

Goodenough closed his eyes. Suddenly I could move again. I sat up.

"I won't forget this, Jack Good."

"Who asked you to forget? Remember, and don't cross me again."

Up Against Things

I went out for a walk one night. When I got back to the school, I saw Mr Tinker's Rolls parked outside, and then I saw the man himself waiting for me. He told me to walk with him, and escorted me to an unoccupied classroom.

"Mr Tinker, have you ever killed anyone?"

He paused. "What right do you have to know about that?"

"I don't have any right to know. Why don't you just tell me anyway?"

"I don't talk about those things. I have something more useful to talk about. Do you know 'Up Against the Wall?'" he asked me.

"Is that a song?"

"Obviously not. It's a hex. Archer and I developed it together, although we have our own variations."

"No, I don't know it."

"Up against the wall," he said calmly, gesturing with his palm.

I found myself flying backward, crashing through desks, and my back struck the classroom wall with great force. I slumped down on the floor, holding my knees, trying to shake out the cobwebs. He loomed over me.

"On your knees!" I shouted.

He smiled. "I don't think so. It's a strong spell, but I was prepared. Up against the wall."

The magic actually lifted me from the floor and pressed me against the wall, spread-eagled: another painful impact.

Scorpion sting!

This one he blinked at for a moment.

"A little better," he said softly. "It hurts, but you should multiply it. A single point of attack is too easy to defend against. Up against the wall."

I was banged against the wall again.

"Up," he said.

I slid upwards along the wall, pressed now in the curve where it met the ceiling. He released the magic. I slid down again, but he caught me with his hands before I struck the ground, easing me to the floor.

I had no saliva in my mouth; it was hard to speak. "How do you do it?"

"Erase the space between. It must be instantaneous."

He offered me a hand, but I wasn't interested in his help. I pressed against the wall to lift myself. "Erase the space? How can you visualize that?"

Mr Tinker said, "According to my wife, you and my daughter are going to Europe to fight again this year. If you can't protect her, I'll have to go myself, and I don't mean to leave my wife, so you had best learn something useful while there's still time."

The classroom door opened, and Dr Archer entered. "What are you doing?" he asked Mr Tinker coldly.

"He's teaching me a hex," I said.

"Giving him a beating does not seem a sensible way to teach," he said.

"I can take it," I told him.

"I know," said Dr Archer.

"I don't like hurting the boy," said Mr Tinker, "but I don't have a third party at hand for the demonstration, unless you're volunteering."

"Goodenough's room is just around the corner," I suggested.

Dr Archer raised an eyebrow. "What hex?"

"'Up against the wall,'" said Mr Tinker. "You still use it, I expect."

"I do."

"Well, how do you visualize space so that you can remove it?" I asked.

"Try a vacuum bottle," he said. "A cylinder between the target and the wall, full of a visible gas. Create an opening atop the bottle; the gas flows out, and the bottle empties. The bottle fades, there is empty space."

We continued the practice for some time. Mr Tinker and Dr Archer scowled at each other and spoke coldly, but as the practice continued, I saw traces of another rhythm they had once had, when they had been friends and allies. They referred to their own school days, and their teachers, and their past exercises, and they clearly knew each other's minds and moods. At the end, after dropping me off by the showers to clean up and pour cold water on my bruises, they went off to eat dinner together, talking as readily as if they had never fought. I heard one exchange from the hallway before I put the water on.

Mr Tinker: "So you know. How long have you known?"

Dr Archer: "A few months."

Mr Tinker: "I'm sorry to hear it. Sincerely, Solomon, I am."

Then they passed out of earshot.

Fresh Cut Flowers

"Simon Magus," said Mr Bannerjee, "you please to report to Dean's office, understanding urgency. Correct?"

As he suddenly said this in the middle of teaching the class magic theory, I knew the Dean had contacted him telepathically. I had often seen the Dean do this with members of his staff, but this was the first time I had been present at the other point of contact.

Leaving class suddenly, and shrugging at Goldberry's questioning look, I went up the stairs and along the hall. The outer door was ajar. My mother was sitting behind the desk, her laptop closed, clearly waiting for me. The Dean stood behind her, hands resting on the back of her chair.

"We have sent the bus for your father," the Dean said.

"You owe all of us an explanation," my mother said.

"I didn't really fight him," I said. "It was the poison. He took it himself. I..."

"I know the details of that," said the Dean. "Your mother has already... scolded me about that incident. It is not why you are here."

I then noticed the Dean's private office door opening slowly. I smelled a perfume like fresh flowers. I knew that smell.

Ana Vorkina.

The moment was not real. Someone had deceived me with magic, with illusion. I was in a far-off world different from my own.

"Good morning," she said in thickly accented English. "It is good to see you again."

"Introduce us," my mother said, not like a friend, but definitely like a mother.

"Uh… Did you meet when she came in?"

"You've been avoiding me since that trip," she said. "Now I know why. Introduce us."

I didn't know what to say. Ana was there. I was in that other world, the one different from my world, the world that had her in it.

"Now, Leicester."

I looked at Ana. "You didn't come back. I thought it was over." I couldn't stop looking at her -- the peasant skirt, plain black shoes, lacy blouse, button nose, hair tied back, eyes with irises that shone like sunlight on the river. "I thought I would never see you again."

"We had a bargain," Ana said, her eyes darting from me to my mother to the Dean. "You fought Pavel Rod. I agreed to visit you here. I have come."

"For…" Still I tried to gather myself. "For how long?" I quickly glanced at my mother, and saw more kindness in her worried expression than I had expected. What was going on between Ana and me was clearly more important to her than what was going on between us Moores.

"My father says I am to stay until you tell me to go. He was angry with me. I understand that. I am also angry with me, and I am sorry." She smiled, lowering her eyes slightly, a new expression of warmth that I was not expecting. "Please, will you introduce me to this lady?"

"Yes. Ana Vorkina, please meet my mother, Mrs Magdalene Moore."

Ana bowed to her and offered a handshake. "I am Ana Vorkina. Your son is brave and powerful. You must be proud of him."

"I am," my mother said. "but how do you know my son?"

Ana looked at me. "I will say?"

I sighed and nodded.

"My father was here not long ago. He invited Simon to visit us in Prague."

"I met your father. Why did he invite my son?"

"He is offering a marriage for your son."

My mother settled deep into her chair, looking at Ana and then at me.

"I am here to be with Simon to see if we will decide to get married."

"My son didn't tell me," my mother said.

"Nor was I informed of this visit, until this morning," said the Dean. "In respect of our new friendship with Arch-Mage Jan Vorkin, I believe that housing and a class schedule for Miss Vorkina can be arranged."

"I didn't know she was coming," I said haltingly. "I didn't think I held up my end of the bargain, because I lost that fight. Ana, I thought you were done with me."

"My father does not think so."

"Yes, but Ana, what do *you* think? That's more important."

She took a long time, maybe struggling for English words, maybe struggling with her feelings. "I was not fair to you before. I should not have thrown you into danger. It is not right to ask a boy to pass a test before you will like him. I have thought about it. There is nothing wrong to stay here for some time.

"Leicester," my mother said. She got up, came to me, touched my forearm gently. "We need to meet her parents. That's how arranged marriages are supposed to be done. You should have told us right away."

"I know," I said, "but I wasn't taking it seriously when I went there. I was planning to get out of it somehow. Then I thought I screwed up and it was over."

My mother looked at the Dean. "Can my son and I use your office?"

"Of course," he said. "Miss Vorkina, come with me. We shall make arrangements for your stay."

When he and Ana were gone, my mother led me to the Dean's office and slammed the door. She sat me down in his chair and perched on the desk.

"Is this what you want, Leicester?" she demanded. "This school has imposed a lot of things on you before." She stopped. "No, that's a stupid question. I saw you light up when that girl came into the room."

"Was it… I mean, was I really obvious?"

"I'm your mother, Leicester." She seemed to be struggling to gather strength. "Oh, God, you're so young."

"And do you think she knows? Can she tell how much I…?"

"I don't know what she's thinking, but I am sure of one thing. Unlike when you went to her home, she hasn't come here to play games. You've made a mess of this thing. You should have talked to me. You never tell me what's going on with you. It's really immature and I'm really tired of it."

"Well, I'm sorry, but I have to take care of my own business."

"You're a child, Leicester. You don't have your own business."

Why did we have to argue about this when Ana was so near to me? Why was I fighting with my mother?

"I told you I didn't want you to work here, interfering with everything. You can't stop me from being with Ana. If she ever wants that, I mean. You can't! I mean…. Please don't." I was gasping for breath, trying not to cry.

My mother got off the desk and came to the chair, putting her arms around me. "I don't want to stop anything, Leicester. I just don't want you to shut me out. I don't want to run your life. I just want to be part of it. Since you started at this school, everything has gone so far from what I ever imagined for your future."

We were quiet for a while.

I wiped my face on my sweatshirt sleeve. "Do you think she likes me?"

"Well, you do have your father's looks. She may be hard to read, but I can tell you this. When people come from a reserved culture, like the Czechs, they don't always say things directly. So I can only say this: she wouldn't be here if there wasn't a chance."

My father came in. She sent me to the outer office while she filled him in. He finally came out and said, "Let's walk."

Making Arrangements

"Arranged marriages are still pretty common in India" my father said. "I grew up with five brothers, and four of them got married that way. Your grandmother tried quite a few times to match me up, which is one of the reasons I came to New York–I wanted to choose for myself."

We were now heading down the stairs.

"You're really too young."

He stopped on the steps and held me by the shoulders. "I know you were shocked when that girl Leah died. I wish I had gotten to meet her. But you have to heal from that, Leicester. Remember her, honour her, but live a normal life. Are you sure you didn't fall too hard for this new girl because you were so upset before you met her?"

"You have to meet her," was all I could say. "You'll understand. I only met her once, and I just knew."

"Once was all it took, huh? Well, your mother affected me like that, but I was thirty-five at the time and had much more life experience. Now I'm fifty, and you're only fifteen. But you are too young for marriage. Be good friends and enjoy yourself."

"Please meet her," I said weakly.

"Of course I will. Believe me, I can tell your feelings are pretty strong, but that's also part of being fifteen. Who are her parents?"

"Her mother is dead. Her father Jan Vorkin is an arch-mage. That means he's the most dangerous man you ever met."

My father smiled. "A man is a man, and if he likes you enough to match you with his daughter, he must be a good judge of character."

We went into the room. Goldberry was sitting at the desk.

"Good morning, Mr Moore," she said. "I need to have a word with your son. He doesn't bother to tell me anything I really need to know."

"This *is* just what his mother is complaining about. Mind if I sit here?" Goldberry took me into a nearby empty classroom and closed the door. "I don't know what happened, but I can tell…"

She had probably done her mental tarot card reading when I was sent out of class.

"You can tell it's serious."

"Bloody well right I can. I may not be at my best, but it doesn't take much to know you're not yourself."

"Ana is here."

"Listen, I didn't tell her much about the school. She doesn't know about our study partner system. So…"

Goldberry was sharp and took the point at once. "So I might look like a rival." "You do understand," I said slowly, "that you are really gorgeous and glamorous, and that makes you a rival for any other girl."

"True enough, but you're not asking me to fade into the background, I hope."

"No! I just mean, we have to be ready to explain."

"Explain that you don't fancy me, and even though I'm wearing your mother's engagement ring, you have totally resisted my charms, and I'm just your chaste little sister. Right?" There was danger in her voice: she didn't want to be pushed to the side by anyone, any time, and I didn't blame her.

"Well, that is all true, but not the way you're making it sound."

"Because as far as I'm concerned, she has a lot to prove to me after what she did to you the last time you saw her."

…………………………………………………………………………

I said "You're my best friend."

"Yes," she said. "Lucky for you. I'll be nice."

It was lunch time. Goldberry lied that she had some last-minute homework to do and left me to go to the dining hall alone. There I found Ana with Ms. Roosevelt-Wilson, the registrar. A number of kids were nearby, observing the newcomer, as kids do. I thanked the registrar and then stood there awkwardly, looking from Ana to the group.

"Charming girl," Ms. Roosevelt-Wilson whispered in my ear.

I was alone with Ana for a few seconds.

"I'm very happy to see you," I said. "I need to explain some…"

Then the crowd came.

The first was Mina, from the divination club. In her black tank top and jeans, black eye shadow, large silver pendant shaped like a bat, she definitely looked like the victim of Dracula that had inspired her magician's name. "Simon Magus, the spirits have bidden me ask you…"

"This is Ana, my friend from Prague. Ana, this is Mina."

Mina offered her usual weak handshake. "It happens that we have room for a new member in our divination club. Would you like to join?"

"All right," Ana said warily.

"Come and eat with us." She was about to pull Ana's hand when the next wave arrived, Robbie and Avery. I made the introductions. They knew all about Ana, but were smart enough (at least Avery was) to pretend otherwise. Soon she had an appointment to summon elementals over the weekend. Then came Rocco. I hadn't told him about Ana, so when I introduced her as my friend from Prague, he said, "Well, if you like, Ana, I'll buy you dinner and show you around the school after."

"No," she said. "I am with Simon."

"Oh. Right. Okay, sure. Have fun." Smiling, he went back to his table, where he was sitting with King planning strategy for the upcoming intramural game. Rocco could be persistent with girls, but right now he had hockey on his mind.

There was a tap on my shoulder. Goodenough was there, and as usual, I hadn't seen him coming. The Jonathans stood a few feet back, close enough to listen, standing together in their grey suits like twin devils.

"Introduction, please," he said, and he mouthed 'Ladybug.'

"Ana, this is William Goodenough. Goodenough, this is Ana Vorkina from Prague."

"Any relation to the Arch-Mage?" he asked smoothly. He must have known the answer.

"I am his daughter." She looked at him puzzled. What was Goodenough up to?

"We have a truce, Jack Good," I reminded him.

"Don't be hostile," he replied. "At your service, Ana Vorkina." He then grabbed Mina's arm – she was his study partner – and dragged her off. The Jonathans followed.

"He is your enemy," Ana said.

"He's my enemy."

"Then he is my enemy." She wasn't declaring, but explaining. If she was associated with me, then my enemies might choose to attack her.

I didn't want to get into that yet. "Did you eat?"

I showed her where to get food. School of the Ages had a regular dining hall and a kosher dining hall, each with its own kitchen, and the kitchen staff, whom we rarely saw or talked to, put out hot food for the three meals and snacks in the evening. We made our own tea and coffee.

Ana and I sat with full plates but didn't eat much. "I can't believe you're here."

She said "The students are strange. All of them want something. I will be careful whom to trust."

"You can trust Robbie and Avery and Rocco and my study partner Goldberry. You'll meet her soon."

Ana nodded. "The Dean explained to me about study partners.

Is she a pretty girl?"

"Yes, she's a very pretty girl, but we're like sister and brother."

"Really? And when did that start?"

"It was always like that."

We walked.

"What about Eduard?" I asked her.

Ana shrugged. "He went to Pardubice for a month. He will live, whether he sees me or not."

We kept walking. We passed a classroom with an open door. Ana stopped, catching my sleeve to stop me, and paused by the door to listen. It was the first year of magic theory. Mr Bannerjee was explaining an exercise to develop universal language. Ana was speaking English pretty well inside the school, but she clearly didn't understand him.

My room door was open.

Robbie, Balaram, and my father were inside. Seeing us, my father stood and came to the door.

"Martin Moore," he said, offering a handshake. "I'm…"

"Simon's father. Yes, I see he looks like you."

"Mostly. I think he's more handsome, but I'm better dressed. Boys, could you excuse us?"

Robbie and Balaram rarely studied together in our room, so my roommate seemed to have brought his partner there specifically to get a look at Ana. It was hard to get rid of them, but my father kept up the gentle requests. Finally they took their books and went into the hall, but they stood in the doorway watching. I started to close the door.

"Wait," Balaram said. "Hey, Ana, I have a magic trick to show you. You interested?"

"What is it?"

"I can tell you what you really want in life."

Balaram had developed this trick as his first-response power the year before at the same time I developed my "on your knees" tactic. He saw images or heard words in a variety of languages and interpreted them pretty skillfully. Ana's forehead wrinkled. "Why do you think I don't know that? Or maybe you want to know? It's not your business."

I closed the door.

"Well, my dear," my father said, "I want you to know that my wife and I are always available, at all hours, if you need anything, or even if you just get tired of school and want a home-cooked meal. Treat us like your own parents. Okay?" He left.

She was sitting in my desk chair. I sat on the bed.

"Anything you want to ask about? I mean, about the school?"

Ana frowned. "It is already a lot for one day."

"Well, then… How's your room?"

"It is dark and cold. Same as this one, but it has a window. How are you used to having no lights?" She looked at the flickering candles on the desk in front of her.

"I don't know. I got used to it. Next year I get a room with a window too."

"How did you get here?"

"Airplane. Your bus collected me at the airport."

"You must be tired."

"I am tired."

I got up. "You can take a nap here."

Ana took off her shoes and lay on the bed. "I think you can leave me and go to your classes."

Classes … yes, I remembered having those. In fact, I was missing a test in one of them. I picked up my school bag. "Ana, I'm really glad you're here. I… I didn't like not seeing you before I left."

Ana yawned and closed her eyes.

Doubts

I went to Arcane Literature class. After class, in the hall on the way to maths, Goldberry stopped me. "Where is she?"

"Sleeping in my room. I'll go wake her up later for dinner. Eat with us."

"Oh, am I welcome?"

"You don't ever need to ask that."

"Things are different now."

"Not between you and me." I looked closely into her hazel eyes. "You're not jealous," I said.

"Truthfully, this situation makes me suspicious, and I wouldn't be a good partner if I didn't tell you so."

"Suspicious how?"

"When you first met her, she nearly got you killed."

"She didn't mean to."

"Suppose she didn't; it was still reckless, wasn't it?"

"It was my fault, too. I wasn't careful enough. I didn't think Pavel Rod would be that dangerous. That wasn't her fault."

"Wasn't it?"

"I fell for her. That's not her fault."

"She didn't want you to?"

"No. No, she had somebody. Goldberry, I told you all this."

"And you didn't question it. Simon," she said sadly, "you are very naïve, you know. People aren't always honest. I learned a lot from William in two years about the kinds of games people play."

Fortunately, there was a classroom nearby. Surprised by my own anger, I dragged her by the arm into the room and slammed the door.

"Explain what you mean. Now!" I demanded of Goldberry.

"First of all, let go of my arm, partner. And don't even think of putting me on my knees."

I did let go. I had left a red mark on her arm. I was really ready to fight, and so was Goldberry. In over two years, we had never been anywhere near coming to blows. She was family, and she was vulnerable after being tormented by Gott im Himmel. I should be protecting her, not hurting her. Something wasn't right in my head. It was time to calm down.

Closing my eyes, I dropped my cylinder of continuous defense. I fell into a chair. I visualized the hourglass, top and bottom cones in opposite rotation, and breathed in and out slowly. I was able to quiet myself, at least physically. "I'm sorry," I said. "What are you trying to tell me?"

Goldberry apparently couldn't sit down; she paced as she spoke. "What I mean to say is that everything you did with her, everything she said, it all could have been planned. What if the trip to that crazy man's house was her father's idea? Look, Simon, we're still at war. This cabal can use people we trust to attack us. They controlled your brother when they attacked me. How would they try to get at you? After the medusa girl beat you, they might have marked you down as weak against girls and set this up."

"All that is too complicated," I said desperately.

"Well, how about this: suppose the Arch-Mage and his daughter are innocent. How do you know this girl inside the building is the same one you met in Prague? She could be an infiltrator of some sort, with a magical disguise, or a wicked spirit in her shape?"

The words stung. On the surface, Goldberry was right that trusted too easily, but…

"Goldberry, you have to understand. I couldn't be fooled. I just feel connected to her. It's like she's perfect."

Goldberry turned away. I continued, "I mean, everything you're saying makes sense, but .. what am I supposed to do?" I could hear a whining tone in my voice. "I like her so much, and you say I can't trust her?"

Goldberry finally came and sat by me. "Well, I don't know for sure. When it comes to a lot of situations, I trust your instincts, but you're too tender with girls. You haven't a clue about them. She may be just as you say, but you have to guard yourself. Get some help figuring her out. It's all very sudden."

"And that bothers you?"

"No, that's not what I mean. Leah fell for you fast. You have a pure heart, Simon. I mean that you always put other people before yourself, and it's not hard to see that about you. That's why Leah liked you right away, and… another girl could be the same way."

I was stunned. I had never heard Goldberry sound so mature.

She said, "Sorry, that wasn't much of a pep talk, but you aren't easy to get through to. It's partly me too, I'm so bloody frustrated that I can't do divination properly."

"My father seemed to trust her, and Ms. Roosevelt-Wilson said she approved. Does that help?"

"Your father is nearly as shrewd as mine, so it does help a bit. Maybe I am worrying a bit much. Simon, it's not that I don't want you to be in love again. I saw you with Leah and I saw how she was too. You take care of people, and you deserve to have someone to take care of y ou." She let go and sat back in her chair. "I wish I could do more to help us. And we have to be careful about asking for help. No one in the club, that's for sure."

"Balaram's trick?"

"Could do. Did he meet her?"

"Not only that, he was offering."

❖ ❖ ❖

Goldberry and I found Balaram in his room. She started things off. "You met this girl Ana. What was your first impression?"

"Seriously? I thought she was pretty. But if I had to pick between her and you, I'd.."

" We're here to be serious. What did your power tell you? What does she really want?"

"That will cost you," he said, grinning.

Goldberry said, "right. What do you want?"

"How about fifty Euros?" I offered.

"My boy's got money," he said. "I figure if you have fifty Euros, you have a hundred. Right, bro?"

"I do, but why are you bargaining so hard, Balaram? Aren't we friends?"

"Sure we are. Which is why you understand that I lose some dollar value when I exchange the currency."

"A hundred Euros, agreed."

"Okay deal. Let me see the money."

" I'll give it to you at meditation."

"Well then," Balaram said giving in, "I do the trick on everyone I meet, sometimes more than once. For her, I did it right away because she's so pretty. What I saw was one of those armoured knights, like in the castles in Europe. You know, King Arthur knights, sort of. Really shiny and bright armour."

"She wants that, or she wants to be that?" I asked.

"Could be either one."

"Did it seem good, positive, you know?"

"Oh yeah," Balaram said. "I didn't get a bad feeling. She's not some monster. Hey, what's this about? I thought she was your girl."

"We're figuring that out now."

"You and her, or you and Goldberry?" He grinned, then shook his head. "Right, I know, none of my business."

New Love and Old

I knocked firmly on the door, heard a muted reply from inside and slowly let myself in. Ana was sitting up, looking at one of my textbooks. She was drinking a bottle of spring water I had lying around.

"This water tasted bad," she said. "I improved it." She handed me the bottle. I took a sip while she and Goldberry eyed each other. The water was very sweet.

"It's much better," I said.

"Good trick," said my partner, entering and offering a handshake. "Goldberry Tinker–Simon's study partner. Come and have dinner, just the two of us."

"All right," Ana said. "You may call me Ana. I know now who you are. My father described to me a beautiful girl he met."

My partner said, "I am hungry, and I can tell by your face that you are too. Let's go."

Why can't I eat with you guys? I thought-traded with her.

Goldberry thought I should stop annoying her and leave them alone together for a while.

Ana had already met most of the important people in my life, but there was one I needed to take the time to talk to. I lay down on the bed and touched the crystal.

Hello, Leah.

I entered a deep trance. The room melted away, and I found

myself sitting in a library of Hebrew holy books, settled comfortably on a bench. Leah was across from me with a book open in front of her. Although her face was older and wiser, she was dressed exactly as she had been the day I met her, and as I saw her in my dreams, in a black dress with white lace cuffs.

"Hello, Simon."

"How is this happening? It isn't like our usual talks."

Leah smiled. "This talk is very important to both of us, and we are each using a little bit of extra magic to make it happen. Let's talk quickly because you will be called back soon."

I got to the point. "Were you with me today? Do you know what's happening?"

"Yes, Simon." Her voice was so sweet, so kind.

"I know I should talk to you more often."

"You don't have to do that. I have many voices that I can hear where I am."

"Leah, I promised you when you died that I would always be faithful to you. I'm sorry. I know I shouldn't be with Ana."

"When I died?" Leah sounded surprised. "That's not what I remember you saying. But it doesn't matter. You don't need to make that sort of promise to me."

"I owe it to you. You sacrificed your life for me."

"I don't think that way at all," she said. "I was meant to have only a short time in a body. I really belong where I am. I am needed here."

There was no answer to this. Time was pressing. I had to move on. "What do you think about Ana? I don't want to do anything if you don't approve."

Leah smiled. "Simon, we are all in God's love. It is right for us to care for each other."

"But Leah, I don't know what to do. I always said I would never love anyone but you, but I can't fight against loving her."

"Oh, Simon. You don't have to feel bad about that. We had such a short time, and we were very young. I always knew you would need someone. You'll be a man soon."

"You won't be angry?"

"Simon, I won't be jealous. Your soul and mine mingled for the purposes of the universe, and that is a greater cause than the love of a girl and a boy. Go back to the world and love Ana. I will always be with you."

Is Death the End?

Ana didn't come back to my room after dinner. Goldberry, where are you guys?

She wanted me to leave them alone.

I walked the halls and finally wound up by the faculty offices, where I saw that Dr Archer's door was ajar, and there was light inside.

"Come in," he said before I knocked.

I entered. I hadn't seen him since we returned from Europe where he had been hurt fighting Dr Beam. There were some large scabs, suggesting his face had been cut or pierced. Behind his wire-rimmed glasses, his eyes were tired, but penetrating.

"I met Ana Vorkina," he said without preamble.

I asked him, "She's not a spy, or someone else in disguise, right?"

He showed me some astrological notes on his desk: a chart drawn like a wagon wheel, with various markings between the spokes. Although the basics had been taught to me in Divination Club my first year, I was hopeless at astrology, just as I was at tarot reading and every other type of fortune-telling.

"I have been researching this case in preparation for your visit. Indeed, it is of great importance, given not only my commitment as your mentor to your successful future, and the Dean's regard for your mother, but also because of the implications for School of the Ages if the Arch-Mage's child should become attached to the community in the long-term. These charts are hastily prepared but I conclude from them, with as much certainty as exists within my professional expertise, that she who is Ana Vorkina in appearance is indeed Ana Vorkina, and that she has represented herself and her motives with complete honesty."

It was as if a burden was lifted and I felt lighter than I had all day.

Dr Archer cautioned. "I believe there to be no deceptive or malign forces directly connected to your relationship. Of course, Gott im Himmel is still a lingering enemy."

"I have to tell you something about that," I said. A bargain was a bargain, and I had to fulfill its terms. "I don't want to go with you next time. Next time, take Goodenough instead of me."

Dr Archer removed his glasses and rubbed his eyes.

"He's more powerful than I am, anyway."

"Measures of power are ridiculous. I do not select companions on the basis of power. William is my protégé, even as you are, and his education is important to me, so that when I take him on a mission, it will be with William's benefit in mind. In every case thus far I have selected you as my companion not due to any frailty of my own, but for purposes of your education and your future. You and Goldberry are quite mistaken in your fears for my safety. I do not need assistance from anyone because that person is 'powerful.' I have given nearly forty years to this school, many of them in the role I currently occupy. My father and grandfather did the same in their turns. I am not especially or particularly vulnerable, any more than other human beings, and what risks I take are calculated and well-researched. Once and for all, put these concerns out of your mind!"

Dr Archer had not been so imperious with me since our first year together, and I had perhaps forgotten what authority he possessed. However, unlike when I had first met him at age thirteen, I didn't easily back off.

"Dr Archer, I'll shut up if you want, but I know I'm not wrong.

If Goldberry and I both think you need help, you should listen to us, since you taught us how to know when things aren't right. Please don't be stubborn. You need help. I can't go this time. Take Goodenough."

"You are ordering me, it seems," he said, putting his glasses back on. "I feel this insistence upon the companionship of William is not entirely of your own devising. He has compelled you to say so."

I nodded.

"And in doing so, he has accidentally served your interest, since you would not at present wish to be parted from Miss Vorkina."

I nodded to that as well. Then I added, "I would go, though, if you needed me to. I'll do anything you ask."

"In that case," Dr Archer said, "attend to your studies. William Goodenough and I are leaving in a week for Amsterdam, for an extended stay, and there we will pursue the magician Kees, whose name Dr Beam revealed."

"You were already planning to go with Goodenough."

"Yes. William's practice at manipulating minds should indeed be of greater use in this instance, since we must extract information from unwilling sources, than your own ability to confront and remove opponents and obstacles. However, I shall require you again later in the year."

"Of course."

Dr Archer fished out another astrological chart from the pile on his desk. "Here is information I have compiled regarding the next month of my life. For the first time in several years, Mercury has become ascendant in the house of my birth. This has a great significance for me because in the past whenever this took place it corresponded to my visits to Johanna Strauss."

"The diviner from Vienna who died?"

"Indeed. She died purportedly of cancer, but I have long suspected that she was, in fact, murdered by a curse from a Gott im Himmel magician. My primary reason for believing this is that her oracular tools were stolen from her home shortly after her death, during the same attack that injured the Dean's son Dempsey, who was guarding the premises. I interpret the chart to mean that since I will not be seeing Johanna herself I will instead be seeing a desirable alternative–the magician most directly responsible for her death."

"Dr Archer, you knew Johanna Strauss for a long time, didn't you?"

"She attended this school and was my wife's best friend."

"So if this Kees killed her, then it's personal."

"Yes."

"Are you going to kill him?"

"Yes."

"How?"

"Pardon?"

"How do you kill someone? What magic do you use to kill a person?"

"I will not speak of this tonight," Dr Archer said. "I believe your parents would not approve were I to impart such knowledge."

"But you know how to do it?"

"Yes. In person, without witnesses, it is not difficult for one magician to kill another."

I had no answer to this.

❖ ❖ ❖

Ana was waiting for me in the hallway by my room. "Walk with me," she said. Her room was up the stairs, at the end of a hallway where graduating seniors usually stayed. Her room was bare except for her suitcase. Sheets, a blanket, pillows, towels, candles, and a box of matches lay on the bed and desk–every student received this collection of basic supplies at the start of the school term.

"You know about meditation in the morning, before breakfast?"

"Yes, the Dean explained."

"Did it go all right with Goldberry?"

"Yes. I understand her. If I hurt you, she will crush me under her foot like an insect. It is the right feeling to have. I would do that for my brothers."

"And I would do that for her," I said. "And… I would do that for you."

Before the Big Game

I couldn't find Ana in the morning, before or after meditation. I went to breakfast and found Goldberry, Avery, and Delphine.

"It went all right at dinner last night?" I asked my partner.

"Yes. I read her palm. Her life has been difficult, but it should be better for a while. It's good for her to be away from home."

"Did you tell her that if she hurts me, you'll hurt her?"

"Absolutely not. I told you I'd be nice. She must have smelled it on me. Water signs can do that."

"You want someone to tell her that?" Avery said. "I'll tell her."

"I don't want anyone to do anything except be as nice to her as possible. If you get mad at her, you can punch me."

Avery laughed. "Then I guess I'm mad at her right now. Stick out your chin."

Delphine got up and stood between us. "Oh! Please don't fight!"

"She's just kidding, Delphine," I said.

Ana came later, and after we said hello, Goldberry took her to get school supplies from the common cabinet. Meanwhile, the rest of us looked over her schedule, which wasn't typical. She had Summoning IV, but her other classes were first-year, including Construction I, basic Hebrew, Magic Theory I, and a tutorial with Mr Phillips. There were no classes with me–probably a good idea, if I was going to concentrate on school at all–but there were several classes with Delphine, who pledged that they would study together and be best friends.

"I thought Mermelstein was your best friend," I said.

"No! He's my big brother."

First class that morning was Construction III with Rabbi Horn. He was planning the year's field trip.

"Let's go to Prague," I suggested. "Anything there? Secret temples, medieval buildings? We have full freedom of operation there now."

"I think if we go to Prague," I said, "we'll be safer than anywhere else in Europe."

"Well, that may be true," Rabbi Horn admitted.

"I'm for going to Prague," Rocco said.

"All right, all right," Rabbi Horn said. "I'll look into it."

At lunch, Rocco rushed to sit by me. "I backed you on that Prague thing," he said. "Now you're going to back me, right?"

"About what?"

"The intramural game tomorrow morning against the Cabala school. I told you about it last month. You need to hex for me."

"Rocco, Ana's here. I need to be with her right now."

"So show off for her. I need your help, Simon."

"It's just a game."

"The whole school will be there, especially if they hear you're going against Mermelstein. Kids have been wanting you to fight him again since first year. They'll all come. I'm going to try something new I've been working on."

"Rocco, it's just a game."

As cheerful as he normally was, Rocco was getting impatient. "You promised me when school started, and I'm holding you to it. What's the big deal? It's like two hours of your life. These guys from the Cabala school are really bullying us, too.

"Simon, you need to understand. You get to run to Europe with Dr Archer, and you're doing stuff with him all the time. Dr Chatterjee didn't take me when he went. I don't have so many chances to get experience or build my reputation. I know intramurals isn't as important, but it gets us ready for league play next year and that's a chance to get noticed by the magic community."

"Getting noticed means making enemies," I pointed out. "For the record, Goldberry and I told Dr Archer he should get you involved. Why don't you go to Dr Chatterjee and volunteer?"

"I did, a couple of times. He said to wait for the right moment. It's getting frustrating." Suddenly his attention shifted. "Oh, great." He looked over his shoulder, and so did I, and there they were: Haim Fox, the Cabala school intramural captain the bullet-headed young Yonah Finkel, and the looming Lowenthal, framed by the entrance to the dining hall. They were carrying sticks and pads and dirty shoes—done with their afternoon prayer, and headed for hockey practice. They found us at our usual table and swaggered over to confront us. Rocco stood forcing me to do the same, and just like that there was a face-off.

"You're in trouble tomorrow, Rocco," Fox said. "No way I'm losing a game in my last year. You've got nobody that can block Benzy."

"What if he trips over his shoelaces or bangs his head on the ceiling," Rocco answered.

"After we blow you guys away," Lowenthal said in a voice that hadn't quite lost its youthful squeakiness, "I'll get a slot at HUN next year." HUN was Hermetic University of the Negev, a large Israeli magic school.

"Big talk," Rocco said, "but we have the edge in hexing."

"You kidding?" Finkel said. "We got Mermelstein. King's not half as good." "King's playing, smart guy," Rocco answered. "My sideline hexer is Simon Magus."

"So what?" Finkel said, giving me a dismissive look. "Everyone knows he can't handle Mermelstein."

"I'm friends with Mermelstein," I said. "We might hex each other, but we're not going to fight. You can try to start something if you want,

Finkel, but it's just a game."

"Well, how about this," Fox said. "You do your worst, and if we win, you both kiss Benzy's foot."

"Guys," I said, "for the last time, it's just a game. I'm not looking for a fight. I don't fight for fun. I only fight for things that matter."

I noticed the Chasidic boys taking a step back, and less than a second later, realized why: the sweet scent of fresh flowers. Ana had come up behind me Orthodox boys were usually a little nervous around pretty girls.

"Who are these boys?" she asked me.

"I'll tell you what matters," Finkel said, raising his voice. "You had lessons with the Rambal last year. I'm in my second year, and I hardly even see him. What's so great about you?" Raising his hand, he pointed his index finger directly in my face.

"Yonah, don't," Fox said. Pointing the finger is forbidden in Orthodox custom; it was probably the strongest disrespect Finkel could imagine, and he was doing it in front of Ana.

"I was messed up last year, and the Rambal gave me some advice. That's all."

He came back at me right away. "Messed up because you got that girl killed. Everyone knows she had it coming for reading Talmud."

I had no time to think; in a split second I had my right hand around his throat. His pointing finger was gone, and with fear in his green eyes, he pushed me away and fell over backwards.

"What is this about?" Ana asked.

"A hockey game," I said. "Fox, you want to back him off?" Rocco said. "Simon's holding back now. If he gets mad, Yonah won't be in any shape to play tomorrow." "Yeah, I'm scared," Finkel sneered.

"Yes you are," Ana said, "I can smell it." She stepped next to me, lightly touching my arm.

King, Robbie, and Avery had just entered the dining hall; seeing what was going on, they joined us. Fox pulled his teammates away from our team. "Finkel shouldn't have mentioned the girl," he said over his shoulder. "I hate bullies," Ana said. "When is this game? I think you should teach them a lesson." "That's right," Rocco added. "That was low. Finkel has it coming."

We explained to Ana what the rules were; she knew about ice hockey, but floor hockey, with tennis shoes on a gym floor was new to her.

"I'm sorry," I told my friends. "I shouldn't have let him get to me. He was trying to psych me out. Rocco, are you sure you can't let me out of this?"

"I need you as a balance for Mermelstein's hexing. It's just one game, okay? Once I debut my new move, everyone will be coming to see that instead, and I won't need you again."

"He will be there," Ana said. We went to lunch.

"You do not have to say," she told me, "but I want to know what is this he said about the girl that made you attack him."

I explained to her briefly–that Leah had been an Orthodox girl reading Talmud, which is unpopular in a lot of the Jewish community, and that she had been regularly attacked magically by the older kids at the Cabala school, who wanted her to stop doing it, and that I had fought about it before. I also told her who Mermelstein was, and how our relationship had changed from enemies to friends in two and a half years. Ana nodded often, asking a lot of questions. It filled a lot of time, till lunch was over and we both had to leave for class.

"I am learning a lot about you," she said at the end of the talk. "Tonight, you do not think of me. You think about this game. Help your friend. Stop the bullies."

The Big Game

While the remainder of the team was practicing on the court and Goldberry was keeping Ana company I'd spent the previous night looking through my school notebooks for hexes, hoping to find some the Cabala school kids wouldn't be expecting. Miss Chatterjee, who was in my room most nights, copied some of my ideas into her own notebook, promising to work on them as well. I came up with a list of about six I was going to try, specifically leaving out "up against the wall," which was brutal, and also my first-response, "on your knees,"—both only for serious situations. Miss Chatterjee helped me assemble some components that might make the hexes more effective.

Games at School of the Ages were held in the morning, to admit lots of sunlight from the gym's windows. As a result, after meditation, both teams only had a light snack before reporting to the gym.

Mr Bannerjee was wearing a referee's shirt and a baseball cap and carrying his usual whistle and clipboard. As for other adults, the Dean and my mother were there, as well as most of the full-time teachers. Every student in the school that I knew was present, except for William Goodenough, who was still in Amsterdam with Dr Archer. Miss Chatterjee, Goldberry and Ana sat together. To my surprise, Corby Crow, Rocco's usually absent study partner sat in the front row.

As we waited, various parents also arrived on both sides. I said hello to the Vitellos, Rocco's parents, and to Dr Pierre, Avery's mother, who sat with the Ravitzes. When it was time Mr Bannerjee called both teams to the center of the court.

Not everyone has seen a hockey game in a gymnasium. Two plastic frames with nets were set up at opposite ends. Because of the school's small student body, teams of five were fielded for intramurals– our interleague team would take players from both teams. The goalkeeper wore a chest plate, shin guards, elbow and knee pads, and a mask. Kids wore athletic clothes of their own choice and used basic hockey sticks. The Chasidic kids played in black pants, white shirts with the *tallis* hanging out.

When the game started, the teams would move back and forth pushing the ball with their sticks. Other than goalkeeper and sideline hexer, there were no fixed positions in this version of the game; everyone had free movement throughout the court. We sideline hexers were established on opposite sides of the court, each of us to stand in a small zone defined by tape on the floor. The official rule was that we could only hex the players and each other. The other kids in the school were not supposed to get involved, but we figured they would.

"Not to cause permanent injury," Mr Bannerjee insisted. "Attacks with hex being only to distract or to cause fumbles. Actual wounds are fouls, two penalty shots result. No hexing against players doing face-off, wait for ball to be in play. Maybe I am not looking, but I know what you are doing. This being clear, I hope. This is a game only, and players we are wanting against other schools next year. Same rules agreed, now being told at Archway Prep, Institute for Creative Hermetics, San Francisco Hospitallers, etc. Careful also not to hit with sticks or body parts. High sticking of course penalty shot. Serious injuries very regrettable because no healing crystal skulls available."

We all nodded. The captains went to the teams. Rocco's team– Robbie, King, Rocco's orthodox roommate Daniel, Avery as goalie, and me– looked weak against Fox, Finkel, the gigantic Lowenthal, and graduating senior Shifrin. Meir Kupferberg was their goalie, probably not as good as Avery, but I doubted he was a weak link, either. Mermelstein was absolutely deadly, of course. I had something to clarify with him first, so I stopped him, offering a handshake, which he accepted. I held onto his hand and spoke as close to his ear as I could– given our height difference. He had to lean over to hear me. "This is just a game, Yakov. It's stupid to get mad over it, right?"

He shrugged. "They asked me, that's all."

"Well, people seem to care which one of us is better at hexes, but I don't care. So whatever we do, it's just for fun."

"Sure," he said. "But if I hit you with something, you should go down." He pulled his hand free. "After the game, back to normal."

We went to our individual taped areas. The goalies got in position. The teams faced off. I reinforced my personal defensive cylinder with a layer of stone. Mr Bannerjee blew the whistle and dropped the ball. The Chasidic fans roared.

First things first: Finkel. I had prepared a full visualization of him the night before, and was able to call it back into my mind quickly. I shouted his name and pointed at him. It was my new hex: Seven Stings. Specifically, it was an extension of the single sting I had learned to use the previous year to disarm a person. This spell was seven simultaneous highly painful, throbbing scorpion stings– left hand, right hand, left knee, right knee, left eye, right eye, gut. He went down like he had been shot. Dazed, he got to his feet, coughing, alternately rubbing his eyes and shaking his hands. Because of the angle at which at which he had fallen, his stick had cracked. The ball had gone past him, and King was moving it towards the goal, but Shifrin cut him off. A kid on the Cabala school side passed a new stick out to Finkel, and he gave me an angry look, but I'd made my point. I wouldn't have any more trouble from him.

Something was burning on my arm, under my sweatshirt. It hurt. I visualized pouring cold water on a fire, and the pain died down. I looked at Mermelstein. He nodded, and as he did he threw out his right hand, and King spun around as if caught in a twister and dropped his stick. The hex against me had been a distraction. Lowenthal crashed into King, knocking him aside, took the ball, and made for the goal. Rocco rushed him, but was overpowered. Shifrin had Daniel blocked. Fox was keeping Robbie tied up. Time for something Lowenthal wasn't expecting. I had my bug toy in my hand– visualized it, multiplied it a dozen times then threw the bugs at his face. There were no real insects, but to Lowenthal it seemed that beetles were crawling all over his cheeks, getting at his eyes. He stumbled. Rocco went for the ball, passed it up-court tc Robbie. King was gathering himself to receive another pass. Robbie drew back the stick to shoot, but then his pants slid halfway down his legs throwing off his balance and he missed the shot.

"Jerk," he shouted at Mermelstein as he pulled his pants up.

Finkel took the ball and headed towards the goal. No way was I going to allow him a shot. Holding a top I had found in a pile of Robbie's junk– I made a spinning motion with my hand and visualized Finkel. In a moment he had run in an arc and was headed down towards his own goal.

"Wrong way!" Fox shouted.

"Look out!" Meir shouted.

Finkel shook it off and stood re-orienting himself, but that gave King a chance to steal the ball and pass it to Rocco, who took a shot. Meir checked it with his stick, passed it wildly and it shot out of bounds. Mr Bannerjee blew his whistle. Rocco went to face-off against Fox, and the other players rearranged to new coverage. Robbie was going to try to cover Lowenthal this time around. He would need help. I kept my visualization of Finkel in mind and began to build Lowenthal in my mind's eye as well. Maintaining mental images of two people at the same time was difficult, but if I could hex them both at once at a key moment, it might mean a chance for my team to score.

....

Play resumed. Fox took the ball and drove up court towards Avery, passing back and forth with Shifrin. Lowenthal went around Robbie, and I got him with the bug toy again. “Oy, stop it,” he growled, missing the pass.

Shifrin shot out from behind Daniel, caught the pass on his stick, shot for a goal. The ball bounced off Avery’s stick and into the net.

“What was that?” Rocco asked Daniel.

“Ow,” Daniel said, holding the back of his neck. Even from where I was, I could see a large red handprint there. A psychic slap in the head from Mermelstein still left welts. I hadn’t been planning to hex Shifrin, who had been nice to me in my first year at school. I would still concentrate on my two targets, the younger players, who would have weaker defenses.

Daniel and Shifrin faced off. Daniel got the ball and passed to King. King drove down the court and passed between Fox’s feet to Rocco. Finkel stole the ball and passed to Lowenthal. I put a scorpion sting in the small of his back– he gave a little jump and ran out of bounds. Robbie shot across court. Meir was ready to block, but then his leg flew up at the ankle, and he fell backwards into the net, and the ball followed him in. Mr Bannerjee blew the whistle again.

“That was good,” Mermelstein called to me.

“Wasn’t me,” I admitted. I looked around at my team, asking with my eyes if they had thrown the hex. No one acknowledged it. Somebody from the sidelines, then. I scanned them, and to my surprise, Corby Crow met my eyes and nodded.

The game went to the end of the first fifteen-minute period. I continued my strategy of harassing Finkel and Lowenthal. Mermelstein nailed everyone except Avery, including numbing Daniel so much he had to be carried to the bench till his legs regained feeling. At one point, Robbie seemed to move down court faster than I could explain. There was no more scoring.

…………………………………………………………………………

We had a short break to plan strategy. Rocco said he would deliver his surprise in the last few minutes of the second half. He told me to lay off Lowenthal, who seemed to be sufficiently psyched-out, and put more heat on Shifrin. I discarded my visual model of Lowenthal and began to build Shifrin, beginning with the big red beard. Daniel was getting killed by the stronger senior, so Rocco switched his coverage with King's.

The second half, I hexed Shifrin over and over. Most of the hexes didn't penetrate his defenses, but he was aware of them, and kept looking over at me. The distraction seemed to help as King was able to steal the ball from him several times. It moved back and forth and both goalies blocked several shots. Again, a few times Robbie seemed to break free of Lowenthal. Knowing he wasn't faster than the tall boy, I wasn't sure how he did it. At a key moment, I used the top trick on Finkel again making him miss a pass and Robbie nearly scored.

There were loud shouts from everywhere in the stands but not for the missed goal attempt. Avery was on fire! Flames ran all along her chest pad. Mr Bannerjee blew the whistle. Players from both sides ran towards her. Although he was at the far end of the court, Robbie got there first, patting out the flames with his hands.

"This hex not permissible," Mr Bannerjee said. "Very dangerous. Yakov Mermelstein, explain."

"I wouldn't do anything like that," he said. "I don't have any problem with her."

"Agreed, nearly past one year since you were close to killing someone," said Mr Bannerjee. "From stands, this one." He peered at the crowd. "Individuals responsible already departed, this I am thinking. Wishing to continue?"

"Try and stop me," Avery said.

"No penalty shots; investigation and punishment later for crowd members. No personal vengeance, Radish, game violation being my purview."

"Got it," Robbie said.

"Hexers to boundary areas, other players to positions, captains face off at center."

Play went back and forth. No scoring; all of us were distracted, wondering who exactly had been behind the attack on Avery.

King took a shot at the goal but Meir tapped it away with his stick. Meir's deflection put the ball close to Rocco, who made a surge, and shouted, "This is it!"

Family History

Being alone with Ana was tough to arrange. As a new kid with an exotic background she was in demand, and I often found myself just saying hello. We talked a little, but class schedules and homework made us too tired for much more. I couldn't say why it was so difficult to spend time with her, because she wasn't avoiding me.

One day I told Ana about my early childhood, living next to the haunted house in Hicksville and spending time with my mother's parents. I told her about my father's parents, Stringfellow and Devi, and my five uncles. I told the story of how I had become a magician. I described falling in love with Leah. I told her about the fight in Alexandria and Leah's death and meeting the grand rabbi Yehoshua ben Perachyah. I told her about studying with the Rambal. I told her about fighting in Paris, about the staircase to Hell and about Level Three's Dream. I told her about meeting Peter Murasaki, about being attacked in my house and about getting revenge on the Connoisseur. Then, finally, out of sequence, holding it back till last, I told her about 9/11.

"You also watched people die in fire," she said. It didn't require an answer. "Now I understand very much. Tell me, if this girl was still alive, you would never have met me. Say it, I will not be angry."

"But she's still with me, bound to the crystal, and I did decide to meet you."

"All right," said Ana. "Show me this crystal. Let me hold it."

I hesitated, I don't know why.

"This you won't trust me?"

There was an angry sensation against the skin of my chest where the crystal touched it. I didn't know what Leah meant by it, but it triggered me to act. Quickly I took the chain with the crystal off my neck and handed it to Ana.

"Teach me to use it. Just say how. I can learn any spirit magic."

"Close your eyes and hold it in your hand and say hello in your thoughts and say her name. When you're finished, say good-bye, and think to yourself that you're hanging up a telephone."

Ana took the crystal and flopped on her bed. She held the crystal against her chest and closed her eyes. I sat looking at her. The sun was coming up, some gray-orange light from the cracks in her window shutters. I watched the light play across her hands and face as she began almost imperceptibly to smile. If only I could tell her about my feelings, but it was impossible. I would frighten her. She was with me because her father had convinced her to give me a chance, but I had no idea if she would ever be able to love me.

Ana finally opened her eyes and stretched. "It was like a good dream," she said. "But it is so strange. This girl is talking about you saying Simon, Simon."

"I think it is not easy to imagine her any other way than as a spirit. She does not feel like a person to me."

"Then what?"

"How do you say in English?"

I turned on universal language. "Say it in Czech."

"This Leah is like an angel."

Wind War II

One day during lunch, a group of us were sitting with our meals when Delphine, who usually ate in the kosher dining hall, came running over to us. "It is so interesting," she said. "There is a big man outside the school in the field. He is a black man, bald, with earrings. He is yelling that he wants someone to come out."

"Oh crap," Avery said.

"Is it your mysterious enemy?" Goldberry asked.

"Yeah. I haven't seen him since I was six," Avery said "but I'm sure it's my dad. I want to get rid of him."

"I'm on it," Robbie said.

"He's too strong for you, dumb-ass."

"No. I mean, maybe he is, but I don't care. I'll take care of it."

He ran out too fast for her to grab him. Avery started to get up to follow.

"Let him go," Ana said. "He is doing right. He is a good boy who will fight for you."

"Yeah, that worked out great with Simon and your enemy," Avery countered. "You almost got him killed, right?"

"That's not fair," I said, but I could see Ana was hurt.

"Then I will fight him myself," she said, "and then you will learn that I am not so bad as you think." Now Ana was up, heading for the door.

Passing into the main entrance hall, with its six pillars representing the six virtues of magicians, we found the school's front double doors open. One person was on the threshold.

My mother.

Dr Archer, the school's defender, would normally have handled this situation, but he was still in Amsterdam. Where was the Dean?

Ana was going to bull right past my mother, but I caught her and held her back. "Wait! We don't know anything about him!"

"I don't care! I am the Arch-Mage's daughter. Who is she to accuse me?"

This stopped Avery in her tracks.

These two were about to fight, there was a dangerous magician outside and my mother was in the doorway. I gave Goldberry a desperate look.

"It's a misunderstanding," Goldberry said, stepping between Avery and Ana. "Let's all go back and let the teachers handle this."

Thankful for my partner's help, I switched my attention momentarily to the drama at the door.

"I can't admit you without the Dean's permission," my mother said. "He is in class now, but he will see you shortly."

"Woman, this is not your business," someone shouted outside. This loud voice, with a touch of some African accent I couldn't identify, cut off all the arguing among the girls. Delphine darted to the door, looked under my mother's arm, turned to us and winced.

Rushing to the doorway with the others, I got my first look at Avery's father. He was a gigantic man, heavy and muscled. His arms and face were painted with various magical symbols, and he wore gold chains, rings, bracelets, any of which could have been enhanced with construction to assist in his magic. He had a large leather shoulder bag and was carrying a wooden rod with a monkey's skull mounted on it. When he spotted us arriving, he declared, "That is my daughter. Come here, Cecile!"

Throwing her arms out, my mother momentarily blocked any of

us from exiting. Avery answered over her elbow. "No way! You had your chance when I was a kid. You dumped my mother, you jerk!"

"That's your mother talking. I explained the family tradition that forced me to go."

"Is that the one that forced you to take all our savings and leave us without money to pay the bills? I don't believe you! Get the hell out of here!"

"Your mother has told you many lies about me," he answered. "Even worse, she has put you in this foolish school. No reason for that anymore. Now I will teach you, as our family has always done."

"No!"

Ana made her move, ducking under my mother's arm. I grabbed her but she shook me off. Avery's father was smart enough to recognize the threat in her eyes, and immediately raised his skull rod and whispered. Ana was frozen in her tracks.

"Let her go," I said, rushing out to stand between them. "She is under my protection. I am called Simon Magus. I am he who humbles heretics, cures madmen, and binds deadly ghosts. I am a master of *tulpas* who sends the wicked to their knees. She is under my protection."

Avery's father gave me his full attention. He was a monstrous man, not to be ignored or taken lightly. "The sky boils at my word," he answered. "Ethereal beasts groan at my command. I am master of the four corners of the world: I am King Wind. I've heard of you, boy, but you're not at your full strength yet, and you're not ready to face me."

"Release the girl. I don't care who you are, King Wind. I'll kill you if you don't."

His eyes narrowed. "Will you, now? That's interesting."

"Go away!" Avery shouted. "Let her go and go away!"

"Let her go," my mother repeated. "You have no business attacking our students."

King Wind lowered his rod. Ana fell backward into my arms and

I eased her to the grass, laying her down gently there. Then I stood in front of her.

"It's time for you to leave," I said. My voice was shaky. Seeing Ana hurt had taken a lot of the steel out of me. I knew it and so did he. "No one enters School of the Ages without an invitation." I sized him up further. What could I use against him? He wasn't going down on his knees. He looked too tough for seven stings. He was very far from the nearest wall.

He again raised his monkey-headed rod. A strong breeze brushed across the façade and stirred our hair. "You stand between me and my daughter, boy?"

"No!" Robbie shouted. "I do!" He shouldered his way past my mother and then ahead of and to the right of me, squaring off with King Wind.

Robbie must have run back to the room to get his equipment. Now he was wearing his new ankle-length leather coat which his parents had brought him from Argentina. He also had on a matching gaucho hat with a chin strap. In one hand he held a pair of wooden staves and in the other was the geode he used for elemental summoning.

King Wind sized him up. "You're the one called Radish," he announced. "I've heard of you, too. My allies say you haven't found your way to real power yet. You're sure you want to fight me?"

"No, he doesn't," Avery said fiercely, trying to pull at his arm. "He wants to go inside. Just go away!"

Avery's father quickly understood the situation. "You like my daughter, hey? No problem. I'll take you along and teach you too." He smiled, showing brown teeth. "Cecile, no more playing now. Now that you're old enough, I am here."

"She's going nowhere." Robbie reached into his coat and took out a piece of rolled poster board. "She's not going to live in fear of you anymore. I'm going to beat you and get rid of you forever!" He unrolled the poster board and set it down with the geode on top and began to hum a summoning ritual.

"The wrong words to say to me, boy," answered King Wind. "You'll regret them." He shook his skull rod and, reaching into his bag, scattered coloured powders on the ground.

"He's just a child!" my mother objected. "You can't!"

A duel of elementalists had begun.

Quickly I pulled Ana off to the side. I was shocked and disturbed but with my adrenalin flowing, I moved fast. My mother ran across the grass to help me.

The island was blanketed in strong, cold winds. I saw the clouds clearing fast overhead. The trees on the far side of the clearing began swaying.

A young man in a track suit came skipping across the grass from around the corner of the building. He took up a position on Robbie's left.

"What's up?" he said bouncing on and off his toes.

"You're here to fight," Robbie said.

The young man looked at their opponent. "Against King Wind? Yeah, right. He's got allies stronger than me."

"Okay, I'll call you some help."

Meanwhile, King Wind's ally came, and the winds with him were warm, pleasant and strong. He came streaking out of the sky and stopped just over King Wind's shoulder. A tall thin man with skin the color of tea, he had long flowing hair and a beaklike nose and was wearing loose multicoloured robes.

Avery said, "Hey, what's up, Mr Z.?" she called nervously.

"Greetings, sweet child," said the wind. "Why go you not with your father? Journey with him, and I will be your ally, as I am his. Has not my Zephyrina long since been friend to you?"

'Yes," Avery said, clearly relieved the wind was friendly. "But my dad's a jerk. Zephyrina must have told you that."

"He is King Wind," answered Zephyrus, the West Wind. He meant that Avery's father was one to obey without question.

Another of Robbie's allies arrived, another young man

"He got two dukes," Avery said to me. "I had no idea."

"Is that good?" I asked her.

"It's awesome, but we're still in trouble."

The West Wind sized up his opposition. "Nicholotus. Nathanotus. Should you not now flee this place? O my nephews, I shall blow you from here to the Sahara, and leave you choking with sand." They ignored him.

With my mother's help, I got Ana to sit up. She looked around, realized where she was, and came to her feet. Seeing this, Zephyrus dropped lower, closer to King Wind's ear, and said, "Do you know who that is? It is the Arch-Mage's child. He commands Boris, and even his children do not lack allies. She's as big a threat as Radish."

Robbie was smart enough to seize the moment. He sent his winds to the attack. Nathanotus spun round once and then speared into Zephyrus, driving him down and back, while Nicholotus came behind him, taking him round the neck in a chinlock. King Wind turned toward Ana, digging in his bag and I advanced to draw his fire. I could hear her running somewhere behind me when his spell came. It was like hands grabbing all my limbs, my neck, and the muscles of my chest, hands covering my eyes and ears and mouth. If I succumbed, I would be paralyzed and insensible, as Ana had been before. But my defensive cylinder was in place. The hands couldn't get a grip.

Goldberry had come out and was hustling my mother inside.

"You can't hoodoo me, King Wind. For the last time, the Arch-Mage's daughter is under my protection," I repeated. "Attack me again and I'll humble you. Attack her again, and they'll find your body floating in the river in the morning."

He laughed. "All right, boy. You make your threats." He waved his rod at me dismissively. At that moment, I had to jump aside.

Nathanotus plummeted out of the sky and crashed to the ground at my feet. Above, the West Wind was dealing a series of body blows to Nicholotus. Rubbing his neck, Nathanotus sprang into the air and zoomed back into the brawl.

Far overhead, more winds were arriving, but they circled, only watching the battle. Closer, leaves and debris whirled here and there as Zephyrus tussled with his nephews. It wasn't an even match–he easily tossed them around–but they were keeping him occupied.

I ran after Ana. She was now squatting by the edge of the island, looking into the water. "Ianeira," she whispered. "Ianassa. Come to me."

"Ana," I said.

"Panope," she said to the river. "Apseudes."

Lying in the grass, I saw King Wind gesture to the other circling winds. They were all girls. Most of them still held back, but four descended into the battle, grappling with Robbie's winds, tying them up. Avery finally remembered that she had power too, and at her gesture, five more of the winds flew down and encircled her, guarding her.

With Nathanotus and Nicholotus occupied, Zephyrus was again free to act. He made sweeping gestures with both hands. From his fingers came one vortex, then a second, like baby tornados. They touched down in the grass and began to move toward Robbie. His eyes widened, but he lifted his staves, crossing them in front of his face, chanting something. Meanwhile, at her command, two of Avery's wind friends threw themselves in the way of the twisters, holding them back. Nicholotus and Nathanotus were pinned in midair unable to free themselves. There was nothing I could do to help; I had absolutely no power against elementals.

"Good," Ana said. She stood erect, her head thrown back. I followed her gaze. Four young girls, long-haired, wearing Greek shifts, were climbing out of the water. Dripping, they strode across the grass and bowed to her. She pointed to King Wind. "Drown him."

The girls nodded and collapsing became like flows of rainwater cutting through the grass.

King Wind didn't see the water.

It flowed up his legs and over his torso, enveloping him. Tthe four girls sprang from the water, two on his chest, two on his back, and they began to slap and strangle him. Wild panic entered his eyes and he gesticulated violently at Zephyrus. The West Wind, focused on controlling the tornadoes, finally noticed what was going on and descended to his master's side. He thrust one arm down King Wind's throat, guaranteeing him air, and with the other hand, he clasped one girl's face and shoved. She flew off into the distance, vanishing into the sky. With a single swipe, he cleaved through the two on King Wind's back with a fierce move that made a boom like a thunderclap and sent spray everywhere. He then backhanded the final one, who went flying backward and crashed into the school façade.

"You forget yourself, girl," the West Wind said sternly to Ana. "Had not your father the services of Boris my brother, I would give you a whipping for your interference in my business."

One of the tornadoes was gone. The other was diminishing in ferocity. Nathanotus broke free of his cousins and flew at Zephyrus, who slapped him aside.

Then the battle stopped. The tornado faded. The winds ceased to struggle. They all let go of each other.

The Dean and another teacher had come out onto the lawn. My mother, Goldberry, and Delphine were behind them.

"Is this really necessary?" asked the Dean calmly. "I believe Ms. Gale informed you I would come shortly."

"The Radish challenged me for rights over my daughter," said King Wind. "I don't back down from a challenge. You don't know, teacher-man, but in my family tradition, at age fourteen, she belongs to me. Her mother made trouble, putting her with you."

"I don't especially care about your family tradition," said the Dean coldly. "We operate in *loco parentis* here, on behalf of her mother who is her legal guardian, and I think going with you is not in her best interest. You have weakened what little claim you might have by fighting our students. You are an adult magician in your prime and should have known better. I believe I have your match here." He gestured at the other teacher.

"I can handle him," Robbie said.

"You are both bold and capable," said the Dean. "School of the Ages is proud of your accomplishments."

The teacher put down his hood and removed from inside his robe a scruffy white toy poodle. He was a handsome, graying man in his late forties with an unlit pipe in his mouth. "I am School of the Ages' master conjurer," he said. "I am called Walter Phillips. You saw that my student is no pushover and if you're foolish enough to try me, I'll give you all you can handle."

"I didn't come here to fight anyone," King Wind said. "I came for my Cecile. I have parental rights."

"Then you should have acted like a father!" Avery shouted.

Mr Phillips looked up at the winds, then stroked his poodle, Murgatroyd, who was cradled in one elbow. Murgatroyd began to bark. Rather than his usual yaps, they were deep and resounding. One by one, the winds pirouetted and then sped off into the sky, Nathanotus and Nicholotus both bowing to Robbie before they did.

Only two winds were left, Zephyrus himself and his daughter Zephyrina, who hovered over Avery stroking her hair gently.

"Zephyrus," said Mr Phillips, "I know you dislike being part of a family squabble. It demeans you."

"Aye, 'tis so," said the West Wind. "In faith, I love the child better than the father, but duty is duty."

Mr Phillips looked at Avery. "Command his neutrality. Use the ancient compact."

"Okay," said Avery. "Zephyrus, by the terms of the ancient compact, I command you never again to attack me or my friends."

"I honour the compact," said the West Wind.

"Oh, and give us some fresh fruit before you go."

Zephyrus made a sweeping gesture with his hand. Fruits of many colours and varieties plunged out of the air and littered the ground at her feet. There was enough to feed the entire school.

"Now get out of here."

"I shall begone."

A strong gale came up, enveloped him, and he melted into it and vanished.

"And now, King Wind," said the Dean, "I ban you from the premises of School of the Ages, in perpetuity, on pain of death. And I give you a further warning. If you assault or meddle with any of my students while they remain minors, we will exact vengeance of the utmost severity."

King Wind frowned. "I understand. But don't think I will forget. I am alone today, but if I come back here, I won't be." He turned to us, addressing Robbie, who was standing with his arm around Avery. "You're not bad, Radish, but as long as I live, you won't be the best, and you won't be safe."

"You won't live forever," Robbie said.

King Wind laughed harshly, turned on his heel and walked towards the woods.

"Thank you," Avery said. "All of you. You didn't have to do all that."

The Ghost in the Crystal

That night, when I went to her room, Ana was weeping. Opening the door, she nodded to me to come in, and when I got closer, she stood beside me, unable to face me. I put my arms around her, and she buried her face in my chest and sobbed.

"They were my friends," she whispered. "We used to swim together, you know?"

"You mean the watergirls?"

"When my mother was dead, I called to them. We swam together in the river at night. They kept me safe."

"But… They're elementals. They'll be okay, right?"

"They took care of me when I was little. Your mother is alive. You don't understand."

"But they'll be okay. Elementals can't die."

Ana stopped. She lowered her voice almost to a whisper. "Go. Go, I will see you tomorrow. Not like this. No more seeing me like this."

I didn't sleep that night.

Long before dawn, I went to the meditation hall. It was a place where there was always peace, where no one could shout or fight and all sounds were muted. Avoiding the uncomfortable pews, I sat on the floor, leaning against a wall, and fell asleep.

When I woke, I saw Maestro Morgan, a tall, thin man with a shock of white hair, going about his usual morning activity, cleaning the platform and polishing the fixtures. Delphine was helping him. She was so young, younger even than Leah had been and even more sweet and innocent, and so cheerful despite the horrible life she had had, with a drunk mother, no father that I knew of and poverty and hunger. Now she was in a safe place, had a great father figure in the Maestro and a great big brother in Yakov Mermelstein, and she was well. My life had run a lot more smoothly than hers for a lot more years. Why couldn't I also be well like that?

"It is interesting that you ask," said Maestro Morgan. "Come and help us."

I hadn't spoken aloud, but Maestro Morgan was always able to know people's thoughts.

"You ask why you are not well." Maestro Morgan came back to the point.

"I didn't," I said softly.

"But you want to know," he said. "It is odd how young people are. There may be no problem on earth that you cannot understand, Simon Magus, except your own. Why is that my girl?"

"Because he's a boy," Delphine said. "Boys never understand their feelings. That's why they need us girls."

"And you understand," I said to her. "*You* understand me."

"I think," she said, "you're in love with Ana and you're afraid to tell her because you think she doesn't love you. Is that right?"

"She *doesn't* love me," I said.

"Okay," Delphine said. "Do you really think she would be here if she didn't? You have to tell her you love her.

"I can't do that," I said.

"You can," said Maestro Morgan. "But there is a great price. You must give something up."

"Maestro, if I knew there was something I could sacrifice to have her, I would do it. Believe me."

……………………………………………………………………………………………

"There is something. I am glad you came here," said the teacher. "This is a place where we can help you to give it up. Do you know what it is? It is weighing you down."

"No, I don't."

"When you know," he said, "come back. I will help you then. Now, go back to your room. Someone is waiting for you there. You are excused from group meditation."

I went back to my room.

My parents were there, both of them, she in my desk chair and he in Robbie's. Robbie himself was sitting on his bed, half covered by the blanket, looking owlishly at the three of us.

"Um..." I struggled to understand what the two of them were doing there at six o'clock in the morning.

"I know you don't like us interfering," my mother said. "But this is important.

"We want you to stop wearing that crystal you're wearing around your neck."

"And do what with it?" I couldn't give it up. Leah was always with me.

"Give it to her mother," my father said. "And move on."

My father held out his hand. "It might be hard for you to see Mrs Ritz. We'll help you. I'll give it to her."

"You have to do it, Leicester," my mother said.

Robbie said, "Mind if I comment?"

"Do you have to?" I asked.

Robbie shifted to a better position. "I think pretty much everyone would agree with your folks."

We loved Leah too. I loved Leah almost as much as you did. But carrying her ghost around with you is creepy."

"Leah saved my life when I was captured by Pavel Rod."

"Yeah, but... look, she used to be your girl. But now Ana's your girl, right? Look at Avery and me. We're a team. Bottom line, it's her and me. It's not her and me and someone else."

I had said it only moments before: if there was something I could sacrifice to have Ana, I would. But not this! Not the crystal!

"Give it to me, Leicester," my father said.

"I have to say goodbye."

"Give it to me."

I took the chain from around my neck, weighing it in my hand. Before I could do anything else, my father took it and clasped it in his fist.

"It's not as if I understand magic like your teachers do," he said. "But is it possible that you haven't really been talking to the girl? It is possible that it's part of your own mind that just won't let her go?"

"There is a spirit world," Robbie said.

"If she's there," my mother said, "then she understands, Leicester. Doesn't she?"

"She promised she would always be with me," I said, my eyes wet.

"But you don't need this thing for that," my father said, waving the crystal at me. "How do most of us deal with people who died? We keep them in our memories, and we move on. Am I right?"

"Of course, but..."

When they were gone. I went back to the meditation hall myself. Maestro Morgan was already conducting the session, but when I entered, he came down the aisle to meet me.

"I gave up the crystal. Leah isn't with me anymore."

"That is not precisely right," he said. "She is with all of us. Has Leah not told you that love is God and so does not die?"

"Yes. Yes, she says that all the time."

"And so," said Maestro Morgan, "you have not given her up. What you have given up is what you alone were clinging to. It is a thing that you required of yourself against all advice, and contrary to any example around you."

He was right, and his words guided me to a realization. "My guilt. I gave up my guilt."

The Maestro nodded. "Now you understand. Meditate here a while, and then you will be ready to do what must be done. Young friend, you must believe better what she told you. Love is with God, and so love heals all injuries."

He went back to the meditation session.

I whispered, Goodbye, Leah.

Goodbye, Simon, she whispered back, and squeezed my hand a final time.

I still could speak with her, but now, I no longer would.

Ana was not difficult to find. She was sitting at a table by herself in the dining hall in the room were Miss Chatterjee buried in a book and Goldberry, engaged in some tasseography with an unmarked teacup. As I passed, she caught my sleeve.

"Simon, Dr Archer and William are back. They came in last night."

"How do you know?"

"William came and woke me up."

"I guess nobody got proper sleep last night."

"Seems not," Goldberry said.

"William said it went splendidly. He brought me some tulip bulbs."

"Simon."

"Yes."

Goldberry spoke loud enough to be heard several tables over. "She's a good girl, that one. I'm sorry I doubted her. She has the partner seal of approval. Right?"

"Thank you."

I went to Ana's side and touched her shoulder.

"What do you want?" she demanded.

"I want to talk."

"Talk to your dead girl."

....

"I can't. I don't want to."

"You can't. Why not? Lost your magic powers?"

"I gave up the crystal. I said goodbye."

Ana looked up at me, just for a moment, and then again turned away. "Why you did that? You loved that girl best."

"I did, once. But it's different now. When I saw you," I said, "you were so beautiful, so perfect, I thought it was impossible you would ever want me."

"Yes. Very good to me, manners, a gentleman. Only that. Like a nice boy who is not interested."

"I was always interested."

When we went back into the school, we had decided we were a couple.

Der Sinneskannibale

I met Goldberry to go to Dr Archer's office. He looked well. He had shaved. The scars on his face were barely visible.

"Word has reached me," he announced, "that your relationship with Ana Vorkina has taken a positive turn. It is the best possible news. Fortunately, I have no ill-news from Europe. The occult shops informed us of a magician in Amsterdam named Kees von Honthorst. We learned that he was a tulip vendor in a shop near the West Church. I am entirely convinced that he used a curse to murder Johanna Strauss, my former closest ally in Europe, as I have discussed with you. He was in possession of numerous items stolen from her after her death in 2002. Another magician must have assisted, since, as you will recall, the Dean's son Dempsey was protecting her home, and he was an able and active combatant, far too capable to succumb to the decrepit and repugnant Kees."

"Did you get revenge?" Goldberry asked. "He had it coming."

"Yes. Von Honthorst is dead, and the stolen artifacts have been recovered. Most were surrendered to Johanna's son, Gustav. No Goldberry, before you ask, I am not Gustav's father."

"Right."

"However, I did secure an item for your use." He pointed to a large leather pouch on the bookshelf near her chair. As she opened the pouch, he added, "It is quite old, and is reported to have been constructed by

Abramelin the Sage." The object was a fist-sized sphere made of some kind of red quartz shot with veins of silvery metal.

"I can scarcely..." Goldberry said as she caressed the cold stone. She fell silent, her mind perhaps drifting along distant pathways of knowledge.

"School of the Ages is grateful for your service," Dr Archer said, "and it is my purpose to establish my protégés as well as I can. When your abilities are fully mature, your two tools, the Akashic Prism and Abramelin's Globe, should make you the equal of any diviner of your own generation."

She didn't register his words; she was focused on the crystal ball.

"What's next?" I asked.

"We are not prepared to journey to Europe again till matters have been arranged here," he said. "I have another name, but I believe that Goldberry's abilities will be necessary to proceed. In short, we must more specifically locate the stone building that she has seen in previous attempts. This shall require some effort to hasten the spiritual healing that she requires. Abramelin's Globe does not heal, but it should assist her with self-healing. With it she can work to recover memory that is lost, which is a part of that process. In the meantime, we shall have the visit from the retired teachers this week, and then a time travel trip. Goldberry."

"Hmm?" She looked up from the crystal ball, finally returning her attention to us.

"There is a problem that has weighed upon my mind periodically as we have been gathering information from our previous leads. That problem is the sequence of attacks that led to the attack by the party of Gott im Himmel members that has left you in this condition. Using the memento created by Simon, I have extensively questioned the Connoisseur's ghost. I now understand the plan to have been as follows. The cabal's goal was to remove our divinatory capabilities. This was first done by eliminating Johanna Strauss. Because you assumed her role, they chose to target you, even given the risk of involving your father, whose reputation I had expected to protect you. The Connoisseur's role was to dispatch a number of operatives to penetrate our defenses and provide some means of isolating you. They attacked Simon in the hope that they would find that means, and they did, by planting upon Peter Murasaki a glamour that would enable another cabal magician to possess him later. That cabal magician, accompanied by two others for purposes of overwhelming you in battle, would then remove your ability to use divination. You were not meant to remember what they had done; your father was never to learn that it had taken place. They had good reason to be concerned about that, as he was of tremendous use to us in the aftermath in the interrogation of our captives. I had many occasions in January to regret how long he and I have been on bad terms, and to wish for the friendship we used to have when we were young students."

"About the captives," I said. "Why did the Connoisseur send Delphine along?"

"Are you certain you wish to know that?" asked Dr Archer. "You will not like what I can tell you. I have not told her, and there is no reason for her ever to learn."

"Yes, do tell us," said Goldberry. "I don't want to waste any time trying to find out for myself."

"When Simon was defeated," Dr Archer said, "Helen the Medusa's gang was meant to murder her and leave her body in the house, in the hope of causing harm to the Moore family."

"Oh, hell!"

"Three terrible miscalculations by Gott im Himmel have given us the opportunity we needed to destroy them. They underestimated Simon; they underestimated you; and they gave us Delphine. As a result, they have lost three, perhaps four of their core members, and we know roughly the names of those who remain. Kaiser Petrus, of course, and the other who possessed your brother, Simon.

"That brings me back to the problem that has weighed upon my mind. Who were the magicians in the car that night?"

"There was an old German woman who was possessing poor Peter," Goldberry said. "There was a man, and there was a woman in a veil."

"Kaiser Petrus was there," I said. "But Dr Beam was in New York. So which one of them was the man in the car? And who was the woman in the veil? And who was the German witch?"

"Difficult problems," said Dr Archer. "There are some answers to work with. Dr Beam was the man in the car. Kaiser Petrus is a controller of spirits and may have remained hidden himself while sending who used the form of a veiled woman. As for the German woman who possessed Peter Murasaki…"

"'*Ich esse ihre Gehirne und Herz*,'" Goldberry quoted. "She said that through his lips. I still hear that in dreams now and again. 'I eat their brains and heart.'"

"A phrase used to instill terror as long ago as the 1940's," said Dr Archer. "When my father was a young man, he encountered this foe, der Sinneskannibale. I recently read of this in his journals; I regret that we did not know earlier whom we faced. While the translation is not precise, in English, usually she has been called the Mind Cannibal."

"He fought her?" I asked.

"Indirectly," Dr Archer said. "No one has ever seen the Mind Cannibal. Like Kees von Honthorst, she is a magician."

"She controls minds," I said.

"Rather, she replaces them with her own. My father worked to identify and free those who were controlled. It was difficult then, and now she is more experienced."

"I'll find her," Goldberry said. "But there's something I want. When we get there, I want to deal with her. No one victimizes me,

Dr Archer. No one. You understand that."

"Agreed," he said. As she has harmed you, now this foe is yours. I shall help you to prepare."

The Magic Ring

Ana's goal in life was criminal science. She wanted to be involved with police or criminal investigation, to bring down bad guys and punish the wicked. Being with Ana meant sharing things. If someone said something, I thought of telling Ana about it. If I learned a new piece of magic, I wanted Ana to learn it too. When we came together between classes, I wanted to know what had happened to her, what the teachers said, what she did and didn't understand, how the other kids had behaved. Mr Phillips was helping her specifically to find elemental allies who would fight for her. And at dusk, right after dinner, she and I went out to the river bank and when it was not too windy, she practiced making waves.

We had a happy time. My enemies left us alone. Goodenough was occupied with trying to rebuild his relationship with Goldberry and didn't bother me. The Jonathans, who were of course to blame for lighting Avery's hockey gear on fire, were sweeping the roof regularly as a punishment from Mr Bannerjee, and they had settled down, although not forever I suspected.

And my dreams were different. Their worst parts, 9/11 and Helen the Medusa were gone. In the same week that Ana and I got together, a group of retired veteran School of the Ages teachers visited. They talked with the Dean and Dr Archer about old times and strategy for the magical war, and then they talked to us. I made sure to meet each of them. Mr Dancer, a white-bearded man took an interest in me.

"You have some stuff in your room," he said. " Some stuff I want to see. Let's go."

He led me directly to my room and sat down at my desk. "Come on, let me see what's in the drawer here."

I opened the drawer. He pointed to a small box I had there. "Open that."

I opened it. A gold ring with rubies and emeralds lay inside—the Consulting Ring I had taken as spoils from the Connoisseur's home.

"Yeah, that's it. It's been yelling at me since I came into the building. What is that?"

"It's a magic ring."

"Did you ever use it?"

"No. I got it from a bad magician. I'm not sure how safe it is to use."

"Well, you better use it. It's storing up vibrations and needs to discharge some energy. What does it do?"

"Lets me talk to people in my dreams. Living and dead people."

"Oh, that's nice."

"You think the ring is safe to use?"

He peered at it, keeping his hand close to it without quite touching it. "Well, I wouldn't use something like that for entertainment, but you can use it if you have a good reason. What else have you got?"

"That's it."

"No, something in your closet, too."

I went to my closet. There was a suit bag there. From inside came a cloud of choking dust. It was the coat that I had last worn on September 11. Leaving it in the bag, I brought it to Mr Dancer."

"He ran his hands through the fur. More dust puffed out onto his hands and face. "Oh, not cool. What is that?"

"It's from the World Trade Center."

"Why didn't you give this to your construction teacher to fix? It's

Yechiel Horn, right?"

"Yes."

"I taught him how to fix stuff like this. He could do it."

"If I give this coat to Rabbi Horn, he'll forget to fix it, and I'll forget he has it." "Okay, I can fix it then," said Mr Dancer. "I won't forget. Sharp as a tack even at age seventy."

"What's the bargain?" I asked, doubtful.

"The bargain is, when it's time for me to die, I'll come to your house and die there, easy and peaceful."

"That's crazy," I said.

"I'll pick a time when I won't get in your way. I never had any kids and I just want to die around some nice people. Come on, today's my birthday. Make the deal."

"It's a bargain," I said.

"Great. Have it for you in a couple of weeks." He zipped up the bag. "Let's go back and see Solly and the other kids."

That night I discussed with Ana whom I should include in my first try with the magic ring.

"You can call me of course."

I went back to my room. After blowing out the candle, I lay down, and, feeling the consultation ring on my middle finger, I whispered, "Ana Vorkina."

In my dream, I was walking in Times Square, on Broadway, by the Disney theater. Ana came running up to me, pushing through crowds of anonymous tourists, and said something in Czech. I looked around, took her hand, but it turned into a bunch of pencils and I let go.

I popped awake, got up quickly and went to Ana's room and rapped on the door.

"What?" she called through the door.

"Do you remember the dream?"

"Dreamed about you. Let me sleep. Talk in the morning."

....

The ring had worked. Should I use it again?

Back in my own bed, the possibilities of this artifact began to unfold for me. I could call people who had died, question enemies, talk to famous people from any time in history. Would they come? Could I get real information from them? Would enemies be able to attack me or even just tell disruptive lies? How would I know the difference between genuine information and dream nonsense?

A name came into my mind that I hadn't thought of in weeks. Something to do with shouting and noise, a name that was now scarcely real to me.

"Rocco," I said. Who was his advisor? "Dr Chatterjee."

I hadn't seen Rocco since the big intramural game. Nor had I thought of him or heard his name. Nor could I remember what had happened in that game after Avery's equipment was ignited. Something was wrong about this. Maybe by consulting, I could find out what had happened.

It was harder to sleep this time, but I did just manage to nod off.

I was in Dr Chatterjee's office. It was cold, not an uncommon thing in School of the Ages either due to lack of central heating and sunlight or due to the presence of spirits. Dr Chatterjee was in his swivel chair. A baby was draped over his shoulder, chin on his shoulder blade.

"Simon," he said, "why are you consulting me?"

"You know what I'm doing?"

"You are dreaming. How may I help you?"

"We need to find Rocco."

"Who is that?"

"The magician Rocco. His real name is Scott Vitello. He's your student."

"Hmm," said Dr Chatterjee. He patted the baby's head. "How are you, little one? Are you Rocco? What's the matter?"

"Thank God," said the baby. "I messed up, Dr Chatterjee. You remember I was working on that invisibility spell?"

"No," said the teacher. "Who are you, exactly?"

"Not power of concealment, not hiding in the shadows, but really invisible, to everyone, walking around and waving my hand in people's faces and no one can see me or my clothes or anything. That's what I was trying to do."

"That is against the physical laws of the universe," said Dr Chatterjee.

"I know, you told me that. I did it, but I can't turn it off! I did it on the court during the big game, and now no one can see or hear me or anything. I try to smack people and they don't feel it. I take food right off people's plates and they don't notice. It's like you all forgot me."

"I have seen your name in my paperwork," said Dr Chatterjee, "but always dismissed it from my mind. What a curious predicament you are in. Why did you not leave me a note?"

"I did. I left notes for you and Daniel and King and Robbie and Simon, everyone. I stuck up a sign on the door of the meditation hall. No one sees them."

Dr Chatterjee looked at me kindly. "Thank you, Simon. I will address this problem when I am awake."

I didn't wake up after that dream; Ana woke me in the morning banging on my door.

"Rocco."

"Who is that? It is enemy magician?"

"No. He's my friend. You met him. He's the captain of the intramural team."

Ana didn't remember.

"He's invisible, even to memories. We have to help him."

Ana frowned. "This ring is dangerous. It is making you invent people. Take it off."

"I'll take it off later. Right now, it might be helping me remember him. I promise, he's real. I've known him over two years. Let's go to meditation and we'll get some help."

At meditation I gathered up everyone I could who knew Rocco. It was mostly the same story.

Daniel: "The kid who roomed with me? I forgot his name. He moved out and left his stuff."

Mermelstein: "I fought this kid last year? I thought that was you."

King: "The name sounds familiar."

Robbie: "He's the intramural captain? I thought King was."

Goldberry: "Right. Whoever that is, I'll help you find him."

Avery: "The name sounds familiar."

Corby Crow: "My study partner? The school never gave me one."

I led this group to Rocco's room where Daniel gave us permission to take some of his stuff, a notebook and his FDNY sweatshirt. Goldberry took over, leading the shrinking group to the divination club meeting room, stopping by her room to fetch the Akashic Prism.

"Oh my God!" said Corby Crow when he saw Goldberry's device. That was a lot of emotion for him.

Mermelstein scratched his head. He had forgotten why he was there. Delphine sat by him.

With Avery's help to steady her hand, Goldberry held the prism up to catch some morning light from the small windows. The sun shone on the notebook, and creeping across the surface of the table were images of Rocco, his normally cheerful face flustered with anxiety.

"That's him," I told Ana. "Remember, from the game?"

"No, I do not remember, but now I know it is true. How to find him? Call spirit to search?"

"That's messy," Avery said.

"Who's got a map?" Goldberry asked. "Go and get your maps, if you can dowse. Who can pendulum dowse? Not you, Simon, you're hopeless."

"I can," said Corby Crow.

Soon, various maps were laid out on the table. A pendulum for daily use would normally be made with a spherical weight, but a paper clip attached to a string would be good enough for a short-term project. My classmates thought of Rocco and moved their paper-clip pendulums over their maps, watching for a clockwise rotation. There was no air moving in the room, so when the pendulum moved, they trusted to their results and marked the spots on the maps. One location was close to all the marks on the various maps: the Refectory, or third-year library.

If you look on the Internet for pictures of the Refectory of Santa Marie delle Grazie in Milan, and then imagine it with bookshelves, you'll get a picture of this room. On the wall across from the entrance, elevated, is a mural reproduction of da Vinci's *Last Supper*. Along the wall of the School of the Ages Refectory were low bookshelves containing a variety of science and historical books, books on world religions, and multiple copies of *grimoires*, spell books, and the like, some unique to the community of magicians and some of the ordinary type you can buy in the bookstore.

The room was supplied with battery-powered lanterns and smokeless coals, which you had to light when you entered. There was no one visible inside when we entered, but the coals were lit. A book was open on one of the long central tables. I went and stood by it.

"Rocco, turn the page."

Now the book was shut, but I hadn't seen it happen. His spell was strong; we couldn't observe his actions.

Avery had some chalk. She began to write on the floor, a magic circle with symbols in it. Ana knelt by her and made suggestions. Ignorant of summoning, Goldberry and I were left with Corby Crow.

"How come you don't live at the school?" I asked him.

"I am caring for six grandmothers. It is them and me in the world."

'Six Grandmothers' sounded like some kind of mystical code. I decided not to question. Finally Avery and Ana stood up and stepped back.

"Step into the circle, Rocco," Avery announced. To us: "Give him a moment." After a minute, we formed a circle, linking hands around the magic circle.

"Step towards the circle," Avery said.

Slowly we drew in our human circle, till we were shoulder to shoulder.

"Step in," Avery instructed.

Now we were all in the magic circle, all six of us. Rocco was in our midst, hemmed in by our linked bodies, visible again.

"Oh my God," he said. "Thank you, guys. But how did you know to break the spell? I've been trying for weeks to get your attention."

"I dreamed about you," I told him. "Do you remember that dream?"

"Yes, a little. A little."

Corby Crow rolled his eyes. "Why did you cast a stupid spell? Invisibility. I told you not to. So did Chatterjee. Hidden, okay. But not invisible. That's a curse."

"I Know," Rocco said. "But I didn't expect to get stuck. I thought I'd just turn visible again when I got ready."

I never found out who had won the game.

Empire State Building

Ana and I were walking by the river one afternoon. We looked across the water at the city. "Why does no one there see your school?"

"I don't know. Professor Bright said the Dutch knew about this island and there were some families here. I guess the island became hard to see when the school was built. Maybe something was fitted into the geometry of the building. The Founder, Elihu Danvers, is in a memento in the building, so maybe his spirit is involved too. "

Ana kept looking at Manhattan. "We will go to the city today. You show me the famous places, the nice ones."

We found Mr Saluto cleaning the bus at the back of the building. He was always with the bus during the day. I asked him to take us to Manhattan.

"I can't take the bus out without orders from the Dean," he said. "The Dean's not here today."

I dialled my mother's cell. "Ms. Gale, do you remember when the Dean gave permission for Ana and me to take the bus to Manhattan today? I need you to tell Mr Saluto."

I mentally crossed my fingers. My mother was definitely smart enough to pick up on the bluff, if she wanted to. "Put him on."

I handed the phone to Mr Saluto. He listened, nodded, smiled. "Yes, ma'am, Ms. Gale." He hung up. "All right, kids, it's all arranged. We just have to pick up Ms. Gale on the way."

....

I groaned. I didn't want a chaperone.

At the speed the bus travelled, Ana didn't see much of Queens before we pulled up in front of our house in Bayside. Looking up, I saw my mother kiss my father goodbye, shut the new front door, and come down the hill in her spring coat. She boarded, pecked me on the head, and moved me out of my seat sitting by Ana. "Herald Square," she told Mr Saluto.

Herald Square was in the heart of Midtown Manhattan, famous for a Macy's a block long and the multi-storey Manhattan Mall. It was jam-packed with tourists and shoppers. Even with a little residual winter chill in the air, the girls were out in their spring fashions. The Smoot Prep bus could not speed through the traffic, but Mr Saluto never missed an opportunity to weave around standing yellow cabs, and he was able to drive straight through police barricades as if they didn't exist. He dropped us off on 34th Street, promising to pick us up when my mother called.

We plunged into the crowd. My mother held our hands tightly, keeping us together, as we visited the monument to New York Herald founder James Gordon Bennett, and read "Give my Regards to Broadway" from its base. Then, it was time for Macy's.

After about three hours in the enormous, world-famous department store, Ana had five new outfits, complete with shoes and jewellery.

I hauled the shopping bags out to the street. My mother called Mr Saluto. She loaded everything onto the bus and told him to head back to the school and unload the stuff in Ana's room.

We walked over to the Empire State Building. Ana was dizzy and faint from the crowds, the noise, flashing lights, and wild geometry of the tall buildings. We ate at a diner before we went up to the observatory.

❖ ❖ ❖

It was a long trip to the top of the Empire State Building. From there we could see a big swath of Manhattan, the overwhelming ups and downs, grey and brown, lights and tiny moving vehicles. I tried not to look at the gap in the skyline where the Twin Towers had been, but Ana asked me where it was. Holding my hand gently, she said, "It is all right. We will look together." So we did.

Back at street level, my mother bought Ana a phone card so she could call home. She spoke in an animated voice, smiled often, even laughed once. Then she handed the receiver to my mother.

"Martin and I hope you will come soon to meet us at our home," my mother said."

It seemed from her expression that he agreed. Then she handed me the receiver.

"Hello, sir," I said.

" Simon, tell me, did you decide about my daughter yet?"

"She's right here, Arch-Mage. I can't say to you what I didn't say to her yet."

"Then say it to her, fool. I'll wait."

I turned to Ana.

"Do you want to get engaged to me?"

Ana sniffed, wiped her eyes on her knuckles. "All right," she said.

"What did she say?" the Arch-Mage demanded over the phone.

"She said yes."

My mother had hung up the phone and was now on her cell. "Martin, they're engaged," she said. "Now what?" She listened to my father's answer, then looked up. "He says he'll get the ring."

None of my teachers agreed to come to the engagement party, but a lot of kids were coming, so the Dean gave us the school bus. The one surprise was that Goldberry was not coming; she made the excuse that she didn't want another marriage proposal from the Arch-Mage.

I had also called Mrs Lopez at her office to invite Lorena and Level Three, but I was told the Lopez family was in Spain for the summer.

At my parents' home, I entered first, then invited in all the magicians who were visiting for the first time. My mother came quickly and led everyone to the sunny back yard, where my father was scraping his big charcoal grill and our wooden picnic table was laid out with abundant snack food.

In the shade of our old elm tree, on a folding chair, sat my grandmother Devi. At age eighty-nine, she was a thin and wizened Indian woman with a walker, white hair tied back, and a smile containing much warmth and few teeth. Although I knew she preferred Western clothes, today she was wearing a simple pink *sari*. I hadn't seen her in many years, and she looked more frail than I remembered. I approached, kneeling to touch her feet.

"*Hello* grandson," she said, touching my cheek. She looked over my friends and focused on Miss Chatterjee. "Is this the girl? So young!"

"Not me," said Miss Chatterjee.

Taking Ana's hand, I introduced her. "Grandmother, this is Ana Vorkina."

I had taught Ana the Indian greeting of folded hands accompanied by the word "*Namaste*." She did it for my grandmother.

"This girl?" Devi said. "Come here, child." She leaned forward slightly, touching Ana's cheek.

"Your name is Ana? Where are you from?"

"I am from Prague."

She took a red box from the folds of her sari. "Take this to give to her later."

The engagement ring.

"Robbie," I said. "Yakov. Rocco. Can I see you guys inside?"

They all followed me. I took them upstairs.

"I want to do a ritual with this ring," I explained. "If you guys help me, you are giving some energy to the ring to help it protect Ana, and we all become brothers and agree to protect her."

"Sure," Robbie said. "You promise to protect Avery the same way."

"She'll probably be protecting me," I said, "but sure, I promise."

"Delphine," Yakov said. "I don't have a sister, but that's the closest I can come."

"Agreed."

"Lorena," Rocco said. They had never officially been together, but he definitely cared about her.

I won't go into the details of the ritual, which I had planned out with help from Rabbi Horn, but we gave the ring the ability to warn Ana of danger, protect her from magical attacks, and be able to find each of us to get help if she was in trouble. If she used the ring's power to call for help, we would hear the call and get at least a clue about where she was.

It took about ten minutes, and as we headed back down the stairs, the doorbell rang. Avoiding the scattering cats in the hallway, I answered. On the other side of the door was a delivery man from a kosher fast-food restaurant.

Robbie, Rocco, and Yakov joined Meir, Delphine, and Avery as they devoured chicken wings and fries.

My grandmother was beckoning to me. I went and sat by her, on the other side from Miss Chatterjee.

"Explain to me what she says," Devi commanded, patting my hand. "What is it your father does, child?"

"He is a master magician," she replied. "He is Simon's teacher."

"And who is Simon?"

"I am," I said. "It's my magician's name."

"Magician," my grandmother said. "Card tricks, and rabbit out of a hat, and saw a lady in half?"

"No," I said. "I do real magic."

My mother hustled me away, and with my father we went to answer the door.

This was the first meeting between the fathers. Jan Vorkin stood towering in his dark silk suit, his grey hair playing around his shoulders.

"I am called Jan Vorkin, Arch-Mage of Prague. I have come to join your family."

"Welcome," I told him. "You are family."

"Our home is your home," my father said. "I'm Martin Moore, and this is Magdalene."

He nodded to my mother; they had met at School of the Ages before. "And here is my Willa. Come!" he called over his shoulder. Willa was a small, light-haired thirteen-year-old. She had a pretty face and small white hands and was wearing a sleeveless flower-print dress. She didn't speak, giving us a fearful look.

"Willa delayed us," said Vorkin. "She insists upon an airplane and will not be carried by winds."

We moved to the garden. Ana joined us. The Arch-Mage took his daughter by the chin, lifting her face to study it. "You are in love. Good. We will secure this match for you today. Simon Magus, I told you she was worth it. Now you know."

"I knew it the first time I saw her."

Vorkin met Robbie. "Word is you handled a major challenge a few weeks ago, and I know your taste in magic is like mine."

"Maybe you can help me with something," Robbie said. "I've been trying for years to summon Lazar-el, Duke of Water, but I never get an answer."

"Lazar-El the Whale God? No one can summon him. He's asleep. He has been for over a hundred years. If you want a duke of water, there are better choices."

As Vorkin explained, I looked around the party. My father, with Rocco's help, had begun grilling burgers, chicken, fish, and corn. My mother was serving salad.

I gave my father the sausages to grill. In a few minutes we were all settled at various tables eating. Ana brought fish and corn to my grandmother, who didn't eat any red meat.

When everyone was done with food, the Arch-Mage cleared his throat loudly. "Where are the Moores? Come sit by me. If your other guests don't mind, we shall talk business briefly to settle the terms, the length of the engagement and the dowry."

"Yes," my mother said as she sat. "Leicester will be eighteen in three years."

"He won't be able to support her now," my father said, "or even when he gets out of school. It's not that we can't manage ourselves, but I believe a man's self-respect demands he care for his wife by his own labour."

"Money is nothing, Moore," said the Arch-Mage. "The dowry will take care of that."

"Three years," my father said.

"We just want to be together," I said, "We can wait for the wedding. I agree with my father."

I could tell Vorkin was getting annoyed. I wasn't going to risk having him back out. "We'll still be at school, so we won't need money yet, and we won't need to set up a house."

"When you want one, it will be ready," he said. "I will go to buy one tomorrow."

My parents looked shocked. "Surely we should do that ourselves," my father began.

"I am going to buy a house for myself," said Vorkin. "When my daughter wants, she can move into it and I will give it to her husband."

The doorbell rang. We weren't expecting anyone else.

"Go get it, would you, dear?" my grandmother asked Miss Chatterjee.

"Let us talk about the dowry," said the Arch-Mage. "I intend to be generous with each of my children, so speak your mind freely, Moore."

My grandmother said in Hindi, "Ask him for a lot."

"Well, Magdalene," my father said jokingly, "I never negotiated a dowry before. Shall we ask him for a million?"

"Dollars?" said Vorkin. "Or Euro?"

The kitchen door swung open, allowing the arrival of a handsome threesome, Clive, Rosemary, and Goldberry Tinker.

"Simon, dear," said Mrs Tinker, "we must see you get engaged.

Clive Tinker and Jan Vorkin sized each other up as they shook hands.

"We're talking about dowries," my father explained. "I think there has been a misunderstanding. I was kidding my wife when I said a million. We aren't interested in money. We love your daughter, and we want her to marry our son. But not now."

"If I may say, Moore," Clive Tinker said, "neither you nor your son seem to understand what an Arch-Mage is capable of."

"Exactly," said Jan Vorkin. "A million dollars for you is not much to ask."

"Ask him for five million," said my grandmother. "Find out what he's made of."

"Shut up!" my father hissed at her.

"Honestly, your daughter is all the blessing we need," my father said.

"We'll discuss it later." The Arch-Mage turned away. "Moore, are you expecting anyone else?"

"No, we're all here," my father said.

"Good, then we will have the ceremony. Your mother is the eldest, so she should be in charge."

"Oh, he remembered that, the big mouth," my grandmother said in Hindi. "Come here, children."

Then my grandmother gave me and Ana a woven colored string each.

"*Om shri Ganeshay namah*. These two agree to get married. All parents agree to the match."

Ana and I tied the strings around each other's right wrists.

....

"Give her the ring," Devi ordered.

"Wait," said the Arch-Mage. He lifted his hand, palm toward the barbecue grill. A bright flame blazed up from the fading coals. In that upsurge of fire, glowing orange and red, there appeared the beautiful face of a young woman, very like Ana.

"My Erzebet would be smiling like that on this day," said Vorkin, his eyes wet. "Now all the parents are watching. Go on."

I took the box from my pocket, opened it took out the ring and slipped it onto her ring finger. Her mother's smiling face from the fire was reflected in the lovely metal.

Everyone applauded. The summer heat swam around me

...and I returned to that crib

... where as I lay flailing useless limbs

.... tangled in warm bedclothes

... a tabby cat with long gleaming whispers

... licked its lips and frowned and said

"UNLUCKY

IN

LOVE!!!"

❖ ❖ ❖

I was drifting now, as if in a dream, as two pairs of strong male hands lifted me. I felt nothing. I was bouncing, jostling as I was carried. I was set gently on a bed. Then I began to make out voices.

"...a magical attack?"

"Why should it be, Magdalene? He was just overstressed."

"Right. I'll manage him if you want to see to the guests. Yakov, Rocco, you two move off also."

"You sure you don't need us?"

"Where's Ana?"

....

"She's with her father."

A cold wet cloth touched my face. I opened my eyes. Goldberry was there.

"I'm cursed," I told her.

"Cursed? You're an idiot is what you are."

"No. In Alexandria, when Robbie summoned Eurus, and he made us recover lost memories, remember that?"

"Yes, I do. Did the trick, but I wouldn't care for another dose."

"I think my memory was true. Some kind of evil spirit was standing on my crib, shaped like a cat, cursing me to be unlucky in love."

"Really?" Goldberry wasn't buying it. "And because of a half-witted fantasy from the layabout East Wind, you think you're cursed. Right."

"Cursed?" Ana said, hearing the end of it as she entered my bedroom. "No one can curse you when you are mine." "All right," she told Goldberry. "You can go."

"Right," Goldberry returned. "You wouldn't want anyone else to be concerned."

"You can be concerned anywhere. This is with him and me, not with you."

"Which is why you took ten minutes to get here, I suppose."

"My father stopped me."

"So did mine, but I didn't listen. Maybe you need to learn."

"I'm not here to learn lessons from you. Simon is mine now. You had your chance."

"It's not like that at all, and you know it."

"Then what? You are his little mother? He doesn't need one. Go away."

"If it was a magical attack, he'll need me here. I'll go as soon as…"

"Get out, will you?"

"Stop," I said.

They faced off. Goldberry was a tall queen in her elegant red party dress matching gold pendant and earrings. Ana was fierce, her beauty like a summer dawn. The tall queen, and the fierce queen, avenger of wrongs. I saw them then not as others would, but as two towers: a tower of pearls glinting softly in the waning light, and a tower of advancing tidal surge, set to crush all in its way.

I sat up, and the wet cloth fell from my forehead. "You guys can't fight. It will kill me."

"I shouldn't have come," Goldberry said finally, turning away from Ana and me, towards the window.

"I didn't want to cause a problem. Really, I didn't. Ana, you have to know: I looked after him a long time. God, you didn't see him all that time, moping about. That mustn't happen anymore. I won't have it. I'll not stand aside, unless you promise."

"Promise?" Ana demanded. "I owe you no…" She looked at me. She looked at Goldberry. "Yes. Yes, I promise you it will not happen."

Mermelstein in Prague

At school the next day, I told Avery about the vision Eurus had given me.

She said, "Simon, you can't worry about this unlucky in love stuff so much. You know what they say that believing in a curse makes you put your own energy into it. You're lucky, man, and you have to remember that. She's got looks, brains, guts, and money, and she's a good person, and your parents like her, and her father likes you. Not a problem in the world. Enjoy it."

A few weeks later, we went to Prague with Rabbi Horn. It's Yakov Mermelstein's story, so here it is as he experienced it.

Yakov Mermelstein could feel Jewish hearts beating in Prague. As he followed our group through the busy Wenceslas Square, with Meir gabbing at him in Yiddish and the rest of the group all circled around the Arch-Mage and his four children, he could see the outlines of Jewish places that were gone, and shapes like cutouts of Jews that had been there before. It was a difficult experience for Yakov. There was too much information for him, and as he looked at the cutouts with the round-brimmed hats, limping along as if pulling the weight of pushcarts that were no more, he questioned them with his mind: where is the *luz*? No answer came. They were repeating their actions of the past, having no mind for what was happening around them. As for Yakov, this made him more than a little dizzy.

He steadied himself with a hand on Meir's shoulder, and rubbed his hand over his face, covering his eyes. With his eyes closed, he saw no more the city he was walking in, yet he was in the midst of a procession of Jewish silhouettes, who turned their heads, and nodded to him as they passed. They began to pass closer and as they drew nearer, they became more distinct, and he started to see the men, hollow dark eyes and sallow skin, shoulders bent with age and work and worry; laughing boys with free-swinging earlocks running with balls and sticks; women in flowing dresses carrying baskets of fruit with their girls clinging to their skirts. All of them turned to him, and looked at him, and then moved on clicking their tongues. He opened his eyes. Meir was tapping his cheek lightly. He asked, "Are you out of it?"

"Don't you see?"

"See what?" Meir asked.

"All around us. The ghosts!"

Yakov stopped. Meir stopped. The rest of the group went on, not realizing.

"A thousand years of *yehudim* walking all around us."

Meir closed his eyes, reached out with his own cabalistic senses. "They're friendly. Come on."

He led Yakov by the arm.

"You really saw them?" Yakov pressed.

"I can feel minds out there," Meir said. "Your vision, that I never had. Come on, let's catch up."

When the boys met the rest of the group in a restaurant, the Jewish ghosts followed them. The Arch-Mage ordered many dishes. Who in this room could understand? Maybe Simon could, he thought, since Simon had been haunted by a Jewish ghost in the past, but the rest of them had no clue. But Simon was busy with his girl.

Yakov sat, and the ghosts passed by, and then the first of them, an old rabbi with his beard below his shoulders, walked up and looked directly into his face, sizing him up.

"Where is the *luz*?" Yakov asked aloud.

"I don't know," said Meir.

"Not you. I'm asking the ghost."

The ghost walked on.

"This is crazy," Meir said. "Perhaps we should skip the tour and get straight to the Jewish quarter. Who do you want to go with us, anyone?"

Yakov forced himself to concentrate on the people at the table. He read the auras of his classmates and companions, and saw the aura he was seeking on Rocco.

"Rocco," he said.

Meir went to get Rocco and tell the others they were leaving. He came back with Rocco, Simon, and the Arch-Mage.

"You will not need my help, young cabalist?" asked Vorkin.

"If I do, I'll find you," Yakov said. "You too, Simon. It's all right. I just need Meir and Rocco."

"Why me?" Rocco asked.

"I can't say, but you look right for this job."

Rocco was obviously surprised to be teaming with Mermelstein instead of going against him.

Mermelstein stopped short. His intelligence, not his magic, told him who else he needed. "Ask her to come also. Goldberry."

Meir went and tapped her on the shoulder. Goldberry was up and with them quickly.

"You'll help me?" Mermelstein asked.

"Definitely. Anything's…" But she stopped.

"Anything is better than watching Simon carry on with his new family," Meir finished. "That's what you were thinking."

"If you know what I'm thinking, no need for me to say," Goldberry snapped.

Yakov's heart beat faster as they made their way along sloping cobbled sidewalks. Now the white forms were crowding closer, giving him light pats on the shoulder as he led the other two along. The route from Wenceslas Square toward Josefov, the Jewish Quarter, would be winding and complex. But each time Yakov was going to turn wrong, a cluster of ghostly bearded figures were in his way.

The four rambled through narrow cobblestone streets lined with tourist shops and jewellery stores. Rocco consulted a map. "This is Old Town Square," he said. "The Jewish Quarter is north of here."

But he saw before him a rosy-cheeked child moving a finger left and right.

"Where?" Mermelstein asked Goldberry.

"You couldn't possibly have asked me this before?" she countered. "Such as in the school, when I had all my tools with me, and time to think?"

"No," he answered.

"Boys don't know how to plan ahead. No strategy at all. "

"It was necessary first to come here. Nothing would work before that."

She considered. "Let me look at some cards."

"Let's call the Vatican," said Meir. "*Shalom*, your holiness, come over and guide us."

"Shut up!" Yakov barked. "Where in this city is good luck?" He put his face in his hands to block out the chaotic images of long-dead Jews all around him. But still he saw.

"I know," Rocco said. "It's in the guidebook. The bridge nearby has a lucky statue. On Charles Bridge, the statue of St. John Nepomuk, the saint who was executed by being thrown off the bridge. Touch the plaque on the right side that shows the saint being thrown off the bridge. It brings you good luck and you get to come back to the city. Here's a picture."

Goldberry took the book and looked at the small black and white photo printed there. "That's close enough. Let's go."

"It makes sense," Meir said as they walked. "A *luz* is full of emanations to make good luck."

"Of what?" Rocco asked.

"Energy from when the universe was created. It is what creates spirits. It is why all of us are joined."

Mermelstein lifted his head. The ghostly processions were starting to diminish as they crossed the square. "This is right," he said. There were many twists and turns in the streets headed for the Charles Bridge. Soon they saw the tall brown archway, framed by tourist shops, that marked the nearest entrance of the bridge.

"The Arch-Mage has a home here; Simon said as much," said Goldberry. "The *luz* has been just under his nose and he's not found it? How could he not notice?"

They had to cross a street with fast-moving cars. Hundreds of people were circulating in front of the entrance to the bridge, visiting souvenir shops, taking photographs, listening to guides, enjoying the distant wafting sounds of a jazz combo.

"How will we operate in a crowd that size?" Meir wondered. He and Yakov were drawing stares; Chasidim did not frequent this city. None of the four had learned advanced concealment, a form of magical hiding that worked on anyone not looking for you, but all were good enough to be unnoticed if there was a big enough distraction.

"I can hide in shadows," Rocco reminded them. He looked around. The sun was overhead, the sky blue as could be. "If I can find any."

"We could come back at night," Meir suggested.

"I want it finished," Mermelstein said. "Isn't there a way now? The ghosts will not even let me sit in peace."

They walked out onto the bridge. The statues, mostly blackened with soot, represented *figures* from Czech history as well as Christian saints. After a short walk, and two pauses to ask the local vendors for directions they were standing in front of a tall statue on the right, which showed a bearded man in an Orthodox priest's hat, with his head tilted in pain or ecstasy, his two hands clasping a miniature cross with crucified Jesus. A wire of gold leaf with stars formed a halo around his head. Tourists were swarming at the base, touching one of two shiny surfaces and taking pictures. Yakov said, "The Rambal also has that look sometimes." He pushed his way closer, looking up at the statue. It didn't feel right. Emanations were everywhere, but he didn't feel what he had expected to feel close to a *luz*.

An old Jewish lady was leaning on the statue Gray-haired, she wore a cloth over her head, a long skirt and an apron.

"Do you see her?" Mermelstein asked his companions. "The woman by the statue. On the side."

No one else saw her. When Yakov approached her and the statue."

"Not here," he said. "The *luz* is not here. She is trying to tell me that."

"Thanks for the information," Meir said to Goldberry, grinning.

Yakov studied the ghost, who tilted her head, returning his stare. She seemed to be trying to confirm he could really see her.

Yakov shouted, "Stop!" He could make no sense of the old woman's expressions. Apparently satisfied she had Yakov's attention, the ghost stepped away from the statue and rested one ethereal hand on a young, thin, dark-skinned man standing nearby.

"I've got it!" Mermelstein shouted. He looked at the ghost.

She nodded and faded out of sight.

The dark-skinned man was now walking along the bridge the way they had come. They followed. Moving with purpose, he seemed unaware of them amid the dense crowd of tourists. Soon he and they had passed back through the arch that capped the eastern entrance to the bridge. It was back to the cobblestone streets with their shops. They came out by another looming brown tower beneath the arch of which cars passed.

"The Powder Tower," Rocco said.

The young man continued through a large square, with a subway entrance, tourist booths, and the entrance to a massive opera house, and proceeded onto a street where small retail stores lay at the base of residential buildings. He entered one of those buildings. The four students stopped to take stock of it.

"You're kidding," Meir said.

The young man had gone into a restaurant.'

"It's here," Yakov said. "The *luz* is here. Let's go."

"What, you'll just go in and tell them to give you the *luz*?" Goldberry asked.

"Let me go in and find it," Rocco said, cutting them off. "What does it look like, Mermelstein?"

"So many of them I have seen that I can tell you how to recognize this one?" Yakov answered. "It is a bone from the skull. It looks like a bone."

"Okay, I'll try." Rocco stepped into the restaurant. The others waited outside. He reappeared.

"They have a big piece of bone in a plastic case on the counter," he explained. "It says 'good luck' on a sticker."

"I will go in to take it," said Mermelstein.

"How?" asked Goldberry.

"They will understand," he replied. "They must." But now he had his doubts. Jewish law forbade him to take things by force. Nor could he take the *luz* by trickery, nor by theft. All were frowned upon. He had two choices–to persuade, or to negotiate a sale. He explained this to his companions, Meir nodding in understanding.

Yakov counted his money. He had about two hundred dollars. "Not enough," he concluded. He saw Goldberry taking out her wallet. "I don't want your money," he told her.

"It's not my money; it's my father's," she said, but she put the wallet away again.

"Not enough cash," Rocco said. "Stealing it would be easy, but we're not doing that, right?" Yakov shook his head. Rocco continued, "Then let's just be nice. Hang on." He went back inside.

They stood outside waiting on the pavement.

Rocco was back. "Okay, I cut us a deal. We can take the bone if we clean the kitchen. Scrub the pots, the counters, the stove, the walls."

"Oh, brilliant," said Goldberry.

"Not you," Rocco said. "You get to work the front counter while we boys scrub."

"You think I can't clean?" she challenged.

Rocco considered. The wrong answer would get him in trouble he didn't need. "You're at the counter because you're the best at universal language," he answered.

Goldberry patted his cheek. "You did save yourself this time."

❖ ❖ ❖

It was by far the filthiest kitchen Yakov had ever seen. Rocco scrubbed and scrubbed, smiling and occasionally singing. Yakov said, "You helped a lot. Thank you."

❖ ❖ ❖

In the end, Yakov slipped into his coat the velvet pouch containing a *luz*, a soul bone. As they walked to Josefov, he felt the life in the bone mingling with his, and his soul grew.

A Malodorous Solution

Goldberry worked daily to regain her powers of divination. Her friends took turns sitting with her. Some nights it was Miss Chatterjee and me; some nights Goodenough; some nights a varying combination of Avery, Ana, and Delphine, occasionally with the Divination club of Mina, Carol, Irene and Lakshmi.

Goldberry touched and peered into Abramelin's Globe, trying to get back what happened to her the night she was attacked. She whispered to the globe, but it showed her instead many events from her childhood. She watched replays also of our adventures together, and cried when she saw 9/11 or Leah, and laughed too, at the sight of, herself arguing with the Gryphon and Mock Turtle in Level Three's dream. She saw flashes of her parents' lives; watched her teenage father walking the same halls where we now walked, already carrying a thundercloud of emotion round with him. All of it helped, and she felt like she was healing, but the elusive missing minutes of her battle with Gott in Himmel would not emerge.

The breakthrough was not due to any of us.

She was in the divination room with Miss Chatterjee and me. The door was slightly ajar. She bent over the Globe. Her eyes were unfocused. She was remembering. The door creaked open, and a cloaked figure entered: Corby Crow.

"Please excuse us," said Miss Chatterjee, who didn't know him.

"This room is presently occupied."

"I know," he said. "Relax. I'm here to help."

"Help with what?" I challenged him. "What do you know?"

"She's trying to get back her divination powers."

"How do you know that?" Who could have told him?

I said, "This is our private business."

"Quit posturing, you two," Goldberry interjected. "I can't concentrate." She looked up at Corby. Her voice and mannerisms were normal, but her eyes were the red quartz and silver colours of the globe.

"Oh God," said Corby.

He reached into his cloak pocket for a large medicine bottle. "A herbal mix from Russia. For psychic health. It may help with recovering lost memory. It tastes terrible, but..."

"But what?"

"Your eyes."

"My eyes what?"

"Their appearance is most remarkably changed," said Miss Chatterjee. We are all concerned."

"Right, Corby, what's the bargain?" asked Goldberry.

Corby set down the medicine bottle. "I don't bargain like you people. I'm just helping. If you don't take my help now, don't ask later."

"You didn't bargain with these two for help, did you?" Corby returned.

"They're my close friends." Goldberry's eyes had returned to their normal shining hazel.

"Got it," he said. He looked hurt. "The medicine's yours, and you don't owe me anything." He slammed the door behind him.

"We don't have time for this," Goldberry said, a bit regretful of her brusqueness.

I opened the bottle to examine the contents. It looked like tea leaves but smelled terrible. Time for a thought-trade.

....

Dr Archer, Corby Crow just gave Goldberry some herbal stuff. Should she use it?

He advised us to ask Dr Chatterjee.

"Let's go to Dr Chatterjee," I said.

After packing the globe, we went to our teacher's office. It was neat, with very few books on the shelves and very few papers. There was an easel on which were stacked many pieces of chart paper containing star charts and other astrological notes. Miss Chatterjee explained to her father what had happened.

"It seems that he is a very unusual person," she continued. "I found him so. But you are his advisor. Perhaps you are able to say how much trust in him is wise."

"He is a loner, and has only helped any of you once before, when his own study partner Rocco was missing," Dr Chatterjee said. "This time he has volunteered the assistance. Simon, your instincts are generally useful in such matters. Do you feel anxious about this substance?"

"I don't feel any worry at all. I don't understand him, but my gut says to trust him."

"Goldberry, what do you say?"

"I should like to be certain what this stuff does."

" I'll try it first," I said.

"Don't be ridiculous, Simon. I don't recall ever asking you to be a food taster."

"Perhaps it is more efficient for me to try the drink," said Miss Chatterjee. "Being younger and a noncombatant, I am presently expendable."

Her father said sharply. "No one is expendable. Corby Crow is not a bad boy. Let us go and make a pot of tea, and we will all have some."

"Right," said Goldberry. She stood and snatched the medicine bottle. "You can all forget it. I'm the one who got beaten and fouled up by the enemy. I'll take the risk."

....

"You are all very brave and loving," said Dr Chatterjee. "Left together, you will surely destroy yourselves with such heated nobility. Fortunately, I am here to stop you, at least tonight. We shall share the risk. We will all taste the drink together. That is the final word on the matter."

In the dining room, we put a kettle on the fire. I went into the kitchen for a tray with a teapot and four cups. When I got back, the water was hot. We filled the tea pot with the foul herbal mix, and poured the hot water over it.

If it had smelled bad in leaf form, the medicine was far worse in the infusion. Finally, Dr Chatterjee poured a small amount of liquid into each teacup. "Sugar and milk will not be efficacious," he said smilingly, raising a cup to his lips. Quickly he gulped the entire contents. Then his face twisted. "Its flavor is repellent beyond my capacity to explain," he managed. "However, it does not harm my stomach. Go on, children."

Miss Chatterjee drank her tea at once.

Neither of the Chatterjees showed any signs of poisoning. Now it was my turn. I took a sip.

It was like a hundred hot coffees, each brewed with a mix of vinegar, ammonia, and olive oil. The pain in my mouth was as if my palate was peeling off in strips. Quickly, I finished my portion, and it was as the teacher had said: no stomach discomfort. In a part of my mind, also, memories were returning–flashes of moments with my grandparents; parts of school lessons I hadn't been paying attention to; the sun-baked skins of Alexandrian Egyptians; the words on signs in Paris streets.

"Well?" asked Goldberry.

"It works. I can remember what Mermelstein's front teeth used to look like."

"That's all?"

"Let's give some to Goodenough," I gasped. "Bake it in brownies to surprise him."

Goldberry took a deep breath, held her nose, and drained her teacup. "Well, that's vile," she said. Her eyes went glassy. She began to breathe rapidly. Her arms flailed around, one hand catching me on the collarbone, the other striking Miss Chatterjee in the right eye.

"Oh!" said Miss Chatterjee.

Goldberry surged out of her chair, shrieked, "I won't! You can't force me!"

We caught her wrists and pulled her down. I called her name.

"I won't let them force me," said Goldberry. "I fought them, all of them. There was no chance to get away. Peter put me in the car. The moment I sat down, two of them slid in by the back doors. Then my door was stuck. I can open any door, it's just probability, but…" She stopped.

"The lost memories are returning," said Dr Chatterjee. She was talking fast and barely seemed to know where she was.

"The man with the beard, must have been Dr Beam. He touched my face. It began to burn. He was a poisoner, probably had something he could give me from his fingertips. Peter got into the driver's seat. The woman in the black veil laughed at him, and she grabbed the back of my neck with one hand. Her grip was a like a vice. 'Kaiser Petrus is here,' she said. 'Does that make your heart stop?' She pulled me by the neck so I was leaning backwards over the seat. I said, 'Help, Peter. Call Simon.' Then Peter talked in this German old-witch voice. I felt like claws were scratching inside my skull. So much pain. They were all laughing. Nothing funny about it, of course. I used a thought hex to make them forget what they were doing, all three of them, but it wasn't enough; they soon enough remembered. The man put his hand over my mouth. He rubbed some other poison on my lips that tasted like walnuts. I didn't get a full dose, but it made breathing hurt, and he left his hand there, so I bit into it. The woman in the veil said… "Oh, God. No, she couldn't have."

....

"Go on," said Dr Chatterjee. "You must harbour nothing if you wish to heal."

"She said, 'Clive's little girl. We'll make her cry and then kill her mother.' Well, that made me mad. I let go the man and tried to climb over the seat at her, but he put his hand on my face and pushed me back."

Goldberry continued. "Well, the poisons got to me after that. I fainted. I woke up lying in the street, sitting up against a wall."

I asked, "How do you feel now?" She was no longer trembling, and I felt it was safe to let go of her wrist.

"That drink is ghastly," she said. "But I'm not weak or disoriented now. Quite the opposite. I'm more myself than I have been since the attack. I'll find the Mind Cannibal straight away." She touched her stomach. "Well, perhaps in the morning. And another thing, too. If you lot thought I was angry before, then I promise you, there are some surprises coming. Excuse me."

Before We Left

Goldberry's father picked her up in his Rolls-Royce. She was gone for three days. When she got back, she was excused from classes, and the Dean substituted for Dr Archer in his courses. The two of them stayed in the divination room, working together with her tools. Avery stayed with her at night; someone else waited outside the door to help out if needed. Usually it was Ana and me, taking turns.

Dr Archer had brought reference photos for the major cities in Europe. Goldberry would start with a landmark in that city, locate it in Abramelin's Globe–that was easy. She would then scan around the city rapidly, trying to spot the stone building she had detected the previous year. European cities were full of such old buildings, but this one, she now knew, was distinctive because it was located on an island on a body of water inside a city.

London and Paris, were quickly eliminated. Prague and Budapest were out of the question–Jan Vorkin had assured the Dean that no magician was operating in those cities without his permission. Dr Archer had recently been all through Amsterdam and could rule it out. Assuming that the building belonged to the Mind Cannibal, who was a German, Dr Archer thought it most likely that it was located in Germany, and he further suspected that, since the Mind Cannibal had been unseen since before World War II, the building had probably been her headquarters as far back as the thirties. He compiled a list of

German cities along with maps of the parts that had survived World War II's bombings, and they began to work through these cities, starting with Berlin. It was the traditional headquarters of Gott im Himmel.

Goldberry did not find the stone building in Berlin. They ranged outward to other major cities nearby. Leipzig–no good. Dresden–no good. Several buildings were similar, but Goldberry ultimately rejected all of them. Hannover–definitely not, the wrong kind of stone, she said. Hamburg?

She found the building in Hamburg. Hamburg was shot through with canals and inland lakes. Somewhere, on one of those, lay the long-time headquarters of the Mind Cannibal.

Abramelin's Globe would not show her the inside of the building, and Goldberry's vision grew fuzzier the nearer she approached the structure. It was protected against magical viewing, and the more she watched, the more her head hurt. She didn't stop trying; she was determined.

"I've got you," she said to herself. "You're mine now. No one makes a victim of me. No one." Exhausted, she covered the Globe and rested her head on the table. After a brief sleep, she suddenly rose as if completely refreshed. "When can we go?" she asked Dr Archer.

"I don't know," he said. "I no longer have an intuitive feeling regarding such matters. I will examine the star charts, and consult with my colleagues."

"So will I," she said.

She gathered her friends for a war council. We met in the basement.

"Simon, you're with us, I assume," Goldberry said. "Butt out when we get to the Mind Cannibal, but you can guard my back."

"Fine," I said.

"Avery?"

"Mr Phillips says I'm ready, so I'm in."

"Robbie?"

"Yes."

"Mermelstein?"

"The Rambal won't let me," he said. "He says he needs me here for something. I don't know what to do. He hardly talks to me at all."

"Rocco?"

"Chatterjee says no. He says wait till next year for a field mission."

"I'll speak to him."

"No," Rocco said. "It's okay. I messed up pretty bad with that invisibility spell. So he's protecting me."

Goldberry looked at Ana. "I know it's your sort of thing," she said. "But at the same time, it's fairly obvious that if you get hurt, the Arch-Mage and School of the Ages will be at odds."

"I am not afraid. I fight to help my friends," Ana said.

"Yes, but, if you don't mind me saying, if anything happened to you, my partner would be no good anymore. I know you're brave, but his happiness is more important to me."

"No," Ana said, "but…"

"You promised," Goldberry said.

"Promised?"

"At the engagement party. You promised never to make him sad again like he used to be. So let him know that you are safe here. Let him go to war clearheaded."

"Wait a minute." I started to interrupt.

"Shut up, partner. Ana, you promised. You remember? I'm holding you to it."

Ana took a deep breath. "Still in some way you will keep him to yourself. Oh, yes. I understand. You will keep a boy with you but not love him."

Hard-faced, Goldberry considered this. Then she shrugged. "Explain it to her," she said to the others. She withdrew rapidly from the room.

………………………………………………………………………………

"I got it," Avery said. "Rest of you guys clear out."

I never found out what Avery and Ana discussed that day.

I returned to my room that night to find my suit bag laid out on my bed. Looking inside, I found the coat I had been given by Mrs Tinker, that had enabled us to save Mr Tinker on 9/11. Mr Dancer, the retired construction teacher, had returned it to me. It was clean. I took it out, put it on, put up the hood. At once, my anxiety fell away; sounds around me were muted, and I felt a kind of comforting calm and peace, an absence of mental and physical noise, different than I had experienced before. It had given me telepathic abilities before, expanding my simple thought-trading to actual exchange of voices.

Mr Dancer, thank you for fixing the coat.

No problem. See you around.

It worked.

I had one more person to talk to about the trip. I went to my mother the next morning.

"We're going to Hamburg," I said. "Goldberry has found the Gott im Himmel magician."

"And how are you involved?" my mother asked.

"I'm going as a back-up. Goldberry's going to fight the Mind Cannibal, not me, but I'll be there in case there's anyone else to handle."

"Just you two?" my mother said.

"No. Dr Archer, Dr Chatterjee, Avery, and Robbie. Don't worry. Mind Cannibal is probably over eighty years old."

"Well, you'll forgive me if I'm not enthusiastic about my son going to meet someone called the Mind Cannibal," my mother said. "Maybe your father and I should go along."

I was expecting her to say this and was prepared with an answer for her. "I know you guys aren't afraid to help out with stuff like that, but I'm worried about Ana. If you're here, you can help me look out for her."

"You're right about that," my mother said. "I know you're

manipulating me, but you still have a point."

"Thank God, Dr Archer has that much sense."

"Well… He didn't decide, actually. He left it up to Goldberry and me. Goldberry told Ana to stay behind."

"Why?"

"To protect me."

My mother nodded. "I understand. She knows you lost Leah Ritz, and doesn't want that to happen to you again."

"Yes."

My mother sighed deeply. "I hope you appreciate that girl."

"Goldberry has never fought an adult magician one on one before," I added. "She was tough enough to survive three of them back in December, but a duel is different. Anyway, she'll feel more confident knowing I'm there to support her. She's more likely to win with confidence."

"I don't like it," my mother said. "That is a sweet, beautiful girl. She shouldn't be fighting at all. Neither should you."

"I know," I said. "But someone has to."

"Leicester," she said, "you're too young to understand what this sort of thing does to a person."

"That's not true," I said. I was surprised at the coldness in my voice as I argued. "I survived 9/11. I saw people die. And the Connoisseur in Paris, and… And I've…" I couldn't finish the sentence.

We stared at each other. My mother pursed her lips. "I understand. Go."

I heard her cursing under her breath before I shut the door.

Dr Archer Explains

It was a large group by the standards of School of the Ages field teams, that arrived in Hamburg that night: Drs Archer and Chatterjee, Goldberry, Robbie, Avery, and me. We were all fully supplied with equipment for a major operation against tough opposition. I had misled my mother: while we believed the Mind Cannibal was physically feeble, she was known to control minds, making her full resources uncertain.

We had three rooms in a hotel a few blocks from the train station. Having settled into the rooms, we met in the second-floor restaurant to review our situation. Dr Archer explained that our nearness to the station gave us the ability to travel quickly to all major parts of the city. Dr Chatterjee urged a period of extended scouting before making the planned attack. We kids could go sightseeing the next day to get a feel of the city. Most of Hamburg had been destroyed in World War II and rebuilt, largely when it was part of communist East Germany, so magical areas were likely to be few, and, if any were found, were more likely going to be of recent creation.

It was a bright, clean city, hot in the summer, but cooler in some places due to the presence of the huge River Elbe, two man-made lakes, and an elaborate canal network. Although some German cities had strong territorial magicians or groups, this city was, like London, a free zone. It was the perfect location for destructive outlaws like Gott im Himmel and the Mind Cannibal.

The Hamburg train station doubled as a shopping mall, so we were able to get takeout food and eat in the hotel. While Robbie and I were there, we noticed a lot of people, mostly men, walking around in costumes, brightly coloured clothes and devil masks. I asked a woman about this. She said there was a Krampus Festival on. At the hotel, we looked up Krampus on the Internet and found that according to German tradition, Santa Claus had a devil called Krampus who rode with him in his sleigh.

"It's not Christmas," Robbie said. "Why are they doing it now?" he asked the desk clerk.

"It is raising money for the poor in Hamburg," the clerk said in clear, German-accented English. From her tone, I could tell it wasn't the first time she'd been asked that question. After lunch I replaced the chip in my phone for use in Germany and called my mother.

Meeting in the hotel conference room we took stock of our preparations and plans. Goldberry had her tools, Abramelin's Globe and the Akashic Prism, and when she went into battle, she was going to borrow my coat, the Calming Coat as we were now calling it. Robbie hadn't brought his conjuring equipment, because the geodes and hand-staves he normally used could not be transported easily on a plane. Instead, he had focus objects enabling him to quickly access some elementals he had already bound. The ones who had helped him to challenge King Wind were not available this time around; he had spent a long time binding them in preparation for that conflict, and had not been able to bind them for a second use. As for Avery, she was a native talent and didn't need as much equipment as he did, but she had some jewellery she had prepared with Construction, especially her big wooden African earrings. I had a lot of gear, including my protective amulet and scarf, the lock pick coin, and my weapon against spirits.

It was a leather belt. My mother had got me an extra-large one, and I had prepared it with construction, painting magic symbols on the inside and doing a series of rituals naming twenty categories of embodied spirit foes listed in Robbie's summoning textbook and in a few books from the Refectory. The belt would seriously harm spirits, could be used repeatedly, was extremely durable, and would go through any airport scanner because it was an article of clothing.

After the meeting. Drs Archer and Chatterjee added more protective spells to the rooms and advised us to sleep. We would start our operation in the morning.

I had only been sleeping an hour or so when a loud ruckus in the street woke me. I was alert at once and went to the window. A group of men in Krampus masks were chasing each other across the cobblestones, leaping and prancing like ballet dancers. One tilted his head back, beat his chest, yelled—and froze when he saw me in the window. He laughed and pointed. I felt cold as I stared down at his masked eyes.

Robbie had slept through the noise, but I was done with sleep. I put on my clothes and went down to the lobby to use the Internet.

Dr Archer was there, sitting on a sofa, lost in thought. I sat by him.

"I felt that someone would join me tonight," he said. "It is fitting that it be you, Simon. I am going out. I will explore the city in search of a fruitful discovery. Please gather your protective equipment if you wish to come along."

I ran upstairs for the equipment. There was a note in his voice that I didn't like, a kind of resignation, a surrender. I half suspected he would leave while I was upstairs but he didn't. He hadn't moved at all.

"Simon," he said as I sat again on the sofa beside him, "perhaps you are entitled to know certain matters I have kept to myself. Secrecy seems unproductive to me now. Ask whatever you wish, and if I am able to answer safely, I will answer."

"Do you know who Kaiser Petrus is?"

"I believe that Mr Dancer, my former teacher was right to warn me of an old enemy. The Dean has said the same all along. I am not short of old enemies. It is a person who knows the style of magic taught at School of the Ages, and who knows precisely what are the capabilities of those of us active in opposition."

"What about H E Myra? Who is that?"

"H E Myra is not a person," said Dr Archer. "That is all I know."

He was still being evasive. I tried something else. "Okay, here's a question you didn't answer before. Why isn't Donovan helping with this war? Other teachers' sons are helping, and he's just as brave, and just as good at magic, right?"

Dr Archer swallowed before answering. "Donovan is not involved because I do not wish him to succeed me as principal defender of School of the Ages. It is a difficult life. Of course, he may choose it regardless of my wishes, but I need not make it an unquestioned course, as it was in my case. My father groomed me for the position, as my grandfather had groomed him. I never considered another role in life. For my son it shall be different. He shall not be plunged into the task before he has learned what other occupations there may be. Nor will he have to watch his own life partner fade while he is consumed with work. My Ada deteriorated in health as I labored at defense. It was what she wanted me to do, for she loved the school. I felt each hour away from my wife was wasted. Donovan knows of my feelings on this subject. He has said, that he is his own man. Largely this is true. He is calmer and wiser than I was at his age, but he speaks also from the optimism of youth."

"Are you saying that anyone who takes your job will have his life destroyed?"

"No." He didn't seem sure, but then said, "Not Cornelius my father, nor yet Theophilus my grandfather felt it so. But consider your own position. You are fighting for the school. Why? Because you love it and you love people in it? Or out of a sense that it is simply your nature to fight for a good cause?"

"Both reasons. It doesn't matter. I don't care why."

He nodded. "That is because you are young. However, I have had many years to wonder, especially during my years as a widower." He didn't look at me as he said it.

"You've been grieving all these years," I said.

"Yes."

"Even Donovan doesn't know that."

"It is the price of parenting that one must conceal a measure of grief in order to be strong for the child."

"But he should know you better. He's a man now. He deserves to know."

"I agree. Leave that to me, Simon. Ask me something else that is on your mind."

"Okay, here's a different question. Am I going to keep fighting for the school? Will I be trapped like you?"

"Before I met you, Simon, I felt certain in that regard. Because of astrology, I felt I could move people about like chess-pieces. I know you now as a student but I have a sense of the man you will be. I would not define my son's role. How am I to define yours? You are also like a son to me."

I had not been expecting him to say that. The shock of it unbalanced me as he continued.

"I do believe in human tendencies, defined by the conditions of birth, but I do not believe in fate or destiny. Madame Leveque was harsh but correct to say that it is the heart that tells and not the stars. For many years, faced with the loss of Ada, I concluded that that loss could be explained through a mystical analysis of star charts and other cosmic influences. I believed in a great divine clock-work in which all things came to pass according to a decision made by God at birth. You see, Simon, I was always aware that I could not have saved Ada from the cancer that consumed her. I did not blame myself for that, mostly because she would not let me. I wished only to believe that there was an understandable reason for it. The Rambal told me, but I would not believe, that…"

"That there are reasons, but we can't understand them," I finished. "God is too big to understand, and we can only be comforted by knowing that it really does make sense some way that's beyond us. He told me that. I had the same conversation with him last year, that…"

"That he and I had when I lost my wife. Yes, Simon. You are more gentle than I was at your age, but we are not dissimilar in other ways. I have fought many wars and I know what hurts they give, and I do not like how this war has hurt you. Because of School of the Ages, you have met your ideal partner in life. I do not wish you to face the loss that I faced. Yet, as with Donovan, I cannot prevent you, and may only attempt to persuade."

"Dr Archer, you aren't giving me a straight answer. You aren't telling me what I need to know."

"I am telling you what you need, though not, perhaps, what you desire to know. I have created a mechanism whereby you will learn more at a later time."

"A mechanism? You can just tell me."

"Yes, I shall do that. Please proceed with your questions."

"There's one more that you wouldn't answer before. How do you kill someone with magic?"

Dr Archer looked at me with pain in his eyes. "Do you mean to say that you do not know, or that you wish only to force me to answer? You know ways to give an injury. You have only to make the injury more grave. Is that clear enough, or ought I to describe specific mutilations? You have not seen me in battle. Faced with enemies that I must destroy, I destroy them without hesitation. It is a work that a man does not properly take pride in. He thinks of the loved ones and causes whose interests he protects, and he thinks, 'To kill is a sacrifice that I make for them. I shall no longer be an untainted person, but it is worth that loss of self to secure what is dear.' That, at least, is what I keep in my mind.

"As to means. What can you not visualize, Simon? See a man -- see his brain—see his brain on fire. Perhaps you cannot create flames, but the result will be the same. That was how I killed the first man whom I fought to the death. He was called Carlos Grau, a Spaniard. I was in Paris with my father Madame Leveque and Ada, and he called me out in the lobby of our hotel. Ada and I were only students, and if I had not fought him, she would have, and if I had not slain him, he would have attacked us again and again until he was satisfied. He wished to make his reputation by challenging me. That did occur, but not in the way he expected."

Dr Archer rose suddenly. "I think it is best that we go while darkness remains."

Blades

Dr Archer and I walked along the narrow cobblestone street that would emerge in the broad avenue by the train station. A cool breeze nudged the hot summer air. I wondered if it was a wind that Avery knew. It was about two a.m. Dinner time in New York. What was Ana doing? Was she thinking of me?

Then my stomach turned over. “Something’s going to happen.”

“Indeed. I had no specific warning, but I have assumed that our arrival here was observed and would provoke a reaction.”

“You mean that we came out here specifically to be attacked?”

Dr Archer nodded. “The place and time are thus of my choosing.”

“Okay,” I said. “Let’s do it.”

We continued, hemmed in by low buildings. Orange street lamps cast our shadows as we passed. We emerged onto the main street, with the train station’s large steel and glass entrance in sight. There were only parked cars on the street. The city was quiet except for the distant hum of traffic.

“There,” said Dr Archer.

At the far end of the concrete plaza in front of the station stood a female, just visible at the edge of the pool of light from a streetlamp, all in black, with a widow’s veil. Not moving, only watching. She had an air of menace that hung around us like a fog.

Footsteps were now approaching us. From each of the four

directions, in front, behind, from either side, a man in a dark suit was walking slowly towards us.

"This is worse than I envisioned," Dr Archer said quietly. "I should not have brought you. I can no longer anticipate events as I used to, and we are in great peril. We must move quickly. If they surround us, we will both die."

"Can we get back to the hotel?"

"I do not prefer to betray our hotel's location. It would draw further attacks. Prepare, Simon. This is no school exercise. It is a fight for your life."

The four men had closed a few yards. Then, all of a sudden, a clang and a shimmer of reflected light, and they were wielding weapons: a curved scimitar, a crescent-moon-shaped sickle, a rapier, and a heavy hunting knife.

"Make for the train station," said Dr Archer. "Run!"

We ran, side by side, giving a wide berth to the man with the rapier, who spun rapidly to follow. I made the mistake of meeting his eyes. He pointed his blade tip at me and nodded, calling me out. There was no humanity in those eyes, and no mercy.

Past the glass doors of the entrance was an atrium full of closed shops, with stilled escalators. While Dr Archer considered what to do, I watched all four men now walking side by side, weapons in ready positions at hip level, and behind them the woman in the black veil, slim, mysterious, deadly.

Dr Archer gestured. The coin in his hand flashed. A lock clicked into place. I took the coin from my pocket and did the same. We locked all the glass doors, blocking the nearest entrance in their faces. It would delay them, but not for long.

We turned to go, and then a violent shock attacked my defensive cylinder. Nothing was visible, but lightning was playing along the outer edge of my magical barrier, striking at my arms, my legs, my face. I stumbled. Dr Archer caught my elbow, helping me to take a few steps. Countering electricity, how? A lightning rod, rubber gloves? Wood was best. Closing my eyes, I changed my cylinder's outer edge into rough pine bark. I was numbed, and felt how little I had slept, but the lightning no longer penetrated.

Dr Archer pulled me towards the escalators. He was wobbly too, so he must also have been attacked. Behind us there arose a loud wrenching sound. Four station doors were buckling from pressure to open. The glass was shattering. The men squeezed through.

"On your knees!" I shouted at them, exerting my will. They kept coming. I had made no psychic impact on them.

"They are not men," said Dr Archer. "They are the Compass Blades, assassins from the spirit world. They represent the four cardinal directions, aligned with the magnetic forces of the Earth. Quickly, let us go to the platform and see if we can find a train running."

It was quiet. I was sure there were no trains running. We circled the escalators and advanced through the empty mall. When I turned, I saw only one man behind us, the one holding the sickle. "They're surrounding us," I told my teacher.

"They have moved to the cardinal points. They always reorient themselves. That is what Chatterjee Major and Dempsey both reported."

We clattered down another escalator into the huge central platform area of the station. It had a high arched ceiling, like an aircraft hangar. There were six tracks arranged along three platforms, some with dark, parked trains and large glass-windowed hutches. A double row of shops was at either end. We proceeded to the central of three platforms. The vast chamber was brightly lit overhead. It was hot. From the position we now occupied, we could see furthest and had the most room to maneuver. I saw the woman in the black veil.

"Who is that?" I asked Dr Archer. "The same one who was in the car, who attacked Goldberry?"

....

"She is controlling the Compass Blades. She is a cabal magician. I cannot give her a name—not yet."

"Let's take her out quickly."

Dr Archer gestured. The woman went flying backwards, out of sight. "That will not stop her for long," he said.

At once the four armed men appeared on the platform, the closest they had been.

"No more talk," said Dr Archer. From his coat he removed a large wooden rod with a knob at the end, heavy and carved: a *shillelagh*. I took the belt off my shoulder.

The rapier-wielding spirit neared me, again pointing the blade-tip.

"*Havaya Tseva-ot*!" I shouted. "Back away!"

The spirit froze, took a step forward, took a step back.

"*Havaya Tseva-Ot*! Begone!"

The spirit with the sickle rushed Dr Archer. I saw that he caught its wrist, staying the down stroke, and thrust with the point of its club into its chest, and cried out his own magic words. The spirit vibrated, hissed, shrieked, and turned into mist.

The other three closed. The rapier-wielder thrust at me. Its blade caught in my scarf, twisted in its hand. Holding it by the buckle, I swung the light end of my belt at its head.

Dr Archer spun now, holding the *shillelagh* extended, and time seemed to slow down. There was a hum in the air of energy. Quickly he leapt at the spirit with the hunting knife, striking at the wrist to disarm it, then at the chest, and it screeched and was dispersed.

Five seconds had passed, and now time sped up again. I came around with the belt quickly and hit the spirit with the scimitar on the shoulder as it prepared to slash at Dr Archer's back. It made a roaring noise and was flung back across the platform. Dr Archer then struck behind me, rapping my opponent on the forearm so that the rapier dropped from its hand and fell to the platform with a clink.

The spirit with the scimitar was on its feet and charging. The one with the rapier held out its naked hand, and a new weapon formed there. I grabbed the rapier on the ground with my left hand, and jerked my wrist to recover the belt so I could swing it forward again.

The spirit struck expertly, caught the guard of the rapier, flicked it from my hand. I fell back, passing Dr Archer where he and the scimitar spirit were swiping at each other. My opponent closed. I took off the scarf, wound it round my left arm as a shield. The spirit thrust. I blocked with my arm, snapped the belt at it, missed.

She was impressed.

This thought-trade from the veiled woman startled me. The rapier-wielder, flicked up at my face and scratched my cheek. He came in low again; I sidestepped, swung wild with the belt, hit the spirit in its cheek. It went flying back, hit a parked train car.

She was very impressed.

I sent back to her: Shut up, murderer.

Letting the belt drag, I rushed at Dr Archer's opponent and swung it.

The spirit squealed, A hole appeared in its chest, and then it fell into pieces which turned into sand on the platform. My belt was on fire. I tossed it away.

The last spirit was now standing again. It looked at the two of us, raised its left hand, formed a second rapier. It nodded and stepped towards us, a sword in each hand.

Dr Archer now grasped the *shillelagh* at both ends and pulled. It expanded, becoming a bow stave. There was no string, but he drew back and released as if there was. Some force I couldn't see caught the enemy and lifted it off the platform and up towards the roof. Midway there, it vanished.

At last we had time to catch our breaths. I leaned against a bench. The Compass Blades and their weapons were gone. Dr Archer put the *shillelagh* away and finally sat down.

....

She congratulated us on our victory.

"You vicious witch!" I shouted. It echoed throughout the empty station. "Tell me your name, coward!"

She was saying goodbye.

"Well done," said Dr Archer. "We have destroyed the Compass Blades. You have helped me to avenge the hurts of my former students."

I was still struggling for breath. "What did she say to you? Did she thought-trade?"

"She boasted that she could kill any of us any time she wished, but for now, she wanted to get some sleep. She threatened to kill my son. Come, let us get back to the hotel. We must tend to the cut on your face, and inform the others."

At the entrance, we found all the doors intact and unlocked. It was as if the magical battle had taken place only half in our world and half in some other place.

Dream of a Holy Land

It was with a great sense of relief that we re-entered the hotel lobby. "We need to talk about the woman in the veil," I said.

"We will. First I must clean your wound." Directing me to sit, he took a first-aid kit from the hotel counter and knelt by me. As he swabbed my face with antiseptic, I asked, "Are you certain you can't tell me who the woman is? The woman in the veil?"

He was quiet.

"She was in the car. She attacked Goldberry. She sent the Compass Blades to try to kill…"

He was focused on the wound.

"Why are you holding back?"

"I have no strength for the question. I do not wish to think about her identity. I have not addressed it in my mind. Were I to do so, there might be harm to my resolve."

"Well, I want to know." The enemy had told my teacher she wanted to go to sleep. Maybe it would work. "Put a spell on me that I'll fall asleep in exactly ten minutes and then sleep until morning."

He nodded.

"And you go to sleep, too."

Up in the room, I put on the ring with rubies and emeralds. Trying to ignore Robbie's snores and the lingering pain of the cut on my face, I lay there waiting for my teacher's spell to put me to sleep. Just as it did,

I said, "I call you to consult with me—the woman in the black veil."

I was walking in a rocky desert. Behind me were low stone structures, the outlying buildings of a fenced-in orchard from which came the sweet fragrance of lemons.

The woman in the veil was standing next to me. She put her arm around me. I felt suckers attached to my shoulders, as if her arm were lined with leeches.

"You are very bold, Simon Magus," she said. She had an accent, but in the dream I couldn't identify it. "Right after we fight, you want to talk, eh? And with Bayard Dupont's ring. How is he, since you killed him?"

"Dead. Who are you? What are you called?"

"That is right, you do not know me. But Solly does. He did not say. That is like him. He always feared me. He will never say my name, never."

"You know Dr Archer?"

"Oh. *Doctor* Archer. That is what they call Solly now. He is a doctor of what field, do you know?"

I didn't. "I don't care," I said. "I want to know your name."

"Stupid child! You must know. Who could I be? I am Kaiser Petrus, for one thing. You knew that long ago. Solly will not admit it to himself as he will not admit how well we know each other."

"You're Kaiser Petrus?" The surprise was too obvious in my voice. I had been thinking of Kaiser Petrus as a man for the last year. "But who are you? What else are you called?"

"Oh, come. What kind of sorcerer are you that you do not know? You tell me who I am."

She was right. I should have known. I stalled for time. "I've never seen this place. Do you know where it is? Is it a real place?"

"The Holy Land," she said. "Israel. How odd that you dream of it when you have never visited. But I don't mind visiting here in my dream. I don't even hate Jews. As you and Solly are killing off my cabal, I'm laughing. They all deserve to die. I am doing a service to my old school."

I should have known who she was. Looking back, it was obvious, but while consulting with the ring was fairly lucid, it was still a dream, and my thinking was clouded.

"Why then?"

"Oh, Simon Magus! My mind is just on revenge. Morality is for fools. We can do what we like on Earth. God doesn't care. I choose to ruin Solly's life, as he did mine. Running him through a maze, as they did to me."

"They? You mean people at the school?"

" Exactly. Certain people."

I should have known who she was! But I kept stalling. "Kaiser Petrus, I challenge you. I'll meet you somewhere in the city and fight you to the death. You leave everyone else alone."

"You're confident," she said. "Maybe you could even beat me, but I don't think so. Sorry, I cannot agree. Also, I cannot make a promise to leave Solly alone. Even if I agreed, he would continue to hunt me for killing you. I think also I would have the arch-mage of elementals after me, am I right?"

"Go and ask him yourself."

"No thank you, Simon Magus. I will make you a different offer. Bow out, and take the other students with you. Let me kill Solly. I'll disappear after that. I'll kill the rest of the cabal myself and go away forever."

"No."

"Why not?"

"Because I won't sacrifice anyone to protect myself. It's the other way around. And something else, too." I broke away from her suckered grip. "You're a vicious, ruthless person. Magicians like that have to be destroyed."

She flared. "Don't be stupid. You can't destroy everyone you want to. There are far worse people in the world than me. Osama bin Ladin, Robert Mugabe, Kim Jong Il. Men in prison who have killed women and children. Can you get rid of them all? The naïveté of young people, my God!"

Something about her way of talking was very familiar, but in the dream I couldn't complete the association.

"Do you know what Solly said to me in that cold, businesslike voice of his? I said to him, 'you ruined my life.' He said, 'Your own mentality has interpreted this event as more significant than it has potential to be.' Then he recommended I seek out a magician he knew in Frankfurt who was also a psychiatrist. He should rot in Hell!"

"It sounds like he messed up," I said. "But you know what? The rest of us are not chess pieces you can just knock over on your way to checkmating my teacher. We matter. Whatever Dr Archer did to you, I wasn't there, and Dempsey wasn't there, and Chatterjee Major wasn't there, and Johanna Strauss wasn't there, and neither was my brother Peter, and neither was my partner Goldberry, who did absolutely nothing to you, and even if the others weren't on the list, just for attacking her you're going to die. Get ready for it."

Kaiser Petrus turned her back to me. "You first, boy." She looked over her shoulder. "Tell Solly again from me that I will kill his son."

I woke in the morning, with the heartless light of the European sun coming through the curtains. Robbie was up, sitting at the desk looking at a *grimoire* and chewing a buttered croissant that was shedding crumbs all over the floor.

"I know who Kaiser Petrus is," I said.

"How?"

"Dr Archer and I fought her last night in the train station, and then I talked to her in my dream." "Kaiser Petrus is a female? You fought her last night. You talked to her in a dream. And you know who she is. Wow, a lot happened while I was sacked out."

....

I filled him in on most of the details. Then we knocked on the girls' door. Avery called us in. She was dressed in black jeans and a black t-shirt and had her hair in a clip. The usual cute perkiness was gone. She looked tough.

Goldberry was in the bathroom.

"What?" she demanded.

I filled in the girls.

"Hates Dr Archer. Calls him by his school nick name. He ruined her life." Goldberry's eyes widened. "Oh, no!"

"Colette Leveque," I said.

Saving Life

Dr Archer wasn't in the hotel. He was closed off to thought-trades and did not answer his phone. Dr Chatterjee said they had spoken when he rose at dawn. "We are to proceed against Mind Cannibal only after dark," he said. "For now, today we will do some sightseeing. Magical combats cannot be conducted in summer sunlight with the streets full of witnesses. At long as we travel in groups, or at least stay near to each other, we will not be overcome."

"Mind Cannibal isn't the only cabal magician in the city," Robbie told him. "Simon and Dr Archer fought another one last night. A very powerful one."

Fighting Colette Leveque was more dangerous than facing the average enemy. As menacing as she was with her cabal, she was also the daughter of Madame Juliet Leveque, the powerful magician of Paris. Anyone who had a hand in battling Colette might face revenge from her mother. Our best bet to avoid that scenario was to pretend we hadn't known who we were fighting. For that reason, we couldn't tell Dr Chatterjee that we knew. But it also wasn't fair not to warn him about the dangerous enemy that might attack us.

"Dr Archer has given me a brief account," he said. "I am pleased that Major has been avenged. Major himself, and Mrs Chatterjee, Minor, and Maya of course, send their thanks. Thank you, Simon. We shall see to this unnamed female foe once Mind Cannibal has been dealt with."

We headed out for sightseeing. We took a boat ride that started on the Binnenalster, the huge inland lake near our hotel, and ran through Speicherstadt, the warehouse district split by canals.

"There," Goldberry said, pointing through the window of the closed canal boat. We were passing a rocky island in the middle of a broad canal. On three sides it was too sheer to walk up; on the fourth side there were some very steep steps cut into the slope, with a small dock at water level. A tiny house, painted white but yellowed with age, sat at the top.

"That's it?" Avery said. "Mind Cannibal's in there?"

"There," said Goldberry. "I can't wait for tonight."

"When we disembark," said Dr Chatterjee, "I shall engage a motorboat. I used to operate them in my youth. A more recent model should be manageable."

While he did that, we went to several art museums and then went shopping. I tried repeatedly to thought-trade with Dr Archer, but he was still closed to me. We returned to the hotel for dinner.

There was no word from Dr Archer by nightfall. We sat together and discussed what to do. The boat rental platform was close to the Rathaus, a giant city hall building which presided over an open square and a train stop. From there, it was about a ten minute motorboat ride to the rocky island we had seen on the canal tour. We printed some satellite pictures of the area from the internet. The canals were blocked by only a few gates; Dr Chatterjee was convinced he could arrange for them to open for us. We discussed whether we should all go on the boat, or whether some should remain on land as a rear guard or back-up. Finally, we decided to stick together as best we could and trust that Dr Archer could find us.

At about 9 PM Robbie went up to the hotel roof with Avery to summon some elementals. At 9:45 he reported that he had been unsuccessful in calling Gjergj the Granite Fist, and Titus the Igniter, and Sweet Ren the Water Lily, and Norikonotus the Storm Katana. He said, red-faced. "That has never happened before. I feel something is wrong. Kaiser Petrus is blocking me."

At about 10 p.m. we walked the twenty minutes from the hotel to the Rathaus, an impressive building with one tower poised between two long wings. We crossed a canal bridge to the far side, where there was a set of steps going down to the boat rental platform. It was deserted; Dr Chatterjee had the boat keys and went down to the platform ahead of us. Goldberry put on my coat, leaving the hood down. Before we could climb down the metal railings, though, we heard two sets of footsteps coming towards us.

I smelled fresh-cut flowers.

Ana flung herself into my arms.

"You shouldn't be here," I said. "We're going to war."

Was it really Ana? It was; I couldn't be mistaken.

Goldberry made a disgusted noise and turned away.

"How did you get here?" I asked. "How did you find us?"

"A plane ticket on my bed," she said. "If you did not leave it, then I don't know who did. I found you using this." She held up her hand, showing me her diamond engagement ring, which had the magic ability to help her locate me, Robbie, Rocco, and Mermelstein. She pressed. "Come away."

I looked at my companions. I looked at Goldberry.

"Go," my partner said coldly. "None of us is dying today."

"I don't want to run out on you," I said.

"I'll live. That's all that matters, isn't it?"

"No, it's not. But…"

"Why must you interfere?" Ana said to her.

"I don't have to at all," Goldberry countered. "Go on. Take him."

I let Ana lead me away. I had let Goldberry down, but she had plenty of other backup. We were best friends; we'd figure it out.

Ana and I passed the Rathaus and headed for the edge of the Binnenalster. A group of three or four men in hideous Krampus masks, making snarling noises, rushed past us headed the way we had come. Those idiots were all over the place. In the distance, I heard the motorboat's engine start, shockingly loud in the quiet night.

When we had reached the western side of the Alster, halfway to the train station, and the motorboat sounds were faint, Ana stopped. She leaned over the railing and looked into the dark water. "I have changed," she said. "When you went, I meant to be strong."

Ana squeezed my hand. "No more this plan. No more danger for us. And no more risk, Simon. No more fighting. No more."

" I'm not going to die. I can't go. I have too much to do. I have people who need me. You need me, and I'll be with you forever, but… I can't just be yours. I have to fight, Ana."

"No. You are mine." She snorted. "It is not the dead girl you love best. It is Goldberry. You say you love me, it is a terrible lie."

What the hell was she saying? How could she have gotten those ideas? A mysterious plane ticket?

William Goodenough.

"He controls minds," I said. "I told you that."

"Who is that?"

"Goodenough."

"I don't talk to him. It is the divination club. They are saying you are in danger and I must save your life."

Divination club was controlled by Mina.

"Mina is Goodenough's study partner. He used her to manipulate you into thinking these bad things about me. It's all a trick."

"A trick. The trick is that you say you love me and then you go away."

I said, "I'll take you to the hotel. There are protective spells there. We'll put you on the next train to Prague. I'll call you there when we're done."

…………………………………………………………………………………

She nodded.

"I have to finish this war. Kaiser Petrus is too dangerous. She's here in the city."

"What?"

Ana let me lead her. The next train to Prague was in the morning, so I got Ana some food, and then we went to the hotel.

Dr Archer was sitting in the lobby. He stood when he saw us. "I have located the lair of Kaiser Petrus. We must go there."

"What about the rest of the team, and the Mind Cannibal?"

"You did not expect them to be with us," he said. He was right.

"How do you know where Kaiser Petrus is?"

"She told me."

"Thought-trading."

"Yes. Colette and I have been speaking thus for the entire day. We grew up together. It is not difficult."

"Okay, let me put Ana safely in the room."

"I will not stay behind," Ana said. "I do not hide from enemies! I attack them."

"You are not prepared for this task, Miss Vorkina."

"Then we will call my father to help."

"If he comes," said Dr Archer, "then Kaiser Petrus will flee. This is my one chance. She has said that she will kill my son. I must prevent this."

"Did you speak to Donovan?" I asked.

"I did. I talked to him for a long time. He is in Cambridge, and there is no indication of peril. I have asked him to spend the night in Dempsey's apartment for mutual protection. Colette's taunts puzzle me extremely. She would be the spider, but I will not be the fly. I will be a larger spider."

I took Ana up to the room. I promised to come back. Going down the stairs, I tried a thought-trade with Goldberry. She was closed off.

"Dr Archer, I can't reach the other team. Do you know what happened to them?"

"No."

"Do they need our help?"

"I don't know. It is a capable group. I have faith in them."

"Just faith?"

"In the end, faith is all that remains."

The Canal Chase

When Ana and I were out of sight Dr Chatterjee turned back to the boat. It had debris and dirty water at the bottom. "Let us get underway." He looked about nervously. The air was oddly cold, even given their nearness to the canal. A wind came up from the direction of Binnenalster. Dr Chatterjee's teeth rattled. "Board quickly."

Robbie hopped into the boat, wobbled, then helped Avery and Goldberry. Dr Chatterjee started to untie the mooring rope, gesturing to Robbie to start the motor. As Robbie was tugging on the starter, Dr Chatterjee suddenly let the rope slip from his hand.

"Go quickly, children," he said. "You may be going into danger, but it is worse here."

As my friends watched, he took several steps towards the little stairs that led down to the dock, and stopped.

Atop the stairs was a woman in a black dress and a black widow's veil.

"Hurry!" the teacher shouted over his shoulder.

"No way!" Avery shouted.

Dr Chatterjee gestured with his fingers. The motor started, and the boat jerked forward. Avery toppled, catching herself on the side of the hull. Goldberry took the wheel.

"You know what you're doing?" Robbie asked.

"No," Goldberry said through her teeth, "but I am just a bit clever. Help if you like."

....

They were underway. Later, mostly using Abramelin's Globe, we learned what happened on the dock afterwards.

"Naresh," said the woman in the veil. She waited for her voice to be recognized. "Peanuts."

It was his old school nickname, so recognition came quickly to Dr Chatterjee. "Colette," he stammered. "But… Why are you attacking me? We're friends. We always were."

"I am Kaiser Petrus."

"You are…?"

"Simon Magus knows. He did not tell you. He is as secretive as Solly."

"Colette, you nearly killed Major. Why would you do that when we were always friends?"

She tapped her stiletto heel on the wet stair. "I did not want to kill him, and so I did not. It is only Solly who must die, but I am going to hurt you now. Cuthbert!" she hissed over her shoulder.

Thick ropes fell from the empty air and crashed atop Dr Chatterjee. Their weight bore him to the ground. He began at once to chant a *mantra* in a husky voice.

"Too slow, Peanuts," said Kaiser Petrus, slowly descending the stairs. "Cuthbert! The bricks!"

A series of heavy red bricks appeared from overhead, striking his shins and shoulders. Still he continued his *mantra*. Already the ropes were loosening, uncoiling. He recited undisturbed by the pounding of the bricks, which missed his head but clunked on his frail, thin body. The ropes were loose, but the bricks weighed him down. He began to squirm, shaking them off.

"Turpin! Chrétien!" said Kaiser Petrus, calling upon two more allied spirits. "Still his tongue!"

Dr Chatterjee stopped his *mantra* and sat up. Peering sharply into the still night, he frowned. From the nearby streets came sounds of male howling and cackling.

"I have answers to your serpents," he said, standing. "You have hurt my child, Colette. That is not easily forgiven."

He stepped towards her. She shivered in turn, then suddenly ducked her head as if something was striking at her from behind. He chanted a *mantra*.

Again she dodged, once left, then right, and the veil came loose and drifted away, exposing her face, her cruelly set jaw and her green eyes hard in the light from the streetlamps, as the barking and shouting in the street neared them.

"You're good, Peanuts," she said "But I have many allies tonight."

They swarmed him and knocked him out, and left him there lying atop the ropes and bricks, and ran on, along the canal, seeking a small motorboat where three magic students were struggling to find their course.

The boat, clumsily steered as Goldberry slowly got the hang of the wheel, was approaching the first stopping point when they first heard sounds of barking and yelling over the chatter of the motor. At the stop was a pair of heavy gates that would have to swing aside using a mechanism somewhere above. The gates were shut.

"Slow down," Avery said.

"How?" Goldberry countered. After some bumbling, she cut the motor and turned the wheel, but this had little effect on the speed of the boat, which crashed violently into the gates, throwing all of them down.

"Go up the ladder and find some way to open these doors," Goldberry ordered as she resumed her seat.

The din of approaching voices and feet slapping on pavement increased as Robbie, shaken and sweating, climbed up a set of rungs built into the stone canal wall. There was a booth at street level, accessible from a pedestrian bridge built over the doors. He said "What's up?" to a man sleeping inside. The gates started to open a moment later.

Goldberry fired the motor again as Robbie jumped back into the boat. Soon they were moving at a slower, safer speed along the canal path past parked houseboats, but the sound of the pursuers was intensifying. It was dark, and my friends were at a low angle and couldn't see what was coming.

"Got to be someone I can summon," Avery said. "I'll find a friend first." She rubbed both her wooden earrings. "Someone help out," she said raising her chin to the left and then to the right, the activating movements for the spell. Then she took one earring off. "Got some winds hooked up here. Let me see."

They were approaching a turn, where it was either go around a bend or have the canal carry them into the gigantic outer lake, the Aubenalster.

"They can't follow us there," Robbie said. "Whatever they are."

"Forget that," Goldberry said, fumbling with the satellite printout of the canal zone in her right hand with the wheel in the left. "I'm going to the Mind Cannibal. That's if I can read this map at all. Get ready, another gate coming. It's open, but I'll slow a bit."

She slowed, going into the turn, but the boat still hit the wall ferociously, nearly dumping Robbie into the water. "I'm driving next time," he said, as he crawled to the front of the boat to help restart the motor.

"Right. Then we'll wind up stranded in the middle of nowhere. No, thank you."

Avery was frustrated, calling out names of winds she had bound to her earring. None of them were responding to her call. "Can't reach *anyone*. It's not Kaiser Petrus; it's my dad. He's told them all not to come."

As Goldberry and Robbie struggled to start the motor, their pursuers could finally be seen in the amber light of the street lamps on the canal walls. They were running along the narrow ledges atop the walls with an inhuman grace and balance: devil-headed men. The Krampus figures of varying sizes were very agile and fast.

"Those aren't costumed guys; they're real spirits," said Avery. "We really need help. Got two more to try." She stroked the brown wood. "Eureroia? Boreëtes? All cut off."

The Krampus were now closing quickly. There were dozens, and they were big, with horns and claws and fangs.

"Who can control so many of these guys at once?" Robbie wondered.

"Kaiser Petrus," Goldberry said. "She must have beaten Dr Chatterjee."

The lead Krampus were now parallel to the boat.

"Do something," my partner told Robbie. "Something besides saying 'What's up,' if you please."

Avery cursed as more wind spirits ignored her summons.

Robbie fished around in the bilge and picked up a small square framed net on a wooden pole, lifting it with both hands.

"The perfect weapon," Goldberry said acidly.

Straining, imbalanced in the jostling boat, Robbie broke the pole over his knee.

"Even better."

Robbie crossed the two pieces in front of his face in an X and spoke words in Hebrew. The nearest Krampus jerked, threw up its hands, and blinked out of existence. The rudimentary staves burst into flame. Robbie whispered something as the flames spread down his arms to his shirt. He showed no pain as he again crossed the staves and recited, and another Krampus dissolved. The staves fell apart into ash and flinders. He patted out the fire on his shirt.

"How am I supposed to get any winds to come with that burning smell?" Avery complained.

Goldberry twisted the wheel sharply to the right. Two Krampus had jumped, one from each canal wall. The boat hit one wall, and the creatures hit each other and fell into the water. They could not swim, and sank out of sight."Would you mind helping?" my partner snapped.

"Yeah, sorry," said Avery.

A Krampus dropped from the wall and landed on the nose of the boat. Its claws were only inches away.

"Mmm, you slipped," Goldberry said, using her probability magic.

The creature's eyes were shining as it lunged forward, slipped, and fell into the water, sinking like a boulder.

Goldberry now swung the boat left through another open gate and into a narrower canal with a row of old stone warehouses on the left. "Lost them, but it won't last, and we're headed wrong."

"Can you work your way around?"

She squinted at the satellite map. "This isn't a main canal. It's blocked up ahead. We need to turn around."

Avery said, "I got one!" A wind was forming in the air above them. It resolved as a tall, thin female spirit with flowing hair and a hatchet face. "Zephyrida."

Zephyrida watched with watery eyes.

"Zephyrida, can you get rid of those devil guys chasing us?"

She shrugged, as she lingered in midair, and finally shook her head.

"Slow down," Avery said.

Goldberry throttled back.

"Okay, Zephyrida, can you turn us around?"

Zephyrida got behind the motorboat, stabilizing it as its own wake bounced it up and down. When the boat was still, the wind flew round to the prow, sprouted two extra arms to get a better grip, and spun it around

Avery said, "Run us right past them, Goldberry. Zephyrida, wrap yourself around my hands."

As Robbie started the motor again, Zephyrida rolled on her back and drifted down onto Avery's extended palms, dissolving her visible shape while forming misty casings on her clenched fists. A moment later,

Goldberry swung left again, putting them back on their original course.

Krampus were standing on both canal walls along their path. Seeing the boat, they poised themselves to leap. Avery stood in the center of the boat with Robbie steadying her around the waist. She made a backhand sweep, and the wind, trailing from her fist, swatted several Krampus off the wall into the water. From the other side, a huge creature leapt. Avery lashed out with her left fist. The wind caught the creature and hurled it back against the wall. Another leapt. She opened her palm, caught it on an updraft and heaved. It went flying into the distance and was impaled on the distant steeple of a Church.

"Oh no," Avery said. "Guess I overdid it. Zephyrida's used up." The mist was gone from her hands. She looked at the others. "I can try some hexes."

"No, I got it,' Robbie said. "Slow down, get close to that side."

"Slow down?" Goldberry snapped. "You're mental."

"Just do it."

She slowed the engine, steering close to the left wall. Their wake carried them forward. Robbie stood shakily in the boat, his palms on the rough stone. "Look over there!" he shouted, pointing across the canal. The girls turned away. When they turned back, he was wobbling on the left wall. He dropped out of sight into the street beyond.

"No way," Avery said.

A Krampus landed on the nose of the slow-moving motorboat. Its claws reflected the moonlight.

"You slipped," Goldberry said. But her face fell. This time her probability magic had failed.

A shadow fell in front of it. The shadow held two upraised metal bicycle locks.

The Krampus dissolved.

"Speed up," Robbie said as he crawled back to the seats. "Goldberry, just steer. Avery, throw hexes. You two don't look at me, or I can't drift."

"You can drift?" Goldberry burst out. This wasn't the drifting of the boat, but the lazy teleporting that only worked when you weren't watching. "When were you going to tell us that?"

"It's not a secret!" he argued. "I did it at the intramural game. You know the one that…"

"That everyone half forgot about."

"Yeah, guess so. Sorry. Anyway."

The chatter of the Krampus was getting louder. They were getting ready to do something.

"Get closer on one side. I'll take one bunch at a time."

Goldberry steered to the right, grunting as she struggled not to hit the wall again. Avery threw hexes at the group that was further away–none of them worked. A moment later, Robbie was balanced on the wall. A line of Krampus rushed at him with claws stretched out. He crossed the bike locks and chanted. One at a time they dissolved, till one got past and swiped at him. Rocking back, he fell sideways into the street. Krampus jumped off the wall after him.

"Oh crap," Avery said. "Stop the boat. I'm going up there."

"And do what?"

"I don't know. Stop the boat!"

Goldberry did what she could to stop. There were screams from out of sight, barks and yaps and cackles and Robbie's war-cry. A moment later, he was in the boat behind them.

"I'm beat," he said. He held up the bike locks, both coated with rust and ash. "But I cleared one side."

The Krampus on the other wall were still growling and shouting, but they were out of jumping range. Then, as one, they lifted their heads, tilted them as if listening, and then gave a start and ran off in another direction.

"That's the first good news in a while," Avery said.

"Could be," said Goldberry. "But where are they going? If Kaiser

Petrus is using them for another job… Hold the wheel steady."

Avery took over. Goldberry closed her eyes. "I checked the others. Simon is seven of wands, he's his usual brave self -- wherever he might be. Ana is seven of cups. It's unpleasant but not dangerous. Chatterjee is nine of swords reversed–he's in a bad way. No surprise. We didn't think he could beat Kaiser Petrus alone—but he's not dead."

"Dr Archer?" Robbie asked.

"The Star," Goldberry said. "It's one of the better cards. So I don't know. My guess is they're going at Simon. Let me warn him." She paused, tried thought-trading to me. "He's closed off. Still with Ana, for all the good that will do. Right, let's get this over with, and head back as soon as we can."

Surprise Arrival

"There it is," Goldberry said. Ahead of them was the spot she had seen earlier, where the canal split around a small island with a sheer rise to a house at the top. A precarious set of stairs was cut into what was effectively a small cliff. It began at a tiny platform at water level.

On the steps stood men in black uniforms.

Goldberry jerked the wheel and cut the motor. The boat continued to drift forward, carried by the wake. It did not travel as far as the island, but bobbed and drifted gently mid-canal.

"The Mind Cannibal," Goldberry said.

Robbie pointed. "That's the door we want, there at the top. I can't drift there, since they're watching. And some of those guys are as big as I am."

"I did 'find a friend' before," Avery said. "No one showed up. Let me try it again." She tilted her chin up then left, then up and right, and rubbed her earrings.

"Did you make contact?" Robbie asked.

"Sure did," Avery said. "Best I ever did. Lots of friends coming."

They sat in the boat, nervous. As they waited, over the splashing of the canal water and sound of distant traffic came a padded tapping and then steady splashing strokes.

"Man's best friend," Avery said. She gestured at the canal water behind them. Many small, shaggy heads bobbed in the water. "Who let the dogs out? I did."There were dozens of dogs of many sizes. They began to climb onto the island, and the sound as they shook out the water from their fur was like machine gun fire.

The men in the uniforms looked down at the army of dogs and began creeping up the stairs backwards.

The dogs formed a semicircular ring at the base of the island. A large Doberman took up a position at the base of the stairs, raised its head, and bayed. The other dogs answered in voices throaty, whiny, deep, and light. There were no house pets tonight: they were a fighting pack. Dobermans, shepherds, wolfhounds, Weimaraners, large poodles, greyhounds, many mutts. They howled, then barked, and then surged upward.

The dogs rushed up the steps, caught a man and dragged him down. He slid along the steps, leaving them blood-slick. More dogs charged the next man.

A few of the men tried to fight back with truncheons, but mostly they looked for a way to escape upward but there was no room and no escape that way. The men began jumping into the water to get away.

Goldberry started the motor. Slowly she guided the boat to the small platform. Robbie climbed onto the dock and tied up the boat. The way was mostly clear. A few dogs were still yanking at a few limply struggling men, but most of the combatants were now in the canal, the men swimming for their lives.

"I didn't know 'find a friend' was so strong," Robbie said.

"It isn't," Avery answered. "I thought one of you guys boosted me."

"Not me," Robbie said.

Goldberry stepped onto the platform. "I'm going up. Don't come inside unless I call for you—and I won't." She put up the hood of the Calming Coat and began to climb.

❖ ❖ ❖

Goldberry doesn't tell her story about what happened. My other friends, waiting at the base, told me what they heard. My partner's voice was loud and strong, with a command they found unnerving. Somehow on the dock they could hear every sound. Perhaps there was a telepathic connection to them through the calming coat.

Goldberry: Look, then. You stupid old woman. You've left the door unlocked. Shouldn't have put out that poison for the pigeons this morning. Getting forgetful, eh?

She pushed the door open. Creak.

Goldberry: My, my. Look how wrinkled you are. One wrinkle for every victim? Get up from that chair, witch. But it seems you can't. Arthritis flaring up, is it?

A very soft voice: I did not want to. They forced me.

Goldberry: Forced you, Mind Cannibal? Who could force you? Aren't you a fierce killer?

The soft voice: Child, we are not so far different. Once I was beautiful like you and angry, like you.

Goldberry: Let me see you. Get up!

A creak. A crash.

Goldberry: Oh, you've fallen. Rather a bad tumble for such an old lady. In fact, I think you've broken your hip. Does it hurt a bit? Here, I'll lift you.

A thin grunt, and another crash, and a cry of pain.

Goldberry: Sorry, you slipped out of my grip. Did you break your other hip? Might be a strain on your heart, all this pain so suddenly. What are the chances your heart could fail?

The soft voice: I was beautiful once.

Goldberry: You never were, and thanks to you, I never will be again. You've lived too long. I think your heart is failing. I can almost feel the pressure building in your shoulder.

A gurgle.

....

Neither Robbie nor Avery heard another boat touch the dock behind them. They were hearing the sounds of someone choking. Their defensive cylinders did not warn them of the one behind them, who was not an enemy. They had no chance to realize what was happening before their wills were sapped.

"I'll go up and get her," said William Goodenough. "Then the four of us are going to the train station."

"Kaiser Petrus is in the city," Robbie said weakly. "We need to help Simon and Dr Archer."

"You're going to guard Goldberry as I get her away from Kaiser Petrus," Goodenough replied. "Aren't you?"

"Yes," Robbie said thickly.

"Yes," Avery echoed.

"You, see Windy?" he said lightly. "The friend you found was me, after all."

Slowly, Goodenough climbed the steps. At the top of the hill, he entered the tiny house. There, in a cramped kitchen, he found Goldberry standing over the wizened form of the Mind Cannibal who lay on the floor. He lowered the hood of the Calming Coat and touched her cheek gently. "We're going home," he said.

Mortal Enemy

We came to an old church. I didn't know the name, but it was only a few blocks from the pedestrian bridge to the touristy part of Speicherstadt, the canal warehouse district. Dr Archer stopped, and we stood on the steps. It was perhaps one in the morning. There was no one in the Hamburg streets. I had never seen a city so empty.

"Meditate," he said. "Begin with the triangle."

Together we completed three years of Maestro Morgan's meditation exercises. He then continued to more challenging ones I could not do.

He seemed to reach a decision. "I have taken this past day to examine my own mind. I spoke to Donovan; I endured Colette's barbs; I examined myself. It was not an easy thing to acknowledge in my mind that my foe is one who was, in turn, a sister and a partner and, regrettably, a romantic connection. Thus, I questioned why I have chosen you for this event. At first, I told myself the purpose was your training. Then I realized that another person than Donovan would be at risk. But that person could have been another adult magician. Why you? I had never questioned it before. From the time we met, I have felt that you were the right companion for me at this moment in my life."

"Yes sir, I am. I want to be here. I'm proud that you picked me."

"You are still a child. As your teacher, I have excessive influence upon you. It is my thought now, having brought you this far, to reverse the course, and send you away. I have been telling myself that such an action is ill-advised because if I fall, Colette will then attack you anyway. She has already overcome Dr Chatterjee, or so she claims, but the other students have escaped harm, and she has lost interest in them. Only the two of us remain for tonight. Better thus to stand together."

"Yes of course, Dr Archer."

"But I am re-considering this also. I think you ought to go. Return to Ana Vorkina. Gather up the other children. Go to Prague and from there, back to New York."

"No sir. Let's finish the war together."

"Yet I have done wrong by bringing you. Many colleagues have said that. Your mother. Clive, Madame Leveque. They are all correct."

"Maybe, but I don't care. Fighting evil people is right."

"It might seem so," he answered. "I have done it all my life, but I think it has not made me a better man."

"Dr Archer–there is no better man than you."

He turned away.

"Look," I continued. "Let's go get this over with. We can talk about right and wrong on the plane ride back."

"Indeed."

Just like that, we were walking. Climbing up some steel steps, we crossed a pedestrian footbridge and down another set of steps. At the foot of the steps was an open dock with a road opening up on the left and a pedestrian railing next to the canal. A few yellow streetlamps showed an unobstructed path.

Soon we stood outside the entrance to a multi-storey building.

"Why here?" I wondered.

"Colette believes that her needs hold priority over all other events in the world."

The door was open. Beyond, we climbed a staircase side by side. A narrow landing at the top opened into a glass door. It was also unlocked. I pushed it open. Dr Archer nodded to me and I stepped over the threshold.

"I am Simon Magus. I have come as your mortal enemy. Show yourself."

There was blackness on the other side, but I heard distant sounds: laughter, and a hissing sound, and a low rumble.

"I am Solomon Archer. I have come invited." He snapped his fingers. An overhead light flicked on.

We were in a gift shop with a square of glass-topped counters. There were two other exits. Together we crossed over to the opposite corner. Another glass door was open.

"Prepare for battle."

"Yes, I'm ready." I had visualizations ready, of the vacuum bottle, of Colette herself in her black widow outfit.

We came into a large room with a low ceiling and a tile floor. Dim overhead lights showed that the room was mostly occupied by exhibits: elaborate, detailed models of European mountain scenes, in bright colours, with train tracks, and even tiny people. There was room between them for about six people to walk side by side.

We advanced into the room. There was no point in creeping along the wall, trying to be secretive. We could neither hide, nor could anyone hide from us. There was a gap leading to another bigger chamber full of displays. The lights were off. There was a low rumble. They clicked on, dimly, and the lights behind us turned red.

The next area was also full of models. Ahead, the central path broadened and forked into two curved paths. Beyond those paths was a wall covered by a heavy curtain.

There now came a clatter of feet and laughter and barking noises, and from the curved paths now rushed two columns of foes. At first I thought they were men in Krampus masks, like those I had seen in the streets over the previous few days, but now I saw they were more than human. Their crisp, balanced movements, the blazing lights in their eyes, the inhuman echoes of their voices: they were embodied spirits.

Later, Robbie and Avery and I were able to reason out that Kaiser Petrus had recalled them from the chase at the canal in preparation for this battle against us.

Dr Archer stood in front of me raising both hands extended at shoulder level. He began to gesture and each gesture had a devastating effect on the charging Krampus. The first pair flew off to the sides, feet scraping across the models, and struck the walls, and split into fragments of broken glass. The next, obeying his upraised palms, were flung against the ceiling and dropped to the floor. The third pair were squashed on the tile floor; the fourth rammed their horned skulls together, smashing them open.

The low rumble was repeated, and the hiss and the laughter of two more human voices, a male and a female, as the curtain parted in the center. I saw them enter. Colette Leveque or Kaiser Petrus, unveiled now, an elegantly-formed woman with no mercy in her face, wearing jeans and a floral print shirt. Beside her was a figure in a wheelchair, his whole body encased in a body cast.

My defensive cylinder warned me of the attack.

A bruising, battering smell of ammonia and roses rushed directly up my nose.

I lost track of where I was. I fell down. Decision-making was difficult. What sort of counter was there to this?

I visualized my defensive cylinder like a wave, undulating and flowing as water did. I was flexible, malleable, adaptable. I had no physique anymore; I was now only spirit carrying energy into fluid forms.

Getting up I realized who had attacked me, who was in the wheelchair. When my eyes cleared, I looked closer to confirm it, but there was too much motion between us as Dr Archer tore apart the attacking Krampus.

"Not this time, Pavel Rod!" I shouted. "Up against the wall!"

My visualized vacuum bottle emptied in a split second, and the wheelchair flew back, as if pushed by an exploding grenade, and slammed into the wall, dumping him out. He shrieked.

Dr Archer defeated the Krampers–all of them.

"You are wise to tire me with your servitors, Colette," he said. "But you have run out of them. Now we will settle the matter between us."

"Solly," she replied, gesturing at the broken form on the floor behind her. "Meet Pavel Rod. He is son."

H E Myra

"Pavel Rod is in his mid twenties," said Dr Archer. "He is older than Donovan. Ergo, he is not my son, since Ada was still alive at that time."

Colette said, "But there are also magical ways for a child to gain a parent."

"You are lying," said Dr Archer.

"There is plenty of strong magic I know that you have never heard about! I needed a powerful and heartless child."

"I did not think you were so angry, back when Ada was alive. I do not understand, Colette."

The spirits told me that you would betray me. They told me to be ready. But it didn't matter -- I was so much in love. I gave you all my love, Solly. I meant to have something of you, and I had it. Poor Ada never knew. She was a good girl. If she had lived, I would have left you alone after that. I loved Ada too. We used to sit in class and knit together.

Panel groaned. "Mother," he said faintly, "I am broken inside. Can't you help me now?"

"Yes, in just a moment, darling." She waved her hand. The heavy curtains slid open. From the blackness behind came a low rumble, a hiss, and with them the scraping of heavy clawed paws and the snap and flap of big wings.

H E Myra came through the opening. H.E. Myra was a chimera.

Two slitted reptilian eyes at the end of a bobbing, coiling snake head.

It had a second head of a goat and a third of a lion.

It settled on its haunches right next to the wheelchair. The snake head nudged at the recumbent form of Pavel Rod.

"My dear Pavel helped me to create H E Myra," she explained. "I needed many angry souls, people cheated of life and love as I was by you. He was able to gather many sad ghosts, to create H E Myra. Say your goodbyes, Solly, to your son, and to this befuddled boy you have brought with you. Mortal enemy? You make me laugh, Simon Magus. A fifteen-year-old thinks so highly of himself to imagine that he can use such a term? The arrogance, the self-righteousness. Only boys and dictators are so stupidly proud."

Dr Archer wanted me to know that these foes were too much for him alone.

I'm with you, Dr Archer.

I needed an idea for use against this unimaginable creature. I needed inspiration from God. What had the Rambal taught me? *Chokhmah, Binah*.... Of course.

"No goodbyes?" said Colette. "Very well, then. Go on, H E Myra, kill him."

"Mother, no!" Pavel Rod shouted. "We are a team, you promised..."

Suddenly heaving to all fours, the creature swiveled, bringing the goat head closest.

Chokhmah, I thought. *Binah*.

The goat head flexed, then the creature bucked and brought its full weight, goat horns first, against the body of Pavel Rod.

He shrieked.

Dr Archer removed his shillelagh from his coat, flexing his hands on it. His gaze shifted from Colette, who was smiling as the monster killed her son; to H E Myra, now levering its other two heads over Pavel Rod's crumpled form; to me. I nodded.

....

The sounds of the chimera attacking Pavel Rod were terrible. I couldn't look.

"You'll know the right moment," I told Dr Archer. "When it comes, go after Colette with everything you have."

The goat head bleated.

Still looking away, I heard Pavel Rod's final cry of death.

"Now it is your turn," said Colette. "Now you both die. Kill them, H E Myra."

Chokhmah. Binah. Come!

Two flashes. Windows in the air released two creatures, big tigers, black stripes on black fur, each purring softly.

"Destroy H E Myra!" I commanded.

Yes, Master.

They sprang at the chimera. One caught the snake head at its root. The other landed with its front feet on the creature's back and its hind feet tangled in the lion's mane. It gave roar and shook its body left and right.

"Very good, Simon Magus," Colette said, but there was no more time to talk. Dr Archer recognized his chance and attacked. He made swatting motions, left hand and right, to strike her with psychic force. Her body jerked this way and that, but she countered his magic, rooting herself, resisting the punishing slaps, waving her own hands to send him stumbling back. At his gesture, model trains flew off their tracks and across the room at her. She deflected them with gestures, called out the name of a spirit I could not hear, brought down her hands from overhead, dropped ropes over his torso, but he kept on his feet.

Chokhmah had fallen from the chimera's back and was circling, looking for an opening. *Binah* had the snake's neck in its jaws, just behind the head, and was clawing the scaly neck with forepaws, rear paws on the floor keeping the tiger balanced. Then the chimera leapt forward. It brushed *Binah* off. *Chokhmah* leapt, raked its back, bit the goat head from behind. The snake head snapped at *Binah* and snared my spirit tiger around the foreleg.

Still caught by the ropes, Dr Archer fell back. He needed my help.

Seven stings!

Mental stab wounds in Colette's eyes, hands, knees, and belly. She cried out, went on one knee, fired back at me with a rain of bricks that knocked me down. None hit my skull, but one slashed open my cheek.

H E Myraspun. Its massive form knocked down another table and dislodged *Chokhmah* from its back. With a sudden forward thrust it pounced on my tiger even as the snake head dragged *Binah* towards the lion head's bigger jaws.

I was on the floor. I could get rocks. Activating the elemental power taught to me, I filled my hands with smooth stones. Standing, I flung one at Colette and missed. Another, and another. One struck her chest, another her hip. I wobbled and tripped over a brick. Next to me, Dr Archer finally shrugged off the ropes and gestured. Colette was again forced backward but rooted herself.

She spun, and gestured at H E Myra. I threw another rock; she swatted it down with her hand. H E Myra caught *Binah* and its forepaws ripped the tiger apart.

I threw my last rock. I fell over backward overcome by the monster who changed at me. Dr Archer rushed between us, holding up his weapon. It reared up on its hind legs. The great three-headed shape hung over my small teacher.

It was this image of his bravery that I would remember forever.

I wanted to run. I could finally name the feeling I was having.

Fear.

Dr Archer raised his shillelagh above his head and drew a circular shield in the air. The monster was deflected and slid to the right. The snake head lashed and caught his right arm below the shoulder, making him drop his weapon.

I was on the ground. I could get rocks, but throwing little stones would do nothing. I needed to push that elemental power somehow, to find a new way to use it. The tigers I'd called *Chokhmah* and *Binah* had been vanquished, but the forces of reality that bore those names were still with me. Speed, and force. With one hand touching the floor, I extended the other towards H E Myra.

A steady stream of stones, a barrage, a machine gun of rock throwing, a current of elemental force flowed into my one hand and through my body. The rocks smashed one horn and finally crushed the entire goat head. Shifting my hand, I sent more rocks at the lion head. A rain of stone bludgeoned its forehead and nose.

H E Myra gave a full-throated roar and released Dr Archer. It landed on the ground for a moment and then swung its body completely around.

My arm was numb. The flow of rocks stopped. I couldn't do it any longer.

Dr Archer's right arm was dripping with blood as he stooped to lift his shillelagh. Again he pulled at its ends, forming it into a bow stave.

"Simon," he said. "You are familiar with the concept of *Divyastra*, divine weapon?"

"No."

"A yoga master may teach it to a pupil. It channels power from God to destroy a foe. I must use this now. Thank you for fighting beside me. You were a good companion at the end."

He raised his bleeding arm, holding his hand in the air above his shoulder, the bow stave idle in his left hand, and he spoke magic words. I could not understand the words but there was something in them, a power that had been given to him that could not be copied or repeated. A bright light appeared in the air, and resolved into a glowing arrow.

He set the arrow against the bow stave —it hung there —pulled back the invisible string, and let the arrow fly directly at H E Myra.

The pure light of the sun was in the room. There was no sound. I saw nothing else but light, felt nothing but warmth. I was swallowed up by beautiful light.

When the light was gone, I found that I was lying on my back and Dr Archer was next to me. He was not moving. His eyes were closed, his face peaceful. He had said "at the end." I knelt over him, touched his neck. No pulse. He was dead. "At the end." He had known he was going to die. Memories flooded back to me of many things he had said and done in the last few months.

It is a fitting use of my life to extirpate their harmful intent from the world.

So you know. How long have you known? A few months.

I have created a mechanism whereby you shall learn more at a later time.

The Connoisseur had told me that sorcerers know when their death is coming because they stop feeling the current of the future and feel only the peace of the end. That had happened to Dr Archer months ago.

I can no longer anticipate events as I used to.

He hadn't warned me, but he had told me things he would want to say to me before dying.

Why hadn't he told me?

Would I have fought beside him if he had? Or just tried as hard as I could to keep alive the man who was a second father to me?

I had never told him I felt that way. Had he known?

I scanned the room. H E Myra was gone. I saw Colette in one corner, kneeling by her son's dead body.

"Up against the wall," I said.

She flew back and crashed against the wall. I saw blood on her as she slid down to the floor. I rushed at her. She wasn't much taller than me, and she weighed almost nothing as I propped her up. She was beaten. Her clothes torn and stained. The wickedness in her eyes had faded.

"The war is over," she said. "Solly is dead. I've won."

....

"I'm not dead," I said.

"But you don't matter. I told you that. You can go."

"I will," I said. "In just a moment. But first… On your knees!"

She went down on her knees. "Yes, I'm sorry," she said. "I had to kill Solomon Archer. You have to understand. I even sacrificed my own son. It had to be done."

"No, it didn't. Up against the wall."

The magic lifted her off her knees and flung her against the wall. There was a snap. Her ankle had struck at the wrong angle and broken. I let her fall.

"Go, Simon," she said weakly. "The fighting is over. No reason to fight anymore."

"No reason?" I said. "You laughed when I said I was your mortal enemy. Didn't you?"

"It's just taunting. It happens in battle."

"Up against the wall."

She struck the wall again. I held her in place with my hands on her shoulders and repeated the magic.

"Up against the wall. Up against the wall. Up against the wall."

Each repetition of the spell drove her with full force into the wall with nothing to cushion the blow. More bones snapped, a wrist, ribs.

"You make my body the mirror of my spirit," she whispered.

"You killed my teacher, and I'm going to kill you. You made me afraid."

She smiled. "Kill me, then. God does not care."

"Up against the wall."

Her neck snapped.

No More Death

My arms were numb and limp. It was difficult to drag Dr Archer's body all the way out of the building and into the street. I couldn't leave his body there with the other dead. He'd meant too much to me for that.

When I got to the street a man joined me. He was wearing a black suit and had a white beard. He took one of Dr Archer's arms and helped me pull him.

"Thank you, Rambal," I said.

"No," he said. "I am not Rav Moshe."

It wasn't the Rambal. The face was familiar, an old Chasidic man I had met before, but who was he?

I heard a pop, and I was suddenly flung sideways. Heat rose from my shoulder and it grew wet. The old man stumbled away. My field of vision narrowed as I scanned the street and found a second man, a tall blond in a uniform of some kind, holding a pistol extended in both hands. A pistol pointed at me. In the dim streetlight I couldn't make out the uniform. It didn't matter. It was him or me.

"Yeishu," I said softly. A hard punch to the side of the neck. His head slipped sideways and he fell face-first to the ground.

There was someone behind him.

The man who had been helping me cried out. "Dead!"

The person behind the uniformed man was Ana Vorkina. She fell to the ground beside him, touched his face, his cheek. His neck was twisted at a peculiar angle. He was definitely dead. She held his head in her lap.

"You have killed him, how could you?" she shouted at me. "You killed Eduard, why?"

"Eduard?" It took me a while to focus. "He shot me," I said. The pain was becoming worse. I felt my knees quivering. I would fall down in a moment and not be able to get up. Who was Eduard? Then it came back to me. "That's your ex-boyfriend?" I said. "Why did he shoot me?"

I started to fall down. The old man had run away but another pair of hands steadied me. I recognized Dr Chatterjee.

"Why is he here?" I asked Ana.

Dr Chatterjee eased away my torn t-shirt, looking at the gunshot wound. "It is not so bad, but you must go to the hospital," he said.

Finally leaving Eduard's body, Ana came to me, but she didn't touch me. "He came to beg me to take him back," she said. "I was coming here to find you, and he followed me all the way. He was a sweet man. I would not go back to him. He was crying like a little boy. He could not have meant to kill you, but you killed him, why?"

"I'm sorry," I said. "He shot me. I just fought for my life in there. I didn't know who he was."

"It is wrong," she said.

"Ana, I just fought for my life. Dr Archer is dead."

"I told you!" she shouted at me. "I told you there would be a bad end to this war. I begged you to stop! Your teacher is dead. Eduard is dead! He was innocent man."

"He shot me!"

"No, it is all too much. Your Ana cannot live with this."

"It's over," I said. Dr Chatterjee let me sit and was now pressing a torn piece of his shirt against the wound to slow the bleeding. "I promised you, no more fighting. You don't have to live with it anymore. We'll go back to New York and start afresh. Later we will get married."

....

"We will not get married," she said. "Every time I see you now, I will see his blood."

"That's not fair," I said. I was wobbling. I would have fallen on my face without my teacher steadying me.

"This dead body and that one. Good people that I knew. And you have all their blood on you with your own. I will see your body dead also. Then I will be alone again. I will not go on waiting for that day."

"Do not decide impulsively," suggested Dr Chatterjee.

"I'm a good person," I whispered. But I remembered making Colette Leveque's bones break. "I try, I want to be. Please Ana I love you."

"No, it is done," she said. "You are covered in blood. No more blood, no more death, for me it is too much. Goodbye." She turned away quickly sobbing. I was starting to pass out as she walked away.

"No Ana wait," I croaked. "We have to talk about it! Ana!"

❖ ❖ ❖

I woke up in a hospital bed. My shoulder was immobilized with a bandage, and it hurt to move it. Dr Chatterjee was sitting by my bedside. He was also bandaged around the wrist and on his forehead and looked weak.

"Ana," I asked him.

"I have not seen her," he said. "I am sorry, Simon."

"Where's my cell phone?"

He took it out of a drawer and handed it to me. I made three calls. The first was to a Manhattan office. The second was to a number they gave me. That call was answered by Mrs Lopez, mother of Level Three and Lorena, who was in Spain for the summer. I told her I needed the favour she had promised me—to help pick up the pieces in Hamburg, including hiding what had happened from my parents. She agreed and promised to arrive the next day. The third call was to

Jan Vorkin. He answered on the first ring.

"Ana has told me that she broke the engagement with you," he said. "This is terrible news. You must tell me the reason."

I told him the entire story.

"Willa has done this," he said. "She went out a few days ago. She must have seen Eduard and told him about you. She has elementals enough to learn where you are and what you are doing. I will deal with her." "I don't care about Willa. Let me talk to Ana."

He was silent for a moment. "Now that I know what has happened, I know that you are blameless. I will use every kind of persuasion I know to talk sense into her," he said. "But at present she has told me that she wishes never to speak to you again. I do want you as my son-in-law. You are a man of honor. Yet, she is my daughter, Simon, and I must in the end accept her decision."

I felt sincerity and regret in his voice, but he was right; he had to put Ana's wishes before mine or his own. "Thank you, sir," I said. "It's been nice knowing you." I hung up. "It has gone badly, then," said Dr Chatterjee.

"Where's Goldberry?" I asked him. "Robbie? Avery? Are they all right? Where did they go?"

"It has been difficult to reconstruct their movements," he explained. "After defeating the Mind Cannibal, they for some reason left at once for Brussels. Their belongings are still in the hotel. As this seems an unlikely course for such a loyal threesome, I assume there was an additional influence. I would like to learn more, but I was also hurt yesterday and I am not at my best."

We would have to wait for more information. We waited, and I told him the story of Dr Archer's final battle.

The Meaning of Power

Lopez arrived the next day, helping with the disposal of Dr Archer's body, with my medical bill, with shipping back my friends' bags, and with other things that had to be done to cover up the end of the War against Love. She was an efficient businesswoman, and while I never saw her doing magic, I was sure she used plenty to clean up the mess.

Although the gunshot wound was only a flesh wound, and the bullet hadn't entered my body, it was still more than a week before I got back to school. I had to talk to my parents before that. I managed to tell them only that the war was over, that Dr Archer was dead, and that Ana had broken off the engagement. My father flew to Hamburg to escort me back, so I had to conceal my injury from him, not showing signs of the pain it caused me to use my right arm.

On my own I remembered the identity of the old Chasidic man. His name was Rabbi Zalman. I had met him on the first day of school of my second year, when I helped save him from being mugged, and he told me he had seen me kill a man in Hamburg. I hadn't believed it, and I had completely forgotten about it when we were headed to Germany, but he had been right. Now he had seen me kill a man in Hamburg. I didn't know why he was in Hamburg, or why he was standing on a dockside road in Speicherstadt at two o'clock in the morning to see it. Perhaps it was part of his life's journey; I never saw or heard about him again.

With Mrs Lopez' and Dr Chatterjee's help, I eventually found out that William Goodenough had arrived in Hamburg on the same plane that Ana took, and that he had taken the train with my friends to Brussels, and that Martha Goodenough had met them there and bought them all tickets for New York. All three of them had shown up at the Goodenoughs' Manhattan home and been guests there for a few days before Rod Goodenough drove them back to school. None of them could give me a good explanation for why they had gone with him, or a detailed story of what they did while they were with him.

When I got back to school, I went looking for William. I found him in his room alone, lying on his bed with a textbook propped against his pillow.

"Well, Ladybug," he said. "How was your?"

"On your knees!"

He fell out of his bed and to his knees.

"Next time you interfere with me," I told him, "in any way, even the smallest way, I will hurt you so badly your mother won't recognize you. Got it?"

"It's not wise to threaten me," he said.

"I just did."

"But you were the one who…"

He wasn't getting a chance to talk. "Look at the dead bodies I left behind me in Hamburg and decide if I can back it up."

He raised his eyebrows. "All right, Simon. I won't mess with you, but you were the one who..."

"Shut up, you bastard." I left.

For the next few weeks I went to class, did my homework, and kept my mouth shut. Looking around, I didn't see in any of the faces of people I knew any recognition of what it meant to have seen and caused death in war. Goldberry should have understood, and it occurred to me that maybe she did, but we could hardly look at each other. Anger was building up in me, and finally I got a chance to vent it.

I was walking down a corridor of classrooms late at night and saw the Rambal sitting in one eyes closed.

I went in and sat across from him. He opened his eyes.

"Rabbi Lichtman, the war against Gott im Himmel was terrible. People died who didn't deserve to. People who were good feel terrible now. Lives were ruined. I know you can just say that's what war is always like, but I don't need to hear that. What I need to hear is about you. It's about what you did. By that I mean what you didn't do."

He continued watching me.

"You saved me from Pavel Rod. Thank you. And other than that, you did nothing. With all your power, you did nothing. Even worse, you held back everyone in the Cabala school from fighting. Mermelstein wanted to fight. I'll bet there are others who would have. But you didn't let them fight. I want you to tell me why. With your power, you could have saved Dr Archer. Didn't you care about him? With your power, you could have told us where all the bad guys were. They were the enemies of your school even more than mine. You didn't help at all, and we who did fight, some of us.... I lost so much."

"Hm," said the Rambal. "It must be hard for you to look at me if you think I am an idler in wartime. The soldier makes the sacrifices, and then he feels that those who stayed behind are ungrateful and cannot understand. Then he comes to his leaders and demands, 'Why? Why?' And most days the leaders will not answer. You are fortunate compared to them. I will answer you, but I will have to start long ago.

"I was born in 1898. Chasidism was young then. There was talk about power—power to fight the Polish oppressors, power to fight the Russians. But even then I did not understand this idea of power. It is an idea from science, and in those times, science denied God. My father's brother even gave up being a Jew. He read Nietzche and said God is dead. He read Marx and said religion is only a tool to make people submit to bad leaders. He decided to go to the city and change his name.

Not long after that was the terrible war. Here in the United States they call it World War One. What was its cause, do you know?"

"No, I don't."

"It was about this thing called power, the power of nations. Each government was afraid that it would not matter anymore, that others would become stronger and the nation would then fail, would lose money, importance and territory. That mattered to them very much. And so all the deaths and torture and ruin and the way of life for those rulers was ended forever. But the nations who were declared the winners took so much for themselves that twenty years later it started again, as any smart person could have foreseen it would. Then we got a war that did have a cause, a war to stop Hitler."

Hitler was the most destructive man who ever lived, and the one who really defeated him, Stalin, was the next worst. If ever I should have killed a man, that man was Hitler, but when I tried, I failed.

"Because you lost your power."

"I cannot kill anyone, Simon. I do not mean to say that I am without blood on my hands. Instead of killing men, I have given guidance to those who are able to kill. I trained Solly, and I trained you, and there were others before. I do not urge those whom I train to use that knowledge in war, but I have lived through wars, as I said, and I have learned that war cannot be ignored. But Simon, in so many years, I still do not understand this idea of power. Power is not real. You know what power comes down to? It comes down to a person feeling small and telling a story to feel big."

It was impossible for me to out-argue the Rambal. No one ever out-reasoned him; you believed him or you didn't. He calmed me down with his voice and his words, and I wasn't able to stay angry in his presence, but I still had a question.

"Rabbi, I understand now why you didn't fight, but why did you stop Mermelstein and the others? Is it because you want them to all be like you?"

"Want? I don't want anything. That answer is very simple. We stay here and keep the school safe. We are its defense. I am over one hundred years old. My spirit is without boundary, but my body cannot do much. The Cabala students and I we protect the school together. Yakov Mermelstein is for the school's protection inside what you are for the school's protection outside. He does not like that, and so he shouts at me that I am wasting what he can do."

"You need Yakov and the others to sit in the building like batteries you can draw power from?"

"Power, power. You will not give up that word. Listen, they are not batteries. They are young men with understanding. Their importance is the same as mine. We are all equals in the task. Yakov himself… Wait, I will call him."

Mermelstein appeared in the doorway. He approached the Rambal, a gigantic creature before the frail elder who had summoned him there.

"We were talking about you. Your friend wants to know why I did not let you fight beside him in the war, when I knew it to be a great desire of yours to be his companion in battle. Do you want to hear once more, as I tell him?"

"Yes, Rebbe."

"Then listen. When you were a boy, you fought all the time against your older brothers who wanted to make you tougher, who in the eyes of your father have not so much potential for wisdom. When you came here, unwillingly, you still used fighting for all your problems. That was too much for me, so I did not much see you. You had to learn about fighting. The first year, you fought Simon. Was it just?"

"No, Rebbe."

"Because now he is your friend, and that is all he wanted when he met you those years ago. And you had to meet Leah Ritz to learn that understanding and wisdom are found in strange places."

"Yes, Rebbe."

"And the second year you fought Rocco because you could not manage your feelings. The love appeared in you and you could not see it properly and so you projected it upon a girl and it went out of proportion, it became like madness."

"Lorena is a good girl, Rabbi Lichtman," I argued. "She's brave and smart. He picked the right one to fall in love with."

"Yes, yes, I understand," said the Rambal. "Let me talk to Yakov, please. You could not see the love properly, and so you created fighting and hatred. But in the end, Rocco is your friend, and he has helped you to get the *Luz*, and the girl is your friend."

"Yes, Rebbe. I don't fight kids in the school anymore."

I asked, "Why didn't you give me that advice before the war?"

The Rambal was ready with his answer. "You would not have listened."

He was right. The Dean had offered me a path of peace, that night in the car by the hospital, and I had chosen war.

"I know you will both fight again," the Rambal said. "My words will remain at the back of your minds, but you will both be caught in the world's snares. Next year you will again fight side by side. I hope later in your lives you will understand." He closed his eyes.

"Rabbi Lichtman," I said.

He began to nod to himself in the rhythm of prayer.

"Rebbe," I said. "Can you… Can you forgive me? I killed people."

His eyes snapped open. "Forgive you? I am not a judge."

"Then it's true what Colette said to me, that God does not care?"

"He cares," said the Rambal."And your name, and mine, and the names of those dead, are all names of God."

First two books of the series
School Of The Ages

School of the Ages Series -I
Ghost in the Crystal

School of the Ages Series -II
Level Three's Dream